The Christian Home
in Victorian America

Religion in North America
Catherine L. Albanese and Stephen J. Stein, editors

The Christian Home
in Victorian America,
1840–1900

COLLEEN MCDANNELL

INDIANA UNIVERSITY PRESS

Bloomington and Indianapolis

1000659845 T

First Midland Book Edition 1994

This book was brought to publication with the aid of a grant from the Andrew W. Mellon Foundation.

Manufactured in the United States of America

Library of Congress Cataloging in Publication Data
McDannell, Colleen.
The Christian home in Victorian America, 1840–1900.
(Religion in North America)
Bibliography: p.
Includes index.
1. Family—United States—Religious life—History—
19th century. 2. United States—Religion—19th Century.
I. Title. II. Series.
BV4526.2.M37   1986   291.1′783585′0973   85-42947
ISBN 0-253-31376-7
ISBN 0- 253-20882-3 (pbk.)

2 3 4 5 6 99 98 97 96 95 94

To John Hurdle

CONTENTS

ILLUSTRATIONS

FOREWORD

In this new study, Colleen McDannell opens the door to a domestic
world that has been largely overlooked. It is a domestic *religious* world
that she shows us, complete with its own sacred space and time,
officiants, ceremonies, and ceremonial objects. This religious world is
Christian: but, as McDannell demonstrates so clearly as she conducts
us through the homes of nineteenth-century Americans, Protestant
and Roman Catholic Christians read and enacted their faith in different ways. Comparing the two traditions, McDannell sheds light on
what theological distinctions meant in terms of ordinary life, and joins
the growing scholarly effort to recover the religious world of the
average person.

The study stands at the intersection of a number of methods and
approaches: religious studies, American studies, material culture
studies, social and family history. Like a seasoned archaeologist,
McDannell digs skillfully into the material remains of the past. Like a
practiced anthropologist, she measures and evaluates her data to
uncover its significance in the underlying meanings of a culture. A
methodological pluralist, she integrates her approaches to produce a
work that suggests important new directions for American religious
studies to pursue.

As Colleen McDannell opens her door to the domestic religious
world of Victorian America, she also opens *our* door to this series on
Religion in North America. Her book will be only the first of a long
series of studies that will look in new ways at the religious life of our
continent. This will be a series in which religion in the United States
begins to be seen in a comparative light, as students of North American religion work to give Canada, Mexico, and other places south
their scrutiny. It will be a series in which history and the social sciences
become proper partners, even as symbolic and literary studies attempt
to capture what eludes these disciplines.

Religion in North America will be a series in which older approaches and topics, too, will find their niche. Some studies will
concern mainstream cultural phenomena, and others specific traditions. Some will present materials from the past; others will aim to
interpret the present. With one of the most plural religious cultures in
the contemporary world before us, we need to discover all that is

there; and we need, too, to discover the *ways* to discover it. As editors of this new series, we encourage scholarship that will do just these things, and we eagerly await the new—and older—scholars who will take up the task.

Catherine L. Albanese
Stephen J. Stein, *Series Editors*

PREFACE

In 1869 Catharine Beecher and her sister Harriet Beecher Stowe included in their book, *The American Woman's Home,* drawings for a house church. This building, which could also serve as a school, had a steeple for a chimney and a movable screen to convert the parlor into a nave. For the practical Beecher sisters the idea that a house was a church seemed natural. They would have agreed with Father Bernard O'Reilly when he wrote a decade later that a true home is "a bright temple filled with the light of God's presence, blessed and protected by God's visiting angels, and fragrant with the odor of paradise." For the good Christians of the nineteenth century the connection between religion and home was natural and inseparable.[1]

The creators of nineteenth-century culture—ministers, priests, reformers, novelists, architects—saw the home as a vehicle for the promotion of values. Both Protestants and Catholics held that domestic values were eternal, unchanging, and God-given. Like the church, the home (as both a physical space and a kinship structure) promoted a religious perspective. By studying the private aspect of American culture we can clarify the impact Victorian Christianity had on shaping attitudes toward domesticity. Conversely, we can evaluate how beliefs in the divine nature of the home created a particular form of American popular piety.

Historians of the nineteenth century explore the nature of sex roles, labor, childhood, demographics, and ethnicity but ignore the relationship between religion and the home. Recent writers on women's history come close to understanding the religious role of the family, but then stop at noting the changing educational role of mothers and the relationship between women and a "feminized" Protestantism. Scholars of religion examine the social dimension of Christianity and the ways individuals experience the sacred, but not the family's position as middle ground between the community and the self. Turning away from one of the richer dimensions of American religion, they have been slow to integrate material culture into their writings. Provocative studies of the relationship between Protestantism and American culture have appeared recently, but few Catholic historians have followed suit. Catholic historical studies continue to center on bishops and their dioceses, educational institutions, priests, and nuns rather

"A Christian House." Catharine Beecher and Harriet Beecher Stowe,
The American Woman's Home, p. 23.

than the laity. Writers have assumed too often that American popular
culture is Protestant while Catholic culture is somehow "European."

By presenting an analysis of the domestic ideology used by Protestants and Catholics, the present study seeks to create a fuller picture
of American Christianity. It focuses on the philosophy which articulated the home's sacred character, the rituals which instilled that philosophy, and the props advertised to elicit religious sentiments.
Protestants and Catholics described their own visions of a "Christian"
America in terms of the spiritual quality of the home. The home was
not only a private sphere unconnected to society but the starting point
for shaping the public world. Victorian Christians drew from a long

tradition of attitudes toward the family, modifying to fit their cultural situation. Contrasts in Protestant and Catholic expression of domestic sentiments form an important part of the study and highlight the issues of cultural assimilation, social change, and religious antagonism.

To what extent families participated in domestic religion is not my major concern. My attention centers on understanding the various cultural systems that Protestants and Catholics believed articulated the proper Christian home. Domestic advice books, novels, and home design manuals were popular during the nineteenth century. They colored the perspectives of their readers, if not their practice. Advertisers in religious newspapers expected to sell their parlor organs, family prayer books, and lithographs of Catholic clergy. Clearly people do not always do what they are told to do, but cultural norms are not easily ignored.

Although Protestantism always supported the religious role of the family, interest in domestic piety increased between 1830 and 1870. This period saw the assertion of the evangelical denominations' vision of a Christian America. The major Protestant churches of the nineteenth century (Methodist, Baptist, Presbyterian) and many of the smaller ones (Congregational, Disciples of Christ, United Brethren) embraced the hope for a Bible-based, Christian America. Even Episcopalian and Lutheran churches had evangelical branches. Evangelical denominations promoted domestic religion as a means of civilizing America, and their popular literature forms the backbone of this study.

Allied with evangelical ministers in their quest for a Christian America were women writers and architectural critics. They sought to overturn the traditional Calvinist notion of sin and salvation by advancing the spiritual dimension of the home. Their writings on domestic moral influence often preceded writings by the clergy, and by the 1880s even the most reluctant Calvinist writer had adopted their perspective. These "scribbling ladies," as Hawthorne called them, along with architectural reformers, functioned as a secular force not speaking for any denomination, but still articulating the evangelical vision of America. Domestic religion and home sentiments had become more fundamental than sectarian concerns.

The Protestant attitude toward the sacredness of the family developed in antebellum America, becoming entrenched by 1880. A comparable Catholic ideology did not appear until the 1870s. Although early Catholic immigrant groups such as the Germans and the French commented on the home, it was the Irish Catholic community that would dominate Victorian Catholicism. Southern and Eastern European Catholics who began to arrive in the 1880s maintained their own culture, language, and family structure and must be considered outside this study. The Irish, who dominated the clergy, newspapers, and popular presses from 1850 to 1900, shaped the character of American Catholic domestic sentiments. As English-speakers and heirs of British colonial rule they could better understand and respond to the Anglo-Saxon sentiments of Victorian American Protestants.

The slow rise of the Irish into the American middle class corresponded to a greater Catholic interest in domesticity and the religious role of the home. Before 1880, few Irish Americans could afford the pleasures of Victorian family life. By the end of the century, Rome turned its attention to the family, presenting it as a bulwark against the evils of modern society. Both late-nineteenth-century Catholic and mid-nineteenth-century Protestant domestic ideology had supported a growing middle-class culture. The demise of the evangelical hope of a Christian nation after World War I brought the decline of Protestant home religion, except for a flurry of interest during the suburban post-World War II years. Catholics, on the other hand, developed a strong domestic ideology and accompanying home rituals. Both the Second Vatican Council of the 1960s and the emphasis on traditional family values of the 1980s encouraged Catholics to bring religious activities into their homes.

The writing process is never solely an individual endeavor but asks support of both kith and kin. I would like to extend my thanks to the staff of the libraries and archives in which I worked and especially those at St. Charles Seminary Library and Archives, the Presbyterian Historical Society, the Philadelphia Athenaeum, and the National Library of Ireland. Temple University graciously funded much of my research, including travel to collect sources in Ireland. I especially would like to thank Allen Davis of the history department, who not only provided intellectual and moral support but encouraged me to read versions of the chapters at professional conferences. Chapter 2 was first presented at the American Academy of Religion national meeting in December 1982 and chapter 3 at the College Theological Society national meeting in June 1983. Chapter 4 was presented at the biannual American Studies Association meeting in November 1983. There have been many others who have read this manuscript in its various stages and have made important contributions: Catherine Albanese and Stephen Stein, the series editors; Margaret Marsh; Gayle Winkler; Jay Dolan, and the editorial staff at Indiana University

Press. In Germany Bernhard Lang helped not only in criticizing the manuscript but scoured the Continent for European sources, translated foreign writings, and helped with the interpretation of Catholic history and theology.

Finally I would like to thank my husband, John Hurdle, to whom this book is dedicated, for his unending support. His care and constant attention—from computer programming to editing to household chores—place me forever in his debt.

The Christian Home
in Victorian America

[1]
Church, Home, and Society

"There are two institutions that have come down to us from Eden," wrote the Reverend Thomas Moore in 1856, "to prepetuate some of its purity and peace." The first of these was the Protestant sabbath and the second was the family. Although few Catholic writers would call on the Old Testament as evidence for the eternal character of the Christian family, they frequently cited the family of Jesus, Mary, and Joseph as the sacred model for domestic life. Catholics and Protestants assumed that God instituted the family and that it had certain spiritual functions to perform. Neither tradition would have acknowledged that the nature of the family or Christianity had undergone radical changes throughout history. Without understanding those changes we cannot gain the proper perspective on the Victorian family and Victorian Christianity.[1]

The relationship between the home and Christianity in mid-nineteenth-century America was the result of a long social and religious development. Before beginning to untangle that relationship I sketch in four sections the development of American domestic Christianity. The first section traces the evolution of the Christian attitude toward the family, starting with the role of the household in early Christianity and ending with the creation of a strong domestic religion in American Puritanism. The second section moves us away from religion and focuses on the social world of the Victorians, both middle-class Protestants and the Irish immigrants who make up the bulk of American Catholicism. Religious questions are taken up in the third and fourth sections, in which specific aspects of American Protestantism and Catholicism are discussed in order to elucidate the character of domestic religiosity.

The Christian Evolution of Domestic Religion

The gathering of the first Christians in the homes of their members modified a well-established pattern of Jewish family worship. New Testament passages which indicated Jesus' disregard for family ties (especially Mt. 10:34–39) broke with that tradition. In other cases (Lk. 10:38–42) Jesus depends on the domesticity of his followers. Jesus might have conducted his ministry without the benefit of family and home, but the early Christians depended heavily on the hospitality of householders. During the first and second centuries, house churches "provided space for preaching of the word, for worship, as well as for social and eucharistic table sharing." Excavations at Dura Europos in the Tigris Valley revealed what could be the earliest Christian church, which according to Roland Bainton was an adaptation of a private home.[2]

There is no evidence that early house churches endowed either house or family with any special qualities. The church groups which met in homes like Prisca and Aquila's included members of their own household and of other households. They came together because of religious, not familial, commitments. Meeting in members' houses was particularly important during periods of persecution, but when Constantine legitimized Christianity in 313 C.E. he encouraged the building of churches separated from homes. These new churches were built as imitations of Roman public buildings. Worship in the new Christian world would be a public and not a private endeavor.[3]

The charismatic nature of the early Christian community and the later development of a monastic ideal worked against the spiritualization of the family and home life. To have family commitments meant being bound to this world and not preparing for the Kingdom of God. The writings of the Church Fathers, most of whom were celibate bishops or monks, did not treat family affairs. They promoted the celibate life as the surest path to God. Virginity was more valued than marriage, just as "heaven is better than earth, [and] as the angels are better than men."[4]

Even the Church Fathers who mention family life, such as John Chrysostom, were primarily interested in its ability to clarify and reinforce prevailing Christian theology and social structure. "In the home there must be a twofold table," wrote Chrysostom, "one for eating and another one for reading." At this table "the husband shall read what has been written, the wife shall learn, the children shall listen, and the servants shall not disturb the reading." Consequently, the father was told to "make your home into a church" and thus be "responsible for the salvation of the children and the servants. As I the bishop am responsible for you, so everyone is responsible for his servant, his wife, and his child." Chrysostom understood the father as one who headed a large household, just as the bishop headed the local church. The "house as a little church" referred less to the liturgical dimension of family life, of which he gives no further details, and more to the home's ability to produce good Christians who understood church order. "If we regulate our own houses," Chrysostom observed, "we shall be also fit for the management of the Church." The concern of the Greek bishop was educating leaders for an emergent Christian community, not creating domestic ideology.[5]

European Christian families were left to develop domestic rites which combined pre-Christian beliefs with Christian rituals. As early as the sixth century, holy water was blessed for use in protecting the home. House blessings by priests increased fertility and protected the home from evil. Priests, unlike monks or bishops, had little theological education, and often married. They adapted their understanding of Christianity to fit their own needs or those of the local community.[6]

For the families of the Middle Ages, social behavior was not determined by the local priest or church law, but by a complicated kinship system. One way that the extended family exercised its influence was through the social and economic ties legitimized by the rites of passage of the church. After the Council of Trent (1545–1563), the Catholic Church took a hard stand against the control of religion by the kin group. By tightening and regulating church organization, the hierarchy sought to emphasize the importance of the individual and not community (as a collection of families) religious activity. Requirements regarding marriage, individual confession, and the prohibition of unorthodox rites functioned to "divert all streams of popular religion into a single parochial channel." The Catholic hierarchy after Trent insisted that the Christian was an obeying individual whose behavior was dictated not by the kin group but by the church.[7]

The Catholic Counter-Reformation had responded to the Protestant Reformation, which promoted its own views on the family and religion. Protestant reformers also believed that communal activities of medieval Christians created social and theological problems. They, too, condemned the feasting and frolicking which accompanied holy days, the less-than-spiritual pilgrimages, and the ties to dead family members in purgatory or heaven. The reformers "swept away a whole set of rites, practices, symbols, beliefs, and institutional organizations" which previously provided social cohesion and psychological stability. Although each individual church and sect acted at different times and to varying degrees, they achieved the placement of important social and psychological activities within the family.[8]

The Protestant Reformation, first under Luther and then more severely under Calvin, caused four major shifts in the relationship between the family and religion. First, it condemned the monastic and celibate virtues of Catholicism and defined the home as a "school of character," or a "school of faith." Second, the "school of faith" *qua* family was not merely an economic institution; it was a divine vocation. Parents, especially mothers, should take parenthood seriously. Third, the debate over the merits of celibacy versus married life prompted the creation of a domestic rhetoric. Polemical treatises on domesticity served to bolster the Reformation spirit among the people, and to begin the romanticization of the home. Finally, by restricting the ritual and social dimension of the church the reformers paved the way for the development of home-centered religion.[9]

Although there is some indication that Catholics in pre-Reformation England participated in home religion, historian John Bossy concludes, "the Counter-Reformation hierarchy seems to have taken it for granted that the household was a seed-bed of subversion." It was the English Puritan writers and ministers who encouraged family religion. Daily family prayer and Bible reading, catechizing children and servants, and even the mutual confession of sins between husband and wife were important activities in Puritan home life. The Protestant private diary replaced the confessional, and the father replaced the priest.[10]

Protestants turned from the kin group, not to the social world of the parish but to the intimacy of the nuclear family. For Lawrence Stone, the "new emphasis on the home and on domestic virtues" found in Anglican and Puritan households "was perhaps the most far-reaching consequence of the Reformation in England." Whereas Catholics tried to replace the kin group with the parish community, Protestants replaced it with the nuclear family. Although both began to prize individualism, the Protestants saw the individual as existing within a family, while the Catholics placed him or her within the Church community.[11]

After the restoration of the British monarchy and the decline of Puritanism, the enthusiasm for family religion subsided in England. Religious individualism, promoted by radical sectarians, helped undermine the need for family religion. According to Lawrence Stone, evidence found in late seventeenth- and early eighteenth-century writings pointed to the decline of family worship and religious instruction. By 1778 James Boswell could lament that "there was no appearance of family religion today . . . how different from what was the usage in my grandfather's day, or my mother's time."[12]

While the Puritan predicament in England worsened with the restoration of the monarchy and the flourishing of individualism, the Puritans who left for the New World found the colonies more hospitable to family religion. A 1642 Massachusetts law, amplified in 1648, required masters of families "once a week (at the least) [to] catechize their children and servants in the grounds and principles of Religion." Children were taught to read, not for their general education but so that they could read the Bible. The lack of Puritan ministers and the possibility of infant damnation made family worship essential. Religious leadership fell to the father, but Cotton Mather did mention in 1699 that it should "be remembered that the fathers are not the only parent obligated thus to pursue the salvation of their children. You that are mothers, have not a little to do for the souls of your children. . . ."[13]

Puritan family worship formed the basis for evangelical Protestant worship during the Victorian period. Although the content of devotion would change during the nineteenth century, its structure remained the same. The family met in the morning and evening to recite prayers, sing psalms, and read from the Bible. The family prayer books the Puritans brought from England included prayers of thanksgiving, confession, and petitions for the success of the Reformed churches. Grace was said before and after meals, and, according to Charles Hambrick-Stowe, "reenacted on a small scale the experience of God's salvation on their souls." For the colonial Puritans, family devotions were closely tied to public and private forms of piety. From his research, Hambrick-Stowe concludes that Puritan family worship, far from being emotionless, was a "means of grace . . . through which the redemptive drama was reenacted and reexperienced."[14]

The patriarchal, agrarian life-style of Calvinist New England was already beginning to change by the end of the seventeenth century. In 1702 the Puritan divine Cotton Mather regretted that "religion brought forth prosperity and the daughter destroyed the mother." Individualism, deism, rationalism, and concern for the new nation turned attention away from religion, and thus from domestic piety. Just as in England, when religious enthusiasm waned, so did family piety. Victorian Protestant writers would look back nostalgically to the colonial period as the time when Christianity truly dwelt in families.[15]

The Social World of Victorian America

By the mid-nineteenth century, although most of America still depended on farming, certain trends revealed an encroaching industrial
economy. As early as 1820 the textile industry of New England became
a model of economic production and innovative factory life. Manufac-
turers saw the Lowell Mills of Massachusetts as the triumph of Yankee
ingenuity over the threat of European industrial squalor. Americans
embraced the possibilities of mechanization, and in the Northeast
mass production slowly replaced traditional cottage industries. Commercial cities utilized more efficient steam-powered machinery to run
a growing number of factories. Consequently, although American
industrialization would not unfold until after the 1860s, antebellum
America felt the impact of changing modes of production on social
life.

The decline of New England agriculture and the increase in man-
ufacturing produced a decrease in the number of small merchants
and artisans. After the Civil War, goods which normally would have
been hand-produced by family members or local artisans appeared
ready-made on the market. As the agricultural and artisan classes
declined, the number of men involved in commercial exchange increased. Mass production necessitated the activities of factory man-
agers, production middlemen, and clerks, not to mention able bodies
to run the factories. The lure of industrial and commercial life, the
decline of arable New England farmland, and the increase in the
number of landless families combined to alter the economic and social
base of the eastern seaboard.

The change from an agrarian life-style to an industrial one was
gradual. In the early stages of industrialization whole families went to
work in factories. The father negotiated with the company for wages,
set the family work pace, and attempted to integrate family time with
industrial time. Such family strategies only forestalled the inevitable
separation of the workplace from the home, the development of a
wage-earning system, and the establishment of an impersonal labor
economy. For the factory worker, as well as for the clerk or manager,
the time clock became a symbol of a style of work which sought
uniformity rather than individuality, efficiency rather than self-fulfillment, and separation rather than integration. The advent of industrialization and the creation of a wage-labor economy moved the focus
of industry from the home to the marketplace.[16]

Important social changes accompanied the alteration of economic
production. For working men the breakdown of traditional networks

left them dependent on their individual skills. Informal networks of
kin or fellow workers were replaced by the impersonal regulations
and relationships of the workplace. Job specialization and the general
professionalization of American society limited the variety of tasks
which men could perform. As men left their homes they became
distanced from domestic activities. The everyday workings of the
home—child rearing, food production and preparation, personal
health care—seemed worlds apart from male activities.[17]

Significant changes also affected women in the family. The mecha-
nized production of household goods reduced the amount of time
women spent on housework—making soap, weaving, sewing clothes,
making shoes, butchering meat, laundering. Purchasing prepared
goods made the family more dependent on the father's wages than on
the mother's productive capabilities. For the middle-class woman the
availability of cheap household help allowed her to shift some of her
chores to a hired girl. Although many families employed one young
girl, usually a recent immigrant, only the wealthy could afford to hire
a domestic staff.[18]

Women who worked outside of the home found that the nineteenth-century specialization of skills often barred them from participating in new industrial occupations and middle-class careers. The
midwife and female healer of the eighteenth century were prohibited
from attending the newly formed medical schools. Women as well as
men were affected by the decline in the number of artisans and small
merchants. According to Mary Ryan's study of the commercial centers
of upstate New York, 28 percent of the women in the garment industry were native-born white women. Many of those worked to finance
the education of their sons and brothers. For women who entered the
factories, industrial activities were as alienating to them as to the
men.[19]

As men and women drifted farther apart in the workplace, the
social roles of the sexes became more distinct. The "cult of true
womanhood," based on the Victorian understanding of woman as the
model of purity, piety, and domesticity, separated women from men
and their world. Women who hoped to accomplish "masculine" goals
such as education or a career were limited by social expectations of
their feminine nature; and men were separated from domestic activities because of their different "character." Although men might
continue to consider themselves patriarchs of the home, they seemed
unable to exercise that authority. The period of the Puritan father
overseeing the family economy with the support of wife, children,
and apprentices had become a distant memory. Now it was the mother

"The mother sways the dominion of the heart, the father that of
the Intellect." Samuel Goodrich, *Fireside Education,* frontispiece.

who, according to cultural norms, would be expected to nurture the
family.[20]

The nineteenth century also saw the decline of the large American
family. In 1800 the average number of children born to a woman
before she reached menopause was 7.04. By mid-century, this number
dropped by 23 percent to 5.42, and by the end of the century, to 3.56.
Many families increased the number of residents in their homes by
housing relatives or boarders, but among white, socially mobile families the domestic goal was not the quantity of children produced but
the quality. Smaller families, the closing off of the workplace from
middle-class white women, and the solidification of the concept of
woman's real "nature" contributed to equating the home with
women.[21]

Industrialization brought about important changes in the structure
of the house itself and availability of household goods. The production of the power saw in the 1820s and the turning lathe and ripsaw in

the late 1830s facilitated the milling of wood for structural and decorative domestic uses. "Balloon framing" (the construction of an interior, supportive wooden framework) replaced more expensive and labor-consuming ways of house building. The price of carpets came within reach of the middle class with the invention of power looms in 1848. Although fireplaces continued to be a common item in the Victorian home, by 1850 furnaces were also affordable. Indoor plumbing became more popular, but by 1855 New York City with a population of 629,904 still had only 1,361 bathtubs and 10,384 water closets.[22]

Improvements in transportation enhanced technological innovation and industrialization. The Erie Canal connected the Hudson River and New York City with the Great Lakes in 1825, prompting the growth of cities in the Ohio Valley and western New England. Railroads followed immediately behind the canal systems. In 1830 there were only 23 miles of American railroads, but by 1870 the mileage had jumped to 52,922. The horse-drawn streetcar improved local transportation. Even though it plugged along at only five or six miles per hour in 1850, the 500 miles of streetcar line enabled some workers to commute between a suburban home and a city workplace. By 1880 streetcar lines had grown to 4,060 miles, and the suburb had become an important part of the American landscape as well as a goal for many families.

Because of technological and transportational innovation, consumer goods dropped significantly in cost. In 1815 cotton fabric cost eighteen cents per yard, but by 1860 its price had fallen to only two cents per yard. Domestic furnishings such as bookcases, clocks, and overstuffed chairs, which only the wealthy could afford at the beginning of the century, had become common items in middle-class homes by 1880. Now that household goods were more plentiful, many nineteenth-century popular publications—from *Godey's Lady's Book* to *Scientific American*—flourished as advisors on how to use the new goods effectively.[23]

The rise in the middle-class standard of living brought on by industrialization, technological innovation, and improvements in transportation faltered during periodic economic depressions. A major depression in 1837 lasted until 1843; another occurred soon after in 1848. Other depressions occurred between 1853 and 1854 and again between 1857 and 1859. In the latter half of the century almost every ten years—in 1873, 1883, and 1893—the nation's economy plummeted. Families of both the laboring and the middle classes faced unemployment, wage reduction, and loss of material wealth. The boom-and-bust economy provided an unstable backdrop for a society undergoing rapid social change.

The social and economic changes which began before the Civil War escalated even faster during the second half of the century. Between 1860 and 1920 the population more than tripled, and the volume of manufactured goods increased somewhere between twelve- and four-teenfold. Industrialization, urbanization, immigration, and tech-nological innovation would not slow down until well into the twentieth century. By 1900, although the "joys" of a middle-class home were available to more Americans, the social and psychological pitfalls of domesticity were pointed out by a vocal group of feminists and social reformers. The cost of middle-class domesticity had been a high one, but few Americans, even those most at the mercy of nineteenth-century capitalism, would be willing to turn away from the dream of a "proper" home and family.

The steady rise of employment possibilities in the mid-nineteenth-century city offered a realistic alternative to the landless son or daugh-ter of New England farmers. Once in the cities, though, the Yankee farmer found stiff competition for jobs. The first wave of immigration had begun by the 1830s, and by 1920 4.7 million Irish had come to the Land of Opportunity. Although the percentage of Irish arriving in relationship to other immigrant groups decreased after the potato-blight famine years of mid-century, the number of Irish in the United States would remain high. From 1840 to 1860 almost 1.7 million Irish came to America. The number of immigrating Irish decreased to a little over one million during the last decade of the nineteenth cen-tury, while the total population of Irish Americans increased from around one million in 1850 to almost five million by 1900.

In spite of the immigrant's dream of a better life in America, life in the New World held little joy for most Irish. Those who stayed in the major east-coast cities faced lives riddled with discrimination, Protes-tant hostility, slum housing, and poverty. According to Patrick Bless-ing, "the Irish were the only immigrant group whose occupational mobility during the late 19th century appeared almost as small as that of American Blacks." Their infant mortality rate was higher than any other early immigrant group's, and as late as the twentieth century even higher than Ireland's. Fleeing poverty and oppression in Ireland, many confronted a similar fate in the United States.[24]

Irish families, like their Protestant neighbors, were affected by changes in American social and economic structures. Eighty percent of the Irish who came to the United States from 1850 to 1920 were

rural, unskilled farmers. They did not own their land but rented it
from absentee landlords. Few had ever worked in a city or even visited
one. Family patterns in Ireland conformed to this social reality: because of the scarcity of land people married late, if at all. Most of the
immigrants arrived unmarried and hoped to send money back to
their families. As in Ireland, late marriages were the norm in the New
World. Many men and women remained unmarried in America, but
those who did marry and bear children did so with enthusiasm. By
1910 the Irish were second only to the French Canadians in their rate
of reproduction.[25]

The prevalence of permanent celibacy in Ireland encouraged the
development of a sex-segregated social structure. Men who waited for
marriage met together at pubs, fairs, or in the fields to drink and
share stories, while women usually gathered within the confines of
relatives' homes. In most cases this same-sex bonding continued after
marriage, men finding more comfort and support among their male
drinking companions and women with their female relatives. Same-
sex bonding increased the fear of women men held, and vice versa.
Sexuality appeared dangerous because of its mysterious and alienating characteristics. Irish women and men separated themselves from
one another not because of an intellectual understanding of the
qualities of their respective "natures" but because of traditional behavior patterns.[26]

Some traditional social patterns disintegrated in the new American
society, while others remained strong. The marriage rate increased,
but same-sex bonding remained. Old ways survived partially because
the Irish tended to marry other Irish (a trend which only broke down
after the third generation) and live near each other. Catholic domestic
reformers, who sought to promote the middle-class nuclear family,
attacked vigorously the Irish tavern, not only because of their fear of
alcoholism but because it took men away from the home. The tavern
provided space for male friendship and contradicted the middle-class
norm of husband-wife companionship in marriage.

Single women arrived in America at the same rate as men, coming
in even greater numbers during several years. Daughters, according
to historian Carol Groneman, may have been more reliable in their
remittance of wages back to the family in Ireland and so were permitted to leave. Women worked primarily as domestic servants and in the
needle trades. In New York City alone over twenty-five percent of the
Irish working population were domestic servants. Pay for both trades
was abysmally low. In 1853 a New York seamstress was paid eight cents
to make a shirt, sewing some three a day. Domestics fared better

because employers supplied room and board along with a salary of four to eight dollars a month. Once women married they left outside jobs, preferring to send their children to work if necessary and to take in boarders. Groneman concluded that even "when forced by necessity to work, they did so in ways which would reinforce, rather than disrupt, their traditional familial values." Catholic advice literature, although recognizing the reality of female labor, assumed that it was temporary.[27]

Second-generation Irish men and women fared somewhat better in the New World. By 1900, five percent of second-generation Irish males were in the professions. Many had been ordained, thus entering the middle class. Irish women, who at mid-century worked as domestics, composed ten percent of all female teachers born of immigrant parents by 1900. Those who moved west moved upward more quickly. In 1880, 20 percent of the Irish in San Francisco held white-collar jobs; only 13 percent held similar jobs in New York. While many of the newly arrived Irish stayed in the "shanty" towns of the East, other Irish moved out into the suburbs, earning the title of "lace-curtain Irish." These Irish—as policemen, politicians, priests, and teachers—would help the "new immigrants" adapt to American ways during the last decades of the century.[28]

Unlike most other immigrants the Irish brought with them one skill which served them well in the New World. Approximately seventy-five percent of all Irish immigrants in 1850 could read and write English. By 1910 this number had climbed to ninety-seven percent. Literacy and fluency in English permitted the Irish access to newspapers, novels, poetry, and magazines, which not only brought news and stories about the Old World but also helped clarify their position in the New. Gaelic, the indigenous Irish language, had been nearly destroyed by the British and the famine. The two million Gaelic speakers in Ireland in 1822 had dwindled to only 164,000 by 1861.[29]

Consequently, although the majority of the Irish remained in the working classes, they were able at least to read about the "other" America. Advertising, especially in Catholic newspapers, was addressed not only to those who could afford to purchase the goods immediately, but also to those who could read about the goods and perhaps one day purchase them. Although the numbers of middle-class Irish Catholics were small, access to middle-class ideology was readily available. For those Irish who hoped to move out of the lower classes, domestic writings supplied strategies for envisioning a new life.

The major institution within Irish-American society serving to maintain Old World traditions while encouraging accommodation to American life was the Catholic church. In 1822, on the eve of foreign immigration, there were only 163,500 Catholics in America, a mere five percent of the total population; by mid-century their numbers had grown dramatically.

American Catholicism: 1840–1900

The early years of Catholicism in the United States did not prepare the church for the experience of immigration. Although Catholics had settled on the eastern seaboard as early as 1634, they made up only a small part of the population. Catholics in the Spanish western territories had no contact with their coreligionists on the East Coast. Hostility toward Catholics during the colonial period fluctuated with attitudes in Britain. Before 1830, Catholics were typically of Anglo-American or French ancestry and integrated into the American social system. A few could trace their families back to such notable Americans as the Carrolls or Calverts.

German Catholics were the first to arrive in the 1830s; a decade later came the Irish. By 1850 Catholics totaled 1.75 million, becoming the "largest religious communion" in the United States. Ten years later their population doubled. Up until 1900 the greatest percentage of Catholics in the United States had Irish roots. Although their style of religious observance differed from "native" Catholicism and from that of the German immigrants, the Irish soon controlled both the Catholic American clergy and the parish.

The Irish of the mid-nineteenth century were not the faithfully devoted churchgoers we now think them to be. According to historian Jay Dolan, in 1860 only about 40 percent of Irish New Yorkers attended Mass on Sunday. Many Irish, to the consternation of their priests, maintained folkways which seemed more pagan than Christian. The basic tenets of Catholicism were unknown to the Irish peasant who landed in the New World. This ignorance, combined with a limited number of churches, an overworked clergy, and the disorientation of marginal living, discouraged active church participation.[30]

Recognizing the problems which Catholicism faced in Ireland and in the Irish communities in England and America, Irish bishops created what Emmett Larkin termed a "devotional revolution." They made great efforts to educate the Irish, to provide strong episcopal leadership, and to increase the number of clergy and religious. Irish men and women who found their religious sentiments heightened joined the priest- and sisterhoods in record numbers. The devotional revolution carried over to America as priests, nuns, and laypeople came to the New World. Irish American religious leaders sought to organize a strong parish center and to involve the laity in a variety of spiritual and social activities. The drama and pageantry of the church service increased, as did the role of the parish in dispensing charity, jobs, and comfort.[31]

The task of reviving the immigrants' faith was a difficult one, although it was aided by American migration. Separated from family and homeland, the immigrant looked to the church as a familiar and trusted institution. Urban life in America cut the Irish off from traditional rural folkways. Priestly magic, pilgrimages to holy wells, and belief in fairies seemed out of place in the hovels of New York and Boston. The clergy worked hard to replace those beliefs with the tenets of Tridentine Catholicism—an organized, Rome-centered religious community which emphasized the parish, the Mass, and the fulfillment of religious duties.

Protestant antagonism toward American Catholics also aided in the solidification of religious activities. If in fact "the blood of the martyrs is the seed of the Church," then the success of Catholicism at the end of the century must be partially due to its continual harassment during the first half. The association of Irish Catholicism with crime, pagan practices, poverty, and drunkenness became a battle cry for those who sought to rid the nation of immigrants and proclaim it a Protestant state. Anti-Catholic riots broke out in several eastern cities. Churches and convents were burned, and Irish Catholics met Protestant hostility with equal distrust and hatred.

At first glance anti-Catholic sentiments seem to have little to do with domestic religion. However, some theologians who spoke for the spiritual importance of the Protestant family also promoted the creation of a pure "American" nation. Horace Bushnell, noted for his support of the family as a means of Christian nurture, explained in 1847 that "our first danger is barbarism [the influx of foreigners], Romanism is next." Historians credit Lyman Beecher, the father of Catharine Beecher and Harriet Beecher Stowe, with inciting the burning of an Ursuline convent in 1834. Anti-Catholic books, such as Maria Monk's *Awful Disclosures of the Hotel-Dieu Nunnery in Montreal*, wove stories of infanticide, sexual promiscuity, and broken homes. Single women and men (nuns and priests) who were not within the confines of family were especially suspect of endangering American society.[32]

At the same time that anti-Catholic sentiments raged, a new appreciation of ritual drama appeared among Protestants. The Oxford Movement, which began in England and spread to the New World, not only resurrected ritually oriented Protestantism but also led the way for increased conversion to Catholicism. Several converts became commentators on domesticity. The novelist Anna Dorsey became a Catholic in 1840; and Orestes Brownson, who commented on the "feminization" of American religion, entered the same church in 1844.[33]

By 1880 Irish American Catholics would face the presence of other ethnic groups who expressed their spirituality through a variety of languages and customs. By that time, however, the Irish bishops had achieved tight control over the institutional church. In 1886, half of the bishops in America were of Irish descent. The Irish American church had embraced Tridentine Catholicism, often to the point of being legalistic, dominated by their bishops and clergy, and giving unquestionable loyalty to Roman authority. Flourishing lay organizations (sodalities, literary societies, temperance leagues) and popular devotions (Forty Hours, novenas, missions) had wedded the people to the church structure. The 1884 Baltimore Council cemented this connection even further by requiring every parish to have its own parochial school and all Catholic parents to send their children to it. From 1880 to 1910, the number of students in the Catholic schools would triple.

Outside of America, events in world Catholicism intensified lay devotion. Four years after the proclamation of the dogma of the Immaculate Conception in 1854, the Virgin Mary was reported to have appeared to a young girl in Lourdes, France. In 1879, Mary, St. Joseph, and St. John were seen on the wall of the parish church in Knock, County Mayo, Ireland. These reported apparitions increased Marian devotions, especially by women who related to the nurturing and healing aspects of the Blessed Mother. Under Leo XIII, whose papal rule spanned the period 1878–1903, devotion to the rosary increased. Each October for many years the pope penned encyclicals which emphasized the spiritual power of the rosary. In his 1896 letter *Fidentem piumque animum* the Pope encouraged whole families to say the rosary together. Leo XIII vitalized devotion to St. Joseph in *Quamquam pluries* (1889), and in 1893 he designated indulgences available to those who prayed in front of the image of the Holy Family.

Leo XIII also commented directly on the role of the family in society. Although his predecessor, Pius IX, had first mentioned the family in the 1864 encyclical *Quanta cura,* Leo XIII more than any other pope before him linked the safety of the family to the safety of the world. Beginning in 1878 with *Inscrutabili,* and then in 1880 *(Arcanum),* 1890 *(Sapientiae christianae),* and 1891 *(Rerum novarum),* he denounced the trends of divorce, family limitation, and state influence in child rearing. Under Leo XIII, for the first time, the family became the guardian of purity of both society and Christianity.

The concern for the family and the condemnation of many modern social trends filtered down from Rome to the American parishes. It could be seen in popular theology and piety, occurring at the same time that the Irish American family was inching into the middle class. By the end of the century, Irish Catholic families—who sent their children to parochial school, financed the new church, and now prayed at home—had become the Catholic shield in the fight against encroaching modernism.

American Protestantism: 1840–1900

The state of Protestantism during the Victorian period also exemplified a high degree of flux and transformation. The separation of church and state was completed in 1833, when Massachusetts broke connections with the Congregational church. Disestablishment forced American Protestants to face not only the proliferation of denominations but also the existence of Catholics, Jews, Deists, and other "heathens." Some theologians did embrace the possibilities of a new pluralistic republic, but most begrudgingly acknowledged the death of the Puritan holy experiment and rushed to fill the vacuum with an evangelical "Protestant consensus."[34]

Some hoped that the revivals, expecially the western revivals of Charles Finney in the 1830s and 1840s, would serve to invigorate the splintered Protestant denominations. Membership did increase— Presbyterian membership alone grew from 18,000 in 1807 to 248,000 in 1834—but ironically divided the churches even more. Enthusiastic new members found the churches which they joined understaffed, fragmented by theological disputes, and unsure of their role in the new republic. Religious fervor had somehow to be integrated into the established Protestant structure.[35] By the mid-1840s the revivals had declined and new forms of religious expression were being sought.

Accompanying the revival spirit came a rise in evangelical benevolent societies. As voluntary associations of men and women from various denominations, the members came together with specific goals in mind: the distribution of Bibles, the support of domestic and foreign missionaries, the promotion of temperance, the condemnation of slavery. Often led by laymen and supported by women, these societies asserted the unity of piety, morality, and civilization. They were convinced that their nondenominational approach to social and spiritual problems would work toward the perfectibility of the nation. Maternal associations, the Sunday School movement, and literature geared to the improvement of the Christian home were all part of the Protestant nonsectarian but evangelical trend.

While nondenominational benevolent societies believed that the progress of the nation was tied to the improvement of individual Christians, other Protestants insisted that fundamental changes in society would occur only by inaugurating God's reign on earth. Utopian communities sought to create small theocracies where the righteous Christian could prepare for the coming millennium. Many mid-century utopians created alternatives to the emergent industrial system by developing communal farming economies. The traditional family was seen as problematic—the Shakers replaced it with a celibate family structure, the Mormons with polygamy, and the Oneida Perfectionists with "complex marriages."

Evangelical Protestants vigorously condemned the utopian experiments, but the concept of creating an ideal society on earth was widespread. Many Protestants expressed millennial hopes and sought to establish an American Christian nation to prepare for the Second Coming. By the latter part of the century, theologians hoped not for the end of the world but for a better one here and now. The Social Gospel movement of Walter Rauschenbusch and Washington Gladden "had a vision of a vastly better human society" and took seriously the complexity of industrialization. According to Robert Handy, though, it was still "the old vision of a religious nation socialized."[36]

Another important influence on the development of Protestant home religion utilized the emotion of the revivals, but had a decidedly European flavor. During the 1830s and 1840s the Lutheran, Reformed, Presbyterian, and Anglican churches underwent what has been termed "churchly" resurgences. Responding to German and English idealism and romanticism, they started to take a more intense interest in past church history and tradition. Ritual and sacramental activities increased. American Episcopalians, influenced by the Oxford Movement in England, supported the construction of Gothic-style cathedrals. Creeds, ecclesiastical leadership, and emphasis on the authority of the institutional church combined to challenge the subjective religiosity encouraged by revivalism, while promoting personal commitment to the tradition.[37]

The impact of churchly resurgence not only encouraged the placement of religious articles in the home, the use of Gothic designs in furniture and housing, and a renewed appreciation of rituals but also motivated many conversions. Several prominent writers on domesticity converted to Episcopalianism after many years of family conflict and personal searching. Sarah Hale, Lydia Sigourney, Catharine Beecher, Harriet Beecher Stowe, and Elizabeth Stuart Phelps eventually found the Episcopal church more conducive to their own personal philosophies than the Reformed tradition.

New England Transcendentalism and the development of "liberal theology" in Congregational and Presbyterian circles also rejected the traditional Calvinist viewpoint. Under the influence of European thinkers such as Friedrich Schleiermacher, Samuel Coleridge, and Thomas Carlyle, American theologians broke with the Calvinist perception of the distant, angry, authoritarian God. As early as 1828 the New Haven theologian Nathaniel Taylor threatened the Calvinist concept of human depravity by asserting that "the sinfulness of the human race does not pertain to human nature as such." The liberal theologian's God was a God of love—intimate, immanent, and concerned about human welfare. Accordingly, feeling, intuition, and emotion were the qualities needed to experience the sacred.[38]

The development of liberal theology in the nineteenth century combined with the cult of domesticity to create what Barbara Welter and Ann Douglas term the "feminization of American religion." As early as the eighteenth century, women outnumbered men in New England congregations. The Puritan association of women with Eve ceased as women asserted their presence in the church. So central were religious concerns to the works of women writers that Douglas claims that female literature replaced traditional male theology as the prime vehicle for transmitting religious values. Women ran (although they did not always head) benevolent societies. In utopian and new religions women achieved a new ascendance. Shaker elderesses received messages from their founder, Ann Lee; Mormons and Christian Scientists worshipped a Mother/Father God; and the Seventh-Day Adventists followed a female prophet. Women preachers, missionaries, and eventually even ministers threatened the male hierarchy of the Protestant churches.[39]

The most influential mainstream Protestant theologian to adopt a "feminine" attitude toward Christianity was Horace Bushnell. In 1847 Bushnell wrote "Discourses on Christian Nurture," which explained how the religion of the heart could be cultivated in the home. Since people were not by nature depraved, he concluded that they could learn how to lead a good and Christian life. The child could learn to love "what is good from his earliest years." "Religion," Bushnell explained, "never thoroughly penetrates life, till it becomes domestic." If children were properly reared in a Christian family, they would not need a conversion experience as adults to confirm their salvation. Consequently the parents, especially the mother, were obligated to create not only a healthful but a spiritual environment for their children.[40]

That the proper Christian home worked toward the salvation of the family was a concept as crucial to Victorian society as it was to Puritan New England. Even the voice of the Social Gospel movement, Walter Rauschenbusch, would write that "the health of society rests on the welfare of the home." That both the family and the church had their roles in the salvation process was an old Protestant conviction, but as the nature of salvation changed so would the character of home religion. Under the impact of industrialization, consumerism, and the growth of urban centers, the quality of domestic Protestantism took on a particularly Victorian form.[41]

[2]

Domestic Architecture
and the Protestant Spirit

The development of an ideology of domestic architecture accompanied the economic, social, and religious changes of the early Victorian period. By examining the architectural philosophy and building designs of mid-nineteenth-century housing reformers, we can see how a particular moral and spiritual order was literally "built," if not with wood, then with words. Architectural critics, of course, held no official position in the Protestant church, yet they functioned as important arbitrators of social values and promoters of an evolving Protestant perspective. As a "secular" body they were crucial in asserting the equation of Protestantism with Christianity, Christianity with civilization, and civilization with America. These architectural critics, along with popular ministers and women novelists, came to create the domestic spirit which all Americans, irrespective of ethnicity or religion, would have to acknowledge.

The Ideology of Domestic Architecture

Before the 1840s, literature on domestic architecture by American authors was confined to building manuals, such as Asher Benjamin's *The Country Builder's Assistant,* published in 1797. Building manuals focused on the bare essentials of house construction, geared primarily for carpenters. Between 1800 and 1840, 20 such pattern books were published in the United States, mostly reprints of European editions. Unlike Europe, America had no developed architectural profession, and only the wealthy could afford to have their homes specially designed.[1]

In the late 1840s a new type of architectural design book was born and immediately became popular. Their number increased rapidly, 60 being published between 1840 and 1860. The new pattern books departed from the purely mechanical and functional by presenting the public with a domestic philosophy and aesthetic. Along with floor plans, house models, and interior designs, the writers included the theories behind their patterns.[2]

These books were not written by men we might now consider architects—those who derive their primary source of income from designing and overseeing the construction of buildings—but by men of mixed background and artistic training. Andrew Jackson Downing began as a horticulturalist, Orson Fowler was a phrenologist, and even the influential John Ruskin never oversaw the realization of one of his drawings. In general, pattern-book writers and critics like Ruskin were more interested in housing design and advice than in the details of actual building.

Although men almost exclusively wrote the pattern books, both men and women read them. Andrew Jackson Downing in *The Architecture of Country Houses* apologized to his "fair readers" for "the seeming intrusion" on their domain of interior decorating as he tried to "point out the shoals" on which some women have foundered because of lack of "native perception" of fashion and taste. In 1847 the influential *Godey's Lady's Book and Lady's Magazine* began to publish patterns of "model cottages" for its female readership. It published 450 house designs between 1847 and 1892, many designed specifically for the magazine. Other women's magazines also published house plans, but only *Godey's* consistently attempted to familiarize women with the details of domestic architecture.[3]

American architects brought to the public the general theories of European architects, tempered with current views on domesticity. Of these Europeans, perhaps John Ruskin was the most influential. He believed that "all architecture proposes an effect on the human mind, not merely a service to the human frame," and that "right states" and "moral feelings" produced good architecture. Architecture, for Ruskin, had an important role in the creation of a moral and productive society.[4]

The dialectic that good architecture produced good people and good people produced good architecture was readily adopted by American architects. "There is so intimate a connection between taste and morals, aesthetics and Christianity," William Ranlett wrote in 1847, "that they, in each instance, mutually modify each other." Oliver Smith went so far as to say that "nothing has more to do with the

The original caption for this engraving reads: "Poverty, Squalor,
Intemperance and Crime. The neighborhood here shown is a
representation and true type of hundreds of localities which exist
all over the face of this fair land. The scene tells its own story a
tale of brutal passion, poverty, base desires, wretchedness and
crime." Engraving (1873), reprinted in John Maass, *The Victorian
Home in America* (New York: Hawthorn Books, Inc. 1972), p. 15.

morals, the civilization, and refinement of a nation, than its prevailing
architecture." For the Victorian domestic architect, art could not exist
"for art's sake," because it was inextricably bound to society and
morality. Architecture served as both a mode of communication and a
reforming enterprise.[5]

Consequently, housing designs performed two duties: they expressed the character of the family, and they shaped that character. If
moral men constructed moral architecture then good families preferred good house designs. Those who are "spirited, ambitious, and
enterprising, whose aspirations are lofty, and minds high-toned, select
eminences, and build high houses." The "coarse and vicious," on the
other hand, content themselves with "rude haunts, as barren of beauty
as their own hearts of virtue."[6]

Not only did a house communicate something of the morality of its
inhabitants, it also demonstrated the character of the family. For

Andrew Downing, the character of the family meant the character of the father—the "common sense man" preferred "a symmetrical, regular house"; the man of sentiment sought a "house in whose aspect there is something to love," a house with nooks, cozy rooms, and shadowy corners. Likewise, "men whose ambition and energy give them no peace" required a picturesque villa with "high roofs, steep gables, unsymmetrical and capricious forms." A man's home translated his individual personality into a material statement.[7]

For Downing, a man's house also communicated the class in which he belonged. Downing's division of houses into cottages, farm houses, and villas became standard categories for many architects. Cottages, occupied by "industrious and intelligent mechanics and working men, the bone and sinew of the land," should "facilitate the simple manner of living." For those involved in agriculture, their homes should demonstrate "breadth rather than height; a certain rustic plainness" which denoted "a class more occupied with the practical and useful than the elegant arts of life." Likewise for those "of competence or wealth sufficient to build and maintain it with some taste and elegance," a villa or country house exemplified "the most refined home of America—the home of its most leisurely and educated class of citizens."[8]

An essential part of "the True in architecture" was its ability to communicate the class of the inhabitants. Downing insisted that to over decorate a simple cottage, such as by adding highly carved bargeboards, always "degrades, rather than elevates, the beauty of the cottage." Each type of housing, like each type of resident, had its own "peculiar beauty," and one should avoid attempting "to give the modest little cottage the ambitious air of the ornate villa."[9]

Through the "possession of lovely gardens and fruitful orchards" Downing believed that the "improvement of human nature" of all classes could occur. In *Village and Farm Cottages*, written by Cleaveland and Backus in 1856, the authors stated that the home was "an important moral influence; one of the means by which men are to be transferred from the government of Sense and Passion, to that of Reason and the Affections." For the pattern-book writers the design of the home was crucial to the production of good citizens.[10]

What were the values which a good home could encourage? The "solitude and freedom of the family home in the country" preserved the "purity of the nation" and invigorated "its intellectual powers." The love of "one's own house and fireside, of garden, tree," rendered "the homes of the people not only nurseries of filial and fraternal affection, but the earliest and best schools of obedience and duty, of patriotism and piety." The family as "the foundation, the beginning of all society," connected "the individual with the community at large," while teaching that "we are mutually dependent and reciprocally responsible." The proper home—as a combination of family and house—encouraged all of the Victorian values: morality, piety, patriotism, order, stability, affection, intellectuality, education, purity, refinement, and discipline.[11]

While most writers avoided describing exactly how home design influenced the family, Orson Fowler presented an explanation: if an "unhandy house" perpetually irritated mothers it would "sour the tempers of their children, even BEFORE BIRTH, thus rendering the whole family bad-dispositioned BY NATURE, whereas a convenient one would have rendered them constitutionally amiable and good." Similarly, for Oliver Smith "our minds and morals are subject to constant influence and modification, gradual yet lasting, by the inanimate walls with which we are surrounded." Both authors were saying that the *physical* construction of the home shapes the "minds and morals" of the family.[12]

The writers of house-pattern books hoped their their designs would be used to construct future American homes. Individual home ownership, they believed, was now within the reach of most Americans. It was the "republican equality of our institutions," William Ranlett wrote, which "offers to all, the opportunity of being the proprietors of their own home." Cleaveland and Backus echoed this sentiment: "a modest home, which he may call his own, is beyond the reach of no capable and industrious man." Orson Fowler (also a food reformer) insisted that since home ownership should be placed above everything else, a family might want to subsist on a diet of boiled wheat and apples in order to save for their important purchase.[13]

Andrew Downing was particularly concerned that the newly rich of America not fall into the trap of hoarding their wealth in palatial estates and then warping "the life and manners of [their] children." True American homes "built by no robbery of the property of another class, maintained by no infringement of a brother's rights" would "minister to all the wants, necessities, and luxuries of a republican." The individual, privately-owned home stood as a fortress against the threats of economic communalism proposed by Fourier by asserting the inherent value of domestic independence.[14]

One important way of securing this domestic independence was by building the family home in the country—not the howling wilderness, but the suburbs. Cleaveland and Backus informed their middle-incomed readers that by using the railroad or steamboat they no longer had to live where they worked. They might have to trade "some associations and friendships, some privileges . . . of church and school, some amusements. . . . But mark what compensation! You have gained a *home*—that which you never truly have in the hired city lodging." In the country the family would be far away from "the dangers and temptations, the unnatural excitements and morbid stimulants, the thousand baits and haunts of vice, with which the city abounds." And, "amid the serenity and peace of sylvan scenes, surrounded by the perennial freshness of nature," mused Downing, "we should look for the happiest social and moral development of our people."[15]

If the quality of one's home determined not only the quality of the family, but the quality of the nation, then the architect's responsibilities were considerable. Gervase Wheeler called his designs "sermons in stone" and understood the architect as having "a great and noble privilege in his power to preach by his works lessons of refinement, harmony, and beauty." House designers were public benefactors who corrected "vicious or improper development of public taste." They sought the uplifting of their architectural profession since it was "upon their judgment, skill, good taste, and knowledge of architecture, [that we depend] for the beauty, grace, and convenience of that dearest spot on earth, the center and sanctuary of our social sympathies—HOME."[16]

The Ideal Victorian House

The Victorian "architects" set out to design homes which embodied the values of domesticity, and in doing so altered the appearance of American architecture. Pattern-book authors set up an ideal of how housing should look, and home owners constructed their homes with that ideal in mind. Obviously not all Victorian homes exemplified the ideals of the architects, but the values which the architects promoted became more and more visible in constructed homes.

A major innovation of the mid-nineteenth century was the promotion among a growing middle class of homes with private, specialized, domestic space. In colonial America all but the very wealthy divided their homes into only one or two rooms. Privacy was neither valued nor available. Housing reformers spread the most aristocratic European predilection for specialized space among the less wealthy. For the architectural critic, each room had its unique purpose and should be separate from other rooms. Toward the end of the century, as household goods became less expensive and more people owned their homes, multiple rooms became common and indicated the "character" of the family. Families now could take seriously the specialists' recommendations.

For the low-income worker, pattern-book writers encouraged simplicity, and divided their interior space into a living room area, kitchen, and bedrooms. As one rose in social rank and financial stability, interior layout and design became more complicated. The living room was broken into a formal parlor for receiving guests, an informal family sitting room, a library for father, and a boudoir for mother. A kitchen, scullery, serving room, pantry, coal pit, china closet, larder, store room, and wood porch now served where a sole kitchen had previously. Rooms were needed for the few servants that the household employed—a housekeeper's room and butler's pantry on the first floor, servants' bedrooms in the attic.

On the upper floors, the two or three bedrooms of a simple cottage might expand into a nursery for the children, special guest rooms, dressing rooms for men and women where "the servant who lights the fire in the morning is not obliged to enter the bedroom," water closets, bathing rooms, and, in the case of Downing's "Lake or River Villa," nine bedrooms. The lower and upper floors would be connected by staircases carefully placed to preserve the privacy of the individuals within the family. Sliding doors on the first floor and hinged doors on the bedrooms separated each space. Add a greenhouse, laundry, verandas, porches and piazzas and you have a home where "the social virtues are more honestly practiced."[17]

Few Victorian homes could boast so many rooms, but the specialization of rooms was firmly established. Men and women had their own areas. Adults were separated from children, just as private family space was separated from public space. Rooms were decorated to point out their purpose— lady's boudoir with chintz and delicate colors, a library with dark oak and leather chairs, and a drawing-room with "more beauty and elegance than any other apartment in the house." Orson Fowler, in his sixty-room octagonal house, had rooms designed specifically as children's playroom, dancing rooms, and a gym for women. For the child who wandered into her father's study or the husband who entered the wife's boudoir the specialized rooms were alien territory.[18]

Areas such as the porch or veranda created a spatial transition which separated the private family world from the public world of the street. Unlike Europeans who used walls to delineate public from domestic space, Victorian Americans preferred spacious lawns and porches. Although seclusion and privacy were important, Frank J.

Scott in *The Art of Beautifying the Home Grounds* insisted that the house should be able to be seen from the sidewalk. Iron or wire fences and low bushes were preferred to heavy fencing and tall hedging. Scott encouraged suburban residents to respect the privacy of their neighbors not by constructing physical barriers, but by teaching their children to stay in their own yard and making sure animals were well-tended. Through instilling a sense of privacy in the family members and by subtle barriers such as the porch, the family asserted its independence while remaining a "good neighbor."[19]

The library and parlor were essential in conveying to the visitor the respectability and status of the family. Because the home had important communicative roles, to present the proper *image* to guests, visitors, and business associates was crucial. A well-stocked library and

The original caption for this engraving reads: "The Neighborhood Where People Live In Harmony. This illustration represents a neighborhood where the people evidently do unto others as they wish others to do unto them. They trust each other. The barriers between them are removed. No animal is allowed to do injury. Enjoying peace and beauty they evidently desire that the neighbor shall share the same. This cooperation, kindness and regard for all, given the beauty, the harmony, the peace, and the evident contentment which are here presented." Engraving (c.1870), reprinted in John Maass, *The Gingerbread Age* (New York: Rinehart and Co., 1957), p. 13.

a tasteful, orderly parlor showed the outsider that the family had education and character, even if the rooms were seldom used. As with the placement of the house in a yard which could be seen from the street, the impression the house made on the outside was important. It would be the architect's responsibility to design a house sufficiently private and yet active in making its statement of character to the public world.[20]

Most pattern-book writers conceived of the home as a refuge from the work-world of the city. They ignored the designs of kitchens, assumed housekeeping would be done by servants, and even restricted gardening to picking flowers rather than raising food. Servants were separated from the family, work space from living space. The lawn, as a totally unproductive expanse, succinctly communicated the leisurely nature of the home. The home was to be a place of relaxation, recreation, and reflection. The notable exception was the writing of Catharine Beecher, who along with her sister Harriet Beecher Stowe showed the home as a working place for women. Unlike the male pattern-book writers who dominated the architectural scene, Beecher and Stowe believed that only by making the home efficient could domestic reform be accomplished.

The Gothic Revival

From 1840 to 1870 a style of architecture appeared in America which dramatically demonstrated the connection between religion, architecture, and domesticity. The Gothic Revival style, although only one of many styles used by Victorian architects, physically embodied many of the attitudes written about by pattern-book authors. Homes built in this style stood within the tradition of medieval Gothic architecture, summarized by Oliver Smith as "the general predominance of the perpendicular over the horizontal." Gothic churches were characterized by their "clustered pillars and vaulted roofs . . . pinnacles, pointed arches and lofty spires" as well as "massive buttresses, [and an] almost endless profusion of decoration." The age of the Gothic cathedral had long passed, but the Romantic fascination with the Middle Ages revived the popularity of pointed arches and vertical heights.[21]

American interest in Gothic style was spurred by three British architects: Augustus Welby Pugin, Sir Gilbert Scott, and John Ruskin. In 1841, A. W. Pugin published *The True Principles of Pointed or Christian Architecture,* stating that only the Gothic style truly expressed the Christian spirit and thus was appropriate for church architecture.

The then-current British architecture, based on the classical style, might be fit for banks and civic buildings but certainly not for Christian churches. Pugin, who converted to Catholicism in 1834, explained that "the Roman Catholic Church is the only true one, and the only one in which the great and sublime style of church architecture can ever be restored."[22]

In spite of the considerable anti-Catholic sentiments in Britain, Pugin became a popular architect. Some said it was he who in 1836 designed the Gothic style Parliament Buildings. Like many Romantic artists he condemned the industrial revolution, vigorously pointing out that smokey towers of British factories now replaced cathedral spires as the dominant feature of the landscape. Pugin insisted that morality and art were directly connected. Good buildings reflected the condition of the society and the conviction of the artist. Pugin died at the age of forty in an insane asylum of "nervous fear," his vision never realized.[23]

The Gothic spirit, however, lived on in England. The Gothic tales of Sir Walter Scott captured the hearts and minds of both British and American readers. The great popularizer of Gothic architecture in England, Sir Gilbert Scott, "stood for the ordinary man who felt an inexplicable need for pointed arches." He constructed over eight hundred Gothic style buildings in Britain, including twenty-three parsonages, fifty workhouses, and forty-three mansions—significantly reshaping the British landscape.[24]

It would be John Ruskin, however, who would de-Romanize Gothic architecture and make it acceptable to the Protestant world. In *The Seven Lamps of Architecture,* while claiming that proper morality produced good architecture, Ruskin vigorously attacked Roman Catholicism. "But of all these fatuities," he said, speaking of inducements to Romanism, "the basest is the being lured into the Romanist Church by the glitter of it, like larks into a trap . . . to be blown into a change of religion by the whine of an organ-pipe; stitched into a new creed by the gold threads on priests' petticoats. . . . I know nothing in the shape of error so dark as this, no imbecility so absolute, no treachery so contemptible." If the truly moral produced the truly good in architecture, then for the beauty of the Gothic cathedral to have been produced by Catholics would be unacceptable. Surprisingly, Ruskin succeeded. His success was due partly to the reworking of the meaning of the Gothic, and partly due to the needs of the Victorians for a Protestant sensual architecture.[25]

In America the Gothic Revival also began with a change in church architecture. The Oxford Movement in England and the American "churchly resurgence" sparked new interest in church architecture. A more affluent America could now afford to create a sense of history. From Richard Upjohn's Trinity Cathedral built between 1841 and 1846 to Washington's National Cathedral begun in 1907, Gothic church architecture became a hallmark of American Victorian spirituality.[26]

The Gothic impact on domestic architecture began on the banks of the river Thames. In 1750, Richard Bentley designed the infamous "Strawberry Hill" for Horace Walpole. This English example of the application of Gothic architecture to home building set the pace for later American developments. Strawberry Hill, called by Kenneth Clark "Gothic Rococo frippery," consisted of room after room of pointed arches, gothicized chimneys, wallpaper, furniture, chapels, and gates. Although Walpole's mansion was a stage for a British gentleman, simplified versions of Strawberry Hill became known as "Carpenter's Gothic" in America because of the attempt to imitate Gothic stone details with wood.

When the Gothic style arrived in America in the early 1830s, the predominant architectural form was the classical style of Jefferson's Monticello and Latrobe's Capitol. Classical architecture suited a new nation which hoped to represent the republican virtues of liberty, rationality, and democracy. It drew from a Greek and Roman heritage of law and civic freedom, and was influenced by the period we now call the "Age of Reason." Classical architecture built into its walls the symmetry of the Newtonian universe and the sensibility of a Lockean rationality. Beauty was inherent in the form of the architecture, not in the mind of the spectator. As long as the building harmonized with an objective sense of beauty it was considered artistic. Simplicity, clarity, horizontal line, and symmetry were the artistic hallmarks of the clasical style during the Federal period.[27]

Federal architecture of well-to-do Americans gave way to a more popularized version: Greek revival. Andrew Downing called the houses of the Greek revival "temple cottages." Built of thin pine boards with classical porticos and wooden columns, they were "entirely destitute of truthfulness." Downing's criticisms conflicted with the ubiquitous character of Greek revival of the 1830s. Northerners slowly lost interest in the style, and the Southern plantation mansion with its stately white facade remains the best known example of the Greek style.[28]

The waning of the Federal and Greek styles of domestic architecture was hastened by the arrival of the Romantic movement from Europe. Emotion and sentiment became acceptable with the decline of the belief in the absolute power of reason. Art historian Mary Foley wrote:

> Circa 1840, standing on the edge of their industrial age, Americans were seized by a nostalgic mood, shaking themselves free of their old, sober, and rational approach to building. In a democratic nation and a prosaic workaday world, they were ready to imagine themselves as bold knights and languishing ladies, heroes and heroines in an antique Gothic tale.[29]

The creation of emotion and sentiment was an important element in the Gothic revival. In 1838 the architect A. J. Davis constructed for William Paulding a Gothic mansion on the banks of the Hudson river. Paulding, a former New York City mayor, wanted a retirement home built in the latest style with the most up-to-date technical conveniences. The house which Davis built and the furniture which he designed captured the Gothic rage then fashionable in England. By using local New York marble Davis created a combination of castle and cathedral for Paulding. The country villa, later christened "Lyndhurst," contained beautiful stained-glass windows and wooden tracery painted to look like stone. Davis altered the original design in 1864 when he doubled its size and added a tower. The library, contrived to look like a chapel complete with altar screen, had high vaulted roofs and stained glass. Most of the furniture, some of which Davis himself designed, was Gothicized; bed headboards had pointed arches, chairs were highly decorated, and porch benches looked like medieval abbey pews. All of the furniture was built by local New York carpenters. The exterior design of Lyndhurst included stained-glass rose windows and decorative battlements.

Like many Gothic revival villas, Lyndhurst had an irregular form which facilitated the construction of additional wings and floors. Its asymmetry and complexity emphasized its individual character and helped create a "Gothic" mood of romance, chivalry, civilization, and antiquity. An important method of creating this mood was to play with light, internal light by using stained and plain glass and external light by creating shadows. In *Gothic Architecture Applied to Modern Residences* David Arnot explained that "light descending in full stream from above, distributed and broken by innumerable angular surfaces, and the brilliant contrast of the dark wood with the mellow hues of the walls and floors" could not "fail to produce one of the most pleasing subjects of internal picture." The architects of the Gothic style produced architectural "pictures," sets for enacting domestic drama. "The effect of the scene," Arnot continued, "may be further height-

Gothic windows at Lyndhurst, a property
of the National Trust for Historic Preservation.

ened by the use of stained glass in the sky-light, being . . . the best
calculated for display."[30]

Davis designed Lyndhurst to tantalize both the imagination and the
senses in order to heighten a domestic aesthetic. Since Victorian
sensibilities combined aesthetics with morality, an emotional/aesthetic
response simultaneously evoked a moral/domestic response. The
good Victorian American might condemn the theater as a den of vice
and iniquity, but it was perfectly accepted—even encouraged—to
create a home which provoked emotion, sentiment, sensuality, and
imagination. What was unacceptable in public could be permitted in
the home.

Lyndhurst stood as the country residence of a wealthy ex-mayor and later railroad magnate. The economic position of the Paulding family and later owners, the Merritt and Gould families, allowed them to indulge in current fashions unaccessible to other Americans. The sentiments conveyed by Lyndhurst, however, appealed to the middle class. More modest Gothic revival homes exemplified similar characteristics. Henry Bowen, co-founder and later owner of the influential Congregational journal *The Independent,* had a Gothic-style home built in Woodstock, Connecticut in 1846. Called "Roseland," it was constructed by Joseph C. Wells who also designed the First Presbyterian Church in New York City.

Like Lyndhurst, Roseland also had windows with wooden tracery, but it depended on board and batten (vertical boards seamed with narrow strips of wood) woodwork to give it a vaguely medieval appearance. Both on the bargeboards and on small attic windows, Wells used a cloverleaf motif found on Gothic cathedrals to represent the Trinity. Steeply pointed gable roofs with finials at their apexes accentuated the vertical dimension. Bay and oriel windows, trellised porches, and molded chimney stacks of glazed stoneware combined to give Roseland a Gothic air. Bowen hired Thomas Brooks of Brooklyn to craft his Gothic furniture: chairs with pointed arched backs and couches in three segments. Roseland in a more subdued manner tried to convey the same sentiments as its grander ancestor, Lyndhurst.

Gothic houses increased in popularity between 1840 and 1860. They caught the imagination of many local builders who, without the help of "expert" architects, constructed delightful houses from pattern books. Downing, who never minced words, called such houses "gingerbread" and claimed that "the sugar castles of confectioners and pastry-cooks are far more admirable as works of art." He reacted to the desire of those of moderate means to imitate the more substantial buildings of their economic and social betters. The builders of "Gingerbread" Gothic homes breached their stations by skirting the issue of "truth" in architecture. They used wood to imitate stone, and paint to make pine look like oak. Downing could not see that the cottage owner wanted a home which could evoke the same domestic emotions as the more expensive models.[31]

When it was impossible to build a new home, Gothic "icing" was added to an older home. A stately late Federal-style house was built in Kennebunk, Maine, in 1826. By 1855, the owners decided to update the house and add Gothic embellishments—wooden spires and buttresses, nailed crenelations, and decorative spandrels. The Gothic trim was removable, a kind of wooden slipcover. The descendents of the owner-carpenter George Bourne have actually taken it off in order to paint the house.

Although Gothic revival reached its height in the northern states, it also spread into the western territories. In the western mining towns of Colorado, newly wealthy families took care to build homes which resembled those of the eastern middle class. The "Lace House" of Black Hawk, Colorado, built in 1860, was perhaps the most famous of these. Its decorative bargeboards, elaborate wood lace on the porch, and pitched roof equaled the best eastern examples of Carpenter's Gothic. The significance of domestic architecture in making a statement about the character of its residents was even more crucial on the frontier where the line between civilization and the wilderness was tenuous.

The popularity of the Gothic style came about during a period of intense distrust of Catholics in America. In 1844, during the height of the Gothic revival in domestic architecture, anti-Catholic riots broke out in Philadelphia and New York. The relations between Catholics and Protestants had reached their nadir. In order to utilize an architectural form which had a strong Catholic tradition, the architects had to be certain that the style's "real" origins lay in the Protestant spirit. Gothic architecture, in the minds of both the educated and uneducated, was disconnected from Catholicism and linked to popular Protestant values.

Along with providing a domestic stage for expressing sentiment and medieval adventure, Gothic revival expressed the popular Protestant need for establishing contact with "nature." One of the important ways in which the architectural writers separated "their" Gothic from the "Papist" Gothic of thirteenth-century Europe was through the use of natural images. For Protestant writers and artists, the Gothic cathedral was not the result of the medieval vision of the heavenly "City of God," but an imitation of nature. Like Emerson, who believed that art must follow nature's lead and be its complement, these writers emphasized the connection of Gothic architecture to the natural world.

A Protestant interpretation of the Gothic cathedral was that the medieval artist recalled ancient Anglo-Saxon worship in the open air, under the trees. The idea of pointed arches and rib-vaulting came from trees bending over in the wind. The sense of interior space originated from the experience of a cave, with decorations looking like stalactites. Even the outside sculpture was supposed to imitate the ice and frost on evergreens. Architectural critics attempted to break off the Gothic from its Catholic roots by insisting that it had natural, not supernatural origins; that it was most at home in the forest, and not the city; and that it captured the Reformation spirit, not the Romanist mind. The painter Thomas Cole captured this idea in his "Architect's Dream," in which a picturesque Gothic church is nestled in an ever-green forest. In order to create a Protestant Gothic style it became necessary to ignore certain facts, such as the existence of Gothic cathedrals at the center of major European cities.[32]

Whether one constructed a church or a house, nature became a source of inspiration and purified sentiment for middle-class Vic-

Interior garden. Catharine Beecher and Harriet
Beecher Stowe, *The American Woman's Home,* p. 97.

torian culture. "The heart has there," Downing recalled, "always within its reach, something on which to bestow its affections." The Gothic revival house grew out of the soil. Its color must blend in with the landscape: stone grey, slate blue, fawn were permitted; white was universally condemned. Porches, piazzas, verandas, and large windows linked interior space with exterior, natural space. In the interior, houseplants, flowered rugs, wax flowers, bouquets of shells, wall pictures made of pheasant's feathers, and stuffed hummingbirds were used to "naturalize" the home.[33]

The Gothic revival house demanded a natural setting. Its angular roofs, exterior decorations, and pointed windows needed the landscape of trees, mountains, and meandering streams as a backdrop. Care was taken to situate the house properly so that it could be viewed from the outside in its bucolic setting. The Gothic cottage reflected the natural order which surrounded it. By reflecting this order, the home exuded a sense of power intrinsic to nature which Downing called "beauty through *power.*" The "picturesque villa—country house with high roofs, steep gables, unsymmetrical and capricious forms," Downing explained, indicated "originality, boldness, energy and a variety of character." By recalling nature, the home captured some of the power of nature—the force of a river, the violence of a thunderstorm.[34]

Gothic domestic architecture presented a feminized version of nature by associating it with domestic expression. Nature was not only power; it was intimacy, affection, warmth. The Gothic house communicated ambition by its steep roofs, but also portrayed feminine virtues by its cozy nooks, bay windows, and delicate bargeboard carvings. For Downing this feminized feeling was demonstrated in decorating the home with natural flora, keeping a flower garden, arranging bouquets, and planting and caring for vines which covered the house. Planting vines was not done by "architects, masons, carpenters, or those who build the cottage but always by those who live in it, and generally by the mother or daughter." This planting and caring for the vines which gently entwined around the porches' pillars was "a labor of love offered up on the domestic altar" and always expressed "domesticity and presence of heart."[35]

Nature, as understood by the writers, had two aspects: a masculine aspect of power, ambition, motion and boldness, and a feminine aspect of intimacy, emotion, and domesticity. For Downing, these two sides of Gothic architecture combined in a curious manner. "The character expressed by the exterior of this design is that of a man or family of domestic tastes, but with strong aspirations after something higher than social pleasures." Downing was unwilling to permit a total feminization of the home and tried to point out how the home communicated the characteristics of the father.[36]

Yet Downing must have been aware that men were spending fewer and fewer hours at home. If father was to commute from the joys of the countryside to his job in the wicked city, then he would be spending even less time creating his own domestic space. Catharine Beecher was aware of the change; in her writings on domesticity, she sought to create a home run for and by women. Beecher designed a Gothic style home which she believed to be the model "Christian Home." This home would not only be constructed and decorated like a church, it would *be* a church. In her *American Woman's Home: Or The Principles of Domestic Science,* written in collaboration with her sister Harriet Beecher Stowe, she carefully designed a home which doubled for a church and a school. "A small church, a school-house, and a comfortable family dwelling may be all united in one building," wrote the sisters. The main room could be transformed into a nave by a movable screen, and "the chimney is finished off outside as a steeple." After giving the details of such a structure, Beecher and Stowe concluded that "the cost of such a building where lumber is $50 a hundred and labor $3 a day, would not much exceed $1200."[37]

In the homes Catharine Beecher designed, the attention given to the "workability" of the home far exceeded the writings of male architects. The architects tried to create a connection between the home and religion by association, inference, and ideology. Beecher in her practical manner tackled the problem directly by unabashedly designing a home which was a church.

By borrowing from the religious architecture of the past, Gothic revival graphically associated the home with traditional religion. Only the wealthy could afford a home such as Lyndhurst, and I know of no actual building of a church/home/school like the Beecher's; these were the extreme examples of Gothic revival. But many houses were built with a lancet window here or there, a stained-glass rose window, vaulted arches in the bedroom, or a cresting with crosses. The Methodists in 1864 built 300 Gothic cottages at their summer retreat in Martha's Vineyard. Gothic houses from Maine to Florida still can be seen, although many have been either destroyed or updated beyond recognition. Between 1846 and 1851, 60 percent of the housing designs published in *Godey's Lady's Book* were more or less Gothic in style. Although the Gothic revival in domestic architecture declined after

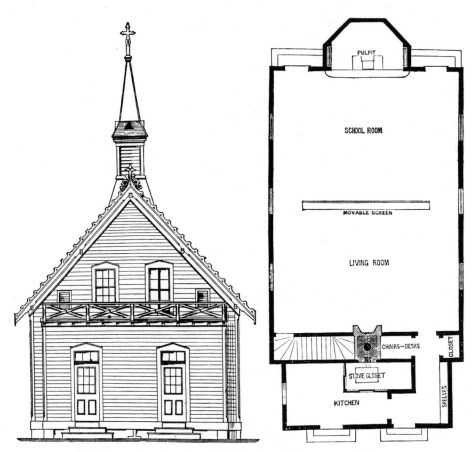

The Christian home. Left: exterior view; right: first floor. Catharine
Beecher and Harriet Beecher Stowe, *The American Woman's Home,*
pp. 454 and 456.

the Civil War, especially with the advent of the mansard roof, remnants of Gothic style—steep pitched roofs, pointed arched windows,
and stained glass—continued into the twentieth century.[38]

Home Decorating in the Protestant Spirit

The space within the Victorian home designed in Gothic or any other
popular form could be made to evoke religious sentiments in several
ways. It could tap into past religious history, tempered by current

attitudes, through architectural associations. In a less direct manner home owners could subscribe to contemporary domestic ideologies which connected good taste with morality. Finally, specific references to Christianity could be voiced through decorations within the home.

Under the influence of Romanticism and the Victorian predilection for conspicuous consumption, Protestant homes departed from the Calvinist distrust of religious art. A woman's (and through her, the family's) domestic sentiments, artistic accomplishments, and spiritual devotion came to be measured by her ability to decorate her home. Religious home decorations had strong Protestant overtones, but were nonsectarian in character. Prior to the 1860s, families demonstrated a restrained attitude toward displaying religious art and artifacts in their homes. Words, either from pious sayings or Scripture, formed the basis of their religious art. After 1860 fashion encouraged stronger iconic expression of religious sentiment.

Perhaps the earliest example of the artistic use of the holy word was the sampler. Young women and girls demonstrated their mastery of embroidery by stitching Bible passages or composing religious poems. These were often signed and dated and hung on bedroom or parlor walls. Along with being a showy accomplishment, samplers displayed a woman's piety. In 1842, fifteen-year-old Ann Britton stitched in her sampler:

> Jesus permit thy gracious name to stand
> As the first efforts of an infant's hand
> And as her fingers on the sampler move
> Engage her tender heart to seek thy love
> With thy dear children may she have her part
> And write thy name thyself upon her heart.[39]

Another craft popular in the mid-nineteenth century was the production of motto-card holders and religious bookmarkers. Directions for making bookmarkers with biblical phrases such as "Forsake me not O Lord" and "God is Our Refuge" appeared in *Godey's Lady's Book*. Mottoes and their cases made from perforated cardboard "could be finished up in most lovely colors and embroidery." Each day a different motto could be set in its case: Monday, "Be diligent in well-doing," Wednesday, "I will lift up mine eyes unto the hills, from whence cometh my help," and Saturday, "Charity suffereth long and is kind." By producing this type of "fancywork" the mother legitimated her leisure activities by associating them with the religious education of her family.[40]

"Praise the Lord." Perforated cardboard bookmark with biblical saying.
Ryan Memorial Library, Archives and Historical Collections,
St. Charles Seminary, Philadelphia.

Departing from the traditional Protestant suspicion of the image, Victorian women made religious symbols out of a variety of materials. Hair art entailed the weaving of strands of human hair (sometimes of a dead relative) into shapes and designs, mounting them on a board, and then covering the surface with glass. Religious symbols, such as crosses or anchors, were made along with birds, hearts, and monograms. Hair art was often used to commemorate dead relatives or friends. Most Victorian mourning art, including that done with hair, did not use traditional Christian symbols of death, but developed its own set. Urns, weeping willows, and mourning figures evoked not only sorrow at the death of a loved one, but thoughts of God's judgment and eternal life (or damnation)[41]

Books which described ladies' fancywork frequently included instructions for making home crosses. These crosses were made of wood decorated to look like marble. The style of the cross could be adjusted seasonally. Christmas crosses had imitation icicles, summer crosses had vines entwining through them, and Easter crosses had lilies. Unfortunately the craft books gave no indication as to how these crosses were used. Probably they were not used in family worship, but served to evoke a general religious sentiment in the home.[42]

Many articles cited in fancywork literature had religious connections. *Godey's Lady's Book* gave instructions on how to fold a dinner napkin into a bishop's hat. Pin cushions were shown in the form of Gothic churches. These items were the more trivial examples of the influence of Romanticism in American Protestantism. On a more serious level, the Romantic spirit allowed Protestant women to build sensuous and emotive religious sentiments into their homes. A section in William's *Ladies' Fancy Work* described the building of shrines "for chaste parlour elegancy." Instructions for constructing prie-dieux found their way into *Godey's*. Gothic designs also became popular on wall brackets for holding Bibles, hymnals, and prayer books.[43]

Just as Protestant artists, poets, and critics reworked the meaning of Gothic to fit their theological and social needs, so Victorian housewives claimed traditionally Catholic images for their use. During the first half of the century, Protestant domestic arts reflected both the evangelical concern for Scripture and the simplicity promoted by domestic reformers such as Catharine Beecher. Samplers or motto-card holders bespoke religious restraint and directness. After the Civil War, with changing patterns of taste and production, the number of articles placed in the parlor or sitting room radically increased. For the gracious lady who read *Godey's* or studied fancywork books the current fashions in domestic taste from Grecian to French antique dictated the style of religious art. The fascination with French design and fashion easily translated into Marian shrines,

Motto-cases. The Athenaeum of Philadelphia.
Williams and Jones, *Household Elegancies*, p. 256.

Left: wooden cross. The Athenaeum of Philadelphia. Williams and
Jones, *Household Elegancies,* p. 181. Right: wax cross. Ryan Memorial
Library, Archives and Historical Collections, St. Charles
Seminary, Philadelphia.

bishop's hat napkins, and prie-dieux. Theology bowed to fashion. By
the 1880s, sandwiched among velvet swags, gilded picture frames,
and crowded étagères were waxed crosses, family Bible stands, and
religious paintings of fashionable Protestants. Popular Protestantism
had gained an iconic dimension which would only be tempered by
reforming trends in religion and design.

Perhaps the most enduring legacy of Protestant iconography in
Victorian households was the parlor organ. In 1860, 12,643 melo-
deons (or small reed organs) were built in the United States. After the
Civil War the simple organs evolved into elaborately carved instru-
ments which still cost less than half the price of a piano. The production of parlor organs peaked between 1870 and 1885, and owning an

Pincushion shaped like a church. The Athenaeum of Philadelphia.
Godey's Lady's Book 90 (1875), p. 560.

Mary shrine. Williams and Jones, *Ladies' Fancy Work*, p. 151.

Prie-dieu. *Godey's Lady's Book* 85 (1872), p. 467.

organ became a symbol of middle-class achievement.[44]

Placed in the parlor or sitting room, the organ dominated the visual space, making a strong statement about the religious and social nature of the family. Following the style of Gothic furniture design, it depended on vertical height to give it presence, while carved pointed arches at the cresting and wooden pinnacles lent it an ecclesiastical air. The major role of the instrument was to provide musical accompaniment for singing hymns and popular songs. The casework of the organ contained special shelves and nooks for placing family mementos, photographs, and miniature paintings. As both a relic holder and a center for hymnody, it could be easily seen as "a domestic shrine to learning, civilization, and familial continuity." As with the creation of religious decoration, playing the organ was a feminine activity which expressed, highlighted, and cemented the mother's role as the spiritual keystone of the family.[45]

Although religious decorations spoke directly about the piety of the family, a good homemaker chose all household art carefully. In an article entitled "The Ethics of Home-Decoration," J. R. Miller reiterated the connection between good art and morality. While a country house with "neatly-painted palings . . . pleasant walks, lovely plants and beds of flowers" has a good moral influence, "the moral effect of interior home-decoration is still greater." Miller warned that many pictures found in Christian homes move the family toward impurity. If a young man desired to rise in his profession he should either have good engravings or nothing on his walls. "The display of undraped figures on canvas," according to Miller, "must exert a harmful influence, especially in the minds of the young." Although Miller seemed aware of criticism of his brand of prudishness (his term), he insisted that "the religion of Christ is chaste, and condemns everything in which lurks even the faintest suggestion of impurity." To maintain a home full of chaste and tasteful art aided spiritual growth and showed the outside world the family's Christian character.[46]

The Home as Sacred Symbol

Once the home became connected with larger visions of morality, aesthetics, class, and civilization, it ceased to be merely a shelter and assumed greater meaning. Domestic housing reformers constructed a symbol system which linked the everyday need for refuge to a higher, more fundamental, moral order. Thus they significantly shaped American culture and religion in three major ways. First, reformers promoted the home as a mediating and unifying sacred symbol. Second, they heightened the domestic nature of American Protestantism. And finally, writers gained newfound legitimacy for emerging middle-class values.

Alan Gowan in *Images of American Living* asserts that the Victorians saw "visual forms in terms of intellectual images" and used them as a "kind of symbolic language." Symbols, according to Mircea Eliade, "identify, assimilate and unify diverse levels and realities that are to all appearances incompatible." As a primary symbol for the Victorians, the home mediated between a variety of social and psychological needs.[47]

Left: John the Baptist and Jesus, leather-work bracket. The Athenaeum
of Philadelphia. Williams and Jones, *Household Elegancies,* p. 125.
Right: figurine of girl praying (mid-nineteenth century). Ryan Memorial
Library, archives and Historical Collections, St. Charles Seminary,
Philadelphia.

The physical layout of the home and the family itself mediated
between the opposing qualities of *public and private.* The home stood
between the outside, public aspect of life and the interior, private
aspect. During this period both the public and the private seemed out
of control. Social and economic changes threatened to fragment society, and heightened American individualism broke men and women
from traditional social networks. Domestic reformers used the home
as a symbolic means to mediate the two extremes.

The home should "stand apart, neither subject to overlooking or
overhearing. . . . The house should be within an enclosure sacred to
it." On the other hand it should be situated such that it could be

viewed from the street. Discreet staircases, sliding doors, and dressing rooms preserved the privacy of the family from servants and guests, but other rooms were specially decorated for visitors. The creation of lawns, porches, and hallways provided space which could regulate the exchange between people's public and private lives. By creating these "middle places" the family could control, in some fashion, their connection with the outside world. Through their control they felt that the outside chaos had been ordered and made safe.[48]

Suburban house construction also sought to mediate between two classical oppositions, *nature and culture*. The domestic architects believed that "experience seems to say that in the country, only, can *men* be reared." The "truly human" could only express itself in the country. This country, however, was not the wild frontier. By "country" the domestic reformers meant the suburban areas a few miles from an urban center. The suburbs mediated between the uncontrolled, howling wilderness and the overcontrolled, decadent city. Nature could be fully experienced in the suburbs through the civilizing channels of proper homes, schools, and civic organizations. The domestic reformers used the suburbs as the means of capturing the vitality of both the growing cities and the westward frontier expansion.[49]

The home was also expected to mediate the divisions of *sex and age*. By creating specialized space within the home, the reformers hoped to promote and justify the differing activities of men, women, and children. Each had their own unique responsibilities, natures, and activities, but lived together under one roof. In spite of the continual shift of men away from the home, the architects persisted in directing their message to men and women. Only Catharine Beecher seemed to see that the home was not a unifying symbol, but a woman's workplace. She was convinced that the home and domesticity held unifying power to heal a divisive nation, but that power would be exercised through women's influence within the home, and not men's.[50]

An important opposition which was *not* mediated by the home was the relationship between *work and leisure*. While Catharine Beecher understood the home primarily as the sphere of work for women, most of the male writers ignored the working aspect of the home. Since they (and the men for whom they wrote) did not do housework, male architects were unable to solve a problem which many women experienced: how to see one's house as an abode for relaxation, repose, and reflection when you spent most of your time working there. When a woman engaged in leisure activities at home, how did those pastimes relate to her domestic duties? For some women this problem was resolved when the popular women's presses began to equate what once might have been considered leisure activities (embroidery, painting, decorating) with women's "work."

The Victorian home was not only a symbol, it was a sacred symbol. "Sacred symbols," writes Clifford Geertz, "relate an ontology and a cosmology to an aesthetics and a morality, their peculiar power comes from their presumed ability to identify fact with value at the most fundamental level." None of the Victorian domestic architects believed that they were creating a new concept of the home. They were firmly convinced that they were stating the obvious, reiterating what any moral, intelligent, and Christian person already knew. They stated these convictions as natural facts. Along with the Victorian clergyman, they knew that the home was "first planted in Eden by God's own hand and has been transplanted into every civilized community."[51]

The Home as Religious Center

The housing reformers insisted that the construction of the home was a fundamentally serious—a religious—undertaking. All that was ordered, meaningful, organized, inhabited, and familiar was given domestic associations. In a society which appeared increasingly more distant, alienating and chaotic, the home was perceived as foundational, eternal, and unchanging. Although Protestantism had always seen home life as crucial to the production of good Christians, the nineteenth century saw the flowering of domestic religion.

Under the influence of liberal theologians such as Horace Bushnell, American Protestantism became more and more home-centered. "The house, having a domestic Spirit of grace dwelling in it," explained Bushnell, "should become the church of childhood, the table and hearth a holy rite, and life an element of saving power." The Victorian home had become the sacred environment where the "three great mysteries" of "birth, of growth, of death" took place.[52]

The ascendancy of the home as a spiritual center coincided with the failure of individual Protestant denominations to uphold what Peter Berger calls the "Sacred Canopy." Pluralism, theological disputation, and secularization broke the holds which the denomination had over society. As early as 1847, Bushnell wrote that the church (meaning the Protestant denominations) "is rent by divisions, burnt up by fanaticism, frozen by the chill of a worldly spirit, petrified in rigid and dead orthodoxy." By the time of the denominational splits over the subject of slavery, it would be obvious to most Americans that the Protestant churches did not give fundamental meaning to life.[53]

The ideology and symbolism of the home served as an alternative to sectarian splintering. Domestic religion acted as the private side to the "Righteous Empire" analyzed by Martin Marty. Just as Washington Gladden and Josiah Strong sought to elude denominational differences and speak directly to American public sentiments, so writers on domesticity tried to present the home as an eternal, unchanging spiritual reality. The privatized "Righteous Empire" was also used to support the evangelical vision of a "Christian" America. Important Victorian values—individuality, personal morality, piety, Anglo-Saxon superiority—thus received not only public acclamation, but also legitimation in the home as well.[54]

Mid-nineteenth-century religious enthusiasm, with which the denominations had a difficult time coping, was not channelled into the domestic sphere. In a spirit of perfectionism the domestic reformers believed that the home could be made perfect and then could function as a guiding light to assist in the salvation of other families. Without even stepping outside of the yard the family could participate in a benevolent activity. The domestic reformers portrayed the home as a type of middle-class utopia—a gathering of mother, father, and children, all working together in an Edenic suburban setting for their mutual betterment and salvation. Each home could be an individual, privately owned, sanctified religious community. The arrival of the Romantic movement with its emphasis on the divinity of nature, the primacy of sentiment, and the legitimacy of aesthetic sensuality helped create the concept of the home as a setting for domestic drama. The house became the center of a new form of liturgy, and the interior furnishings its sacred props.[55]

Domesticity and Middle-Class Values

By the mid-nineteenth century the East Coast Victorian could pick from a variety of goods and services in a burgeoning America. Mass production of furniture, balloon framing, newly accessible suburban land, and a cash economy resulted in a flourishing market for consumer goods. Any remnants of Puritan frugality were quickly dispelled. By linking morality and religion with the purchase and maintenance of a Christian home, the Victorians legitimized acquisition and display of domestic goods. Since the home symbolized the fundamental values of the Victorians—Christianity, civilization, morality, aesthetics, stability, sentiment—one was not building a shelter, but a sanctuary.

"I love the man who earns his money with the special design of spending it," wrote Reverend Titcomb in 1858, "building up their homes, making them abodes of beauty and plenty." Domestic consumerism was legitimated by marshalling material household goods as evidence of Christian civilization and thus of salvation. The overt display of wealth through the acceptable channel of domesticity became fashionable. A well-appointed home was not seen as a foolish expenditure (or as Veblen termed it, "conspicuous consumption"), but rather a conscious effort to create an environment appropriate for Christian nurture. American architects reversed Pugin's and Ruskin's paradigm that good men produced good architecture and offered in its place the materialistic concept that good architecture produced good men.[56]

The attitude that domestic consumerism enabled the home to accomplish the salvation of the family was closely aligned to the importance of environment. Consumerism was only justified when what was consumed actually had an *effect* on the human character. Whereas the conversion experience of Calvinism needed only a receptive adult mind, Christian nurture depended on "the spirit of the house." The domestic environment combined the physical space of the house with the personalities of the family members. "We conceive the manners, personal views, prejudices, practical motives," wrote Bushnell, and the "spirit of the house as an atmosphere which passes into all and pervades all, as naturally as the air they breathe." The housing reformers understood the house and the family as a single environmental quality which acted "naturally."[57]

The endowment of environmental influence and consumerism with religious overtones had important consequences for the development of American class consciousness. Acquiring goods was not only the result of leading a good life. Since "Vice and Deformity are in constant association," and "the slack, low-minded and 'shiftless' aspire only to some hut or hovel," then physical surroundings both demonstrated one's low class and kept one in that class. "The parents," explained Bushnell, "propagate their own evil in the child, not by design, but under a law of moral infection." These "morally infected" children would in turn become parents themselves.[58]

This attitude helped produce a defined class structure. Middle-class Victorians had created an image of stability in a society of flux. A never-ending spiral emerged—the poor were poor because they had no sense of morality, civilization, or aesthetics, and they could never achieve those values because they did not have them. The middle class circled upward into righteousness, the poor downward into degradation. Progressive reformers tried to break the circle by teaching the poor the rudiments of middle-class attitudes toward religion, housing, and work.[59]

Along with promoting the "natural" existence of domestic consumerism and class division, architects emphasized the need for role specialization. The specialization of the household by sex and age served to justify the divisions of external society by sex and age. Understood as the "foundation of society," the home separated naturally into lady's boudoir, children's nursery, and gentleman's library. In the proper Victorian home, everyone did have "a room of one's own." As men moved up the economic ladder, the more specialized their jobs became, the more specialized the rooms in their homes became, and the more distinct the differences between the sexes became.

The development of a domestic ideology based on family structure and home design assumed families to have at least the economic resources to express their domestic sentiments through the manipulation of physical space. Good families exhibited strong control over their physical environment and thus worked for the betterment of their families. Control over home environment was a privilege of only a certain class of Americans. For the Irish Catholics fleeing famine-plagued Ireland, such control was out of reach.

[3]

Catholic Domesticity

It took almost fifty years before Irish Catholic immigrants developed a Victorian domesticity similar to Protestant sensibilities. Due to their social and economic situation, Irish Catholics directed their attentions toward nondomestic issues: work, religious freedom, anti-Catholic sentiments, and Irish politics during the first half of the century. Severe poverty, constant relocation, and tenement life created a situation in which even "an angel from heaven would soon be made as black as the devil." Many families sent only their single sons or daughters to America expecting that the children would send money home. Those sons and daughters either delayed their marriages or remained single. Women, on whom domestic sentiments frequently centered, were busy working as servants, in cottage industries, or factories. Very few women had the leisure or finances to pursue the "cult of true womanhood" popular among the wealthier classes.[1]

Consequently, prior to 1880 only a select few Irish Americans attempted to create a Catholic domestic ideology appropriate for the New World. These few established models which were adapted to a late Victorian world. By the end of the century, when domestic comforts could be reached by more Catholics, numerous local commentators on home life arose. These writers were joined by the Catholic clergy, both at home and abroad, who found in the family ways to promote their particular perspective on modern life.

Sources of Catholic Domesticity

Catholic novelists were the earliest arbiters of Irish American home life. As members of the educated middle class even before the Civil War, novelists played a crucial role in the development of Catholic domesticity. While the majority of Irish Catholics lived in poverty, these literary elites detailed what they believed was proper home life. Sitting between rich and poor they created a middle-class world view by appropriating characteristics chosen from the rich and the poor. They imagined an aristocratic Catholic upper class—Europeans who lived in Old World charm in America—and an old-fashioned Irish working class, one step out of the bog. From these two groups they collected values which supported their own middle-class life-style. Their values were understood as universal and eternal because they appeared in all "good" families irrespective of economic status.

Novelist, translator, and social critic Mary Ann Madden Sadlier stands as a perfect example of the early arbiters of Catholic life. She was born in Cootehill, County Cavan, in 1820, where her father was a prosperous merchant who eventually suffered financial problems in the 1840s. After her father's death, like many young Irish women, Sadlier immigrated to the United States. Two years later she married James Sadlier who was a manager of the Canadian branch of a Catholic publishing house founded by his brother. Unlike many Protestant women writers who were single or had small families, Mary Sadlier had six children. In 1860 the family moved back to New York, and Mrs. Sadlier continued the writing she had begun as a girl in Ireland.

Although she maintained a summer home and commanded the attention of Catholic notables like Orestes Brownson, Sadlier never entered the hallowed halls of the New York moneyed because of her Irish origin. Religion and ethnicity kept her from experiencing the life of the well-to-do, while her economic and educated status kept her from feeling the bite of poverty. She left economic instability in Ireland but could not feel totally comfortable in her new American life. Like most Catholic writers, she saw her middle perspective as giving her permission to comment on both rich and poor, and she did so in almost 50 novels. Through the prism of the upwardly mobile middle class, Sadlier created domestic situations which were both descriptive and prescriptive.[2]

It is difficult to determine how middle-class attitudes toward the home filtered through the Catholic American community. In 1850, when Mary Sadlier published *Willy Burke; or, the Irish Orphan in America,* an incredible 7000 copies were sold in the first week. Orestes Brownson in his *Quarterly* encouraged the production of Catholic literature, although he often disapproved of what was written. Writers like Con O'Leary wrote at the behest of their publishers who knew what was most likely to sell. Father O'Reilly's advice book, *Mirror of True Womanhood* (1876), went through seventeen editions by 1892. It was followed two years later with *True Men as We Need Them*. Most Catholic fiction and nonfiction underwent several editions during the century. The novels and advice books served as models for later domestic writing which appeared in magazines and newspapers. Although *Mirror of True Womanhood* was written in 1876, it was frequently plagiarized by newspaper writers in the 1890s. As long as Irish Americans could relate to the characters of the novels, publishers continued to reprint their somewhat limited supply of Catholic fiction.[3]

An indication of who read Catholic domestic literature can be deduced from its price. The Sadlier novel about orphan Willy Burke cost 60 cents in 1876, while the more upper-class *The Valiant Woman* by Monsignor Landriot cost $1.50. A poor man could afford to buy the *Poor Man's Catechism*, since it sold for only a quarter in 1875. In the same year, a subscription to the literary *Catholic World* was $5. In general, books about the working classes were targeted for the working classes. European reprints, which spoke to the "better classes," had better-class price tags. Novels were more expensive than didactic works. Katherine Conway's *The Way of the World and Other Ways, A Story of Our Set* was twice as expensive as *Bettering Ourselves*, from her "Family Sitting-Room" series. Advice books and the lives of the saints were often given as gifts and awards. Rose Donahue received a copy of *The Mirror of True Womanhood* as a graduating senior in 1892 because of her "General Excellence. Exactness, Needlework."[4]

Catholic books encouraged families to support a particular set of domestic attitudes and virtues. In general, mid-century novels were designed to teach religious and social strategies to their readers. Since life in the New World was radically different from life in the Old, authors like Sadlier painted vivid pictures of what they believed should be proper life in America. Mary Sadlier, Anna Dorsey, Sister Mary Carroll, and Con O' Leary sought to instruct their readers and so instruct later scholars. Further on in the century Catholic novelists took domestic sentiments for granted, and sought to entertain. These later authors, Katherine Conway, Pearl Cragie, Christian Reid, Lelia Harding Bugg, and Ella Dorsey, are less helpful to historians because they assumed a certain type of domesticity is understood by their readers. Consequently, although only a few Catholics had achieved middle-class status by 1880, novelists writing before that date give the clearest portrayal of Catholic domestic sentiments. After 1880 local sources such as newspapers and journals provide the best sources.

Catholics also discussed their domestic concerns in newspapers and journals. Prior to the mid-1870s newspapers focused their attention on politics in Ireland, at home, and in the church. Women might assert their economic power at home and in the community, but politics was the domain of men. Consequently, local newspapers occasionally contained domestic fiction, but their primary features were political and ecclesiastical news. If "household columns" appeared, they were informative rather than didactic. In an Irish world where sex-segregation was the norm, novels were for women and newspapers for men.[5]

For the more literary-minded, journals like *Catholic World* or Brownson's *Quarterly* dealt with theological and intellectual concerns. These areas were also the domain of men and had little connection to domestic affairs. After 1880, however, Catholic women asserted their literary interests more fiercely and gained space in both journals and newspapers. In one volume of *Catholic World* (1882–1883), we see the writings of Jane Dickens, Mary Alice Seymour, Julia Smalley, Christine Faber, Ella Edes, Margaret Sullivan, Elizabeth Raymond-Barker, Henrietta Brownell, and Anna Sadlier. Articles such as "In The Next House" (1882–1883), "The Glenribbon Baby" (1885), and "Homes of the Poor" (1887) illustrate an increasingly domestic slant.[6]

Local diocesan newspapers also reflected the late Victorian change from politics to domesticity. While politics still loomed large, newspapers began to include articles praising the home and describing what "good" Catholics should be doing. They reprinted the sermons of bishops who spoke on domestic concerns. Advertisements for home religious decorations from furniture to holy water fonts expanded as Catholics became more affluent. Popular fiction increased. "Children's corners" and "Woman's World" columns became more detailed, indicating either that more children and women were reading the paper or that they now had more "appropriate" articles for them. Although newspapers would remain male-oriented, they did bow slightly to changing social conditions.

Prior to the 1880s there were no successful Catholic newspapers or magazines devoted to family or women's concerns. There was no Catholic version of *Godey's Lady's Book* until the publication of Boston's *Sacred Heart Review* in 1888. Running until 1918, it once boasted a circulation of 40,000. Almost double the best readership of another popular devotional journal *Ave Maria* (which in 1892 had a circulation of 22,000), *Sacred Heart Review* exceeded the meager circulation of the 1897 *Catholic World* of 2,250. The *Sacred Heart Review's* stated purpose was not to present "news of the world in general, not the occurrences of every-day life in the parish" but rather to "enter the Christian home" with "cheering, hopeful words, and words of counsel and instruction." The *Sacred Heart Review* was the most successful of the "family" Catholic newspapers geared to the emerging Catholic middle class.[7]

Along with the writings of priests and lay people, Catholic publishing houses translated and distributed the works of European domestic commentators. Primarily of French origin, these writings were either the advice of wealthy women or the counsels of pious priests and bishops. Advice books were the outgrowth of movements in France to instill a greater piety in the laity. At first the emphasis was on cultivating a strong relationship between confessor and penitent—usually a woman and her priestly confidant. Later, as this aristocratic practice filtered into the middle classes, personal direction was replaced by a literary work. If one could not have Bishop Dupanloup's personal counsel on child rearing, one could purchase his book *The Child*. Although such works spoke to a social climate different from that of most Irish American families, they were continuously published by popular Catholic presses.[8]

Catholic Attitudes toward Domesticity

Mid-nineteenth-century Catholic novelists, late-century newspaper writers, and European commentators echoed a central theme regarding domesticity. Without a strong family, they exclaimed, economic and political structure would crumble. The family was "the nursery of the nation," and the nation was nothing "save a large family." Social, spiritual, and personal ills could be averted if the family coped with hardship and maintained its integrity. Victorian domestic ideology depended on the concept that the family, as the mid-point between the society and the individual, promoted the "right" spiritual and social values.[9]

The family could perform this function because it was established by God. Writers described this in a variety of ways. The "true" home imitated the perfect harmony experienced in Eden and heaven. Home was a foretaste of "the joys of Heaven"; a "sweet image of God's Home on high." Mrs. I. J. Hale wrote in *Catholic Home Journal* that "Home is the sphere of harmony and peace/The spot where angels find a resting place/When, bearing blessings, they descend to earth." Other writers believed that from the Holy Family of Jesus, Mary, and Joseph "we may learn how to regulate our own homes, and make them abodes of virtue and peace." In a similar manner, Monsignor Maurice d'Hulst insisted that the family replicated the Trinity. "The majesty of the heavenly Father," he wrote, "has descended upon the head of the family circle; the beauty of the mother is illuminated by the splendor of the Son; and love, the work of the Holy Spirit, unites the father and mother, and brings forth the fruit that will cement their union."[10]

By insisting that the family—father, mother and child—was established and maintained by God, Catholic writers presented the family as eternal, natural, and unchanging. Faced with the economic realities of child labor, female-headed households, and industrialization, American Catholic writers had to do some fancy footwork to demonstrate the unchanging quality of the family. Women and children worked only in order to maintain the integrity of the family. Mrs. Keane and her children of "A Washerwoman's Household" were pitied because they had to work after the death of Mr. Keane, but praised because the family stayed together. Single women employed as domestics either married and retired or moved back to Ireland in these stories. Catholic novelists reinforced the eternal and unchanging nature of the family by resolving their stories with the "true" family ethos. Erring characters die (either physically or spiritually), good Protestants convert, and good Catholics are rewarded, not always financially, but always emotionally. If God had established families, then surely they were meant to endure.[11]

Some writers went as far as to say that nothing was more sacred than the family—even the Church—and that the Church was created for families. Miss Barry wrote in 1890 that "all institutions and ordinances which God has created in civil society, and bestowed upon his Church, have for their main purpose to secure the existence, the honor, and the happiness of every home." Creating the perfect home, rather than perfecting the soul, became the goal of family members. Lay women especially saw their domestic roles as increasingly important and emphasized them in articles, novels, and stories. The editor of an article on "French Home Life," which appeared in the 1877 issue of *Catholic World,* tempered the enthusiasm for domesticity by reasserting the traditional Catholic theological preference for celibacy. The article, a translation of *La Vie Domestique* by Charles de Ribbe, quoted a Madame de Lamartine who compared her married life to that of a Sister of Mercy. The editor quickly pointed out in a footnote that "in regard to the heroic virtue that can be practised in the married state there can be no question. As little can there be any question that in the scale of perfection the religious is the higher state." Writers on domesticity displayed little sympathy for this orthodox perspective on the virtue of celibacy.[12]

Like the Protestant pattern-book writers, Catholic promoters of the family saw a close connection between the family as a kinship system and the home as a physical environment. Writers like Anna Dorsey and Mary Sadlier were aware that most Catholics at mid-century could not afford to purchase and decorate a house in order to express their family's character. To remedy this they created in their early novels aristocratic, pseudo-European families who showed the crass Americans what constituted real taste. By the 1880s more Catholics could afford their own homes and home decorations. Advertisements for local department store furniture, stained-glass windows, and parlor organs appeared in diocesan newspapers. The author of "Comfort at Home" wrote in 1889 that "in these days of cheap house furnishings there is no excuse whatever for ugliness." The article concluded by warning that "a good deal of marital unhappiness which culminated in crime has grown out of uncomfortable home life."[13]

By the 1890s in Philadelphia the local Catholic newspaper and Catholic parish calendars carried advertisements for homes in both the city and the suburbs. The builder William Roberts advertised "cozy homes" where families did not "have to settle miles away from a Catholic church." Two-story row houses built by Thomas Twibill in the southern part of the city sold for between $1400 and $1600, but the more wealthy could buy a ten-room home in the West Philadelphia suburbs for $7500. To finance purchases, The Philadelphia Home Purchasing and Investment Company (incorporated 1885) advertised their services to Catholics. As Catholics became more financially secure and domestic sentiments better articulated, builders catered to their desire for homes "a few minutes walk from St. Ann's."[14]

Catholic Domestic Virtues

By looking at the sources of popular Catholic thought—fiction, advice books, newspapers, journals—we can reconstruct a portrait of the ideal Catholic home. It was this home which would be "the resting place of angels." Nine qualities appeared most frequently in Catholic writings and seem to delineate Victorian Catholic attitudes toward home virtues: order, purity, cheerfulness, work, authority, class stability, religion, refinement, and ethnicity. Although the list is not all-inclusive, it does suffice to give an idea of Catholic middle-class domestic ideology during this period.

Since the ideal home imitated the celestial realms of Eden and paradise, as well as the divine home of Nazareth, it was crucial that the home be well-ordered. Order in heaven dictated order on earth. To have control over one's environment demonstrated control over personal passions and societal flux. Catholic writers used a theory of correspondence to assert that a well-ordered home created well-ordered citizens, which created a well-ordered nation. The home should always be neat and tidy. Cleanliness and order went hand-in-hand as the way families controlled their domestic space, and thus their personal and political space.[15]

Cleanliness could not be taken too seriously. The true family realized that cleanliness was "proved by sense of smell, rather than by the sense of sight." Even if the outside appeared tidy, the "rat and roach could tell of hidden drawers and undisturbed nooks where the straightening-out process is culpably neglected." Families needed to take great care because although they might be inured to their household odors, visitors could instantly detect these smells "above the odor of the flowers in the parlor." Such disorder—attested to by all the senses—would affect the family, especially the father who would go to "his business vexed and disturbed, because some necessary article has been misplaced."[16]

Poverty was no excuse for disorder and uncleanliness. The neat and tidy Irish cottage stood as a perpetual symbol of the righteousness of old-world homes. Mrs. Keane, the fictitious washerwoman, lived in a picturesque cottage in a suburb, and her house was "small, very small, but so exquisitely neat, and so attractive in appearance, that the beholder readily attributes to its presiding genius a superior mind." The Sylvie Kiely family, cited in an 1890 article entitled "A Peasant Home," lived in a detached cottage near an orchard. Their peasant house had uncarpeted floor boards "white as a hound's tooth," a book case with a "nice collection of books," wallpapered walls, and a "not expensive but pretty" tea service sitting on a tablecloth "white as snow." Domestic writers had little sympathy for the family which did not present a clean and orderly home.[17]

Women bore the brunt of demonstrating domestic virtues. Their bodies, homes, and life-styles were to manifest orderliness. This is not to say that men were exempt from these values. Good fathers were just as concerned about the orderliness of their homes as good mothers. The good men in Catholic fiction had to stand as paragons of virtue in order to counter the common attitude that Irish men were drunken brawlers. The author of an 1867 *Boston Pilot* article most likely had men in mind when writing that the good parish "is remarkable for its orderly, well-dressed people, who take pride in appearing decent, and of being proper in their homes and conversations, and no

Masthead for the Chicago *Catholic Home*, 1886.

brawls or tumults are ever heard within its walls." O'Hanlon's *Irish Emigrant's Guide for the United States* encouraged each man to "endeavour to raise himself in the social scale" which would require "scrupulous neatness and cleanliness . . . both in person, dress, and house management."[18]

Closely associated with the virtue of order was the more personal value of purity. As other students of the Victorian period have analyzed this important subject from a variety of perspectives, I confine myself to mentioning its appearance in Catholic literature briefly. John Maguire in *The Irish in America* (1868) contended that Irish women never gave up their old-world purity no matter how refined they became. The more patriarchal Monsignor Matignon believed it was the father's purity which gave him the "hold over the souls entrusted to him." "The more spotless he is," wrote Matignon, "the more does the light of his life shine and reflect itself on the family." Even the more female-oriented *Sacred Heart Review* encouraged fathers not to leave to women "the great and holy work of the preservation of purity in their [children's] souls." Fathers and mothers were to see that the "house holds no pictures, statues, nor books unworthy of meeting the eye of innocent children, and chaste souled youth."[19]

An orderly house produced a *cheerful* home. Brawls and tumults disturbed the harmony and peace on which the home thrived. "When will the people come to understand," asked *St. Agatha's Parish Calendar,* "that the poorest home may be made bright and cheerful, and the abode of love and peace?" This love would "manifest itself in kindly, cheerful and unselfish devotion to the common interests and comforts." The novelists drew pictures of the family in a parlor or sitting room, enjoying each other's company, but not directly interacting.

Father might be reading, mother sewing, and the children playing or studying. No one is demanding too much attention from the others, nor sitting apart in isolation.[20]

Authors quickly pointed out that a cheerful home provided a necessary haven for the father. In an 1894 sermon Cardinal Gibbons colorfully described the model home. "Christian women, when your husbands and sons return to you in the evening after buffeting with the waves of the world," he pleaded, "let them find in your homes a haven of rest. Do not pour into the bleeding wounds of their hearts the gall of bitter words, but rather the oil of gladness and consolation." Note that Gibbons included sons as laborers, possibly referring to male children, but he ignored working daughters. The male work world was chaotic, threatening, and exhausting—only in the ordered space of the home could men find true restoration. Women, naturally more domestic, somehow could cope better with work-related stress.[21]

The logic inherent in the system was that if father was happy and restored, then he would stay in his cheery home, and not go out to the cheery pub. A poem which appeared in the 1881 *Baltimore Catholic Mirror* put this sentiment very precisely. Entitled "Make Home Happy," it advised:

> Make your home both neat and tasteful . . .
>   There the heart will rest contented
> Seldom wishing far to roam . . .
>   Such a home makes men the better,
> Sure and lasting the control
>   Home with pure and bright surroundings
> Leaves its impression on the soul.[22]

Thus, the cheerful, neat, and ordered home would keep men from associating with other men and make them more responsive to the family's needs.

Although the home was to be a place of rest and repose, it also was supposed to show the *work* ethic of the family. Catholic writers maintained the tradition that the home had a productive role, and women were not to become leisured, idle objects. "If half the time and money wasted on music, dancing and embroidery," chided the *Baltimore Mirror*, "were employed in teaching daughters the useful art of making shirts and mending stockings and managing household affairs, then . . . the number of happy homes would be multiplied." In *Old and New; Taste Versus Fashion,* the new, but tasteless, Gallagher family had

seminary-educated daughters who could only play the piano, make
wax flowers, and speak a few words of French. They were, however,
unwilling to do housework.[23]

Working was acceptable as long as it kept women within the domestic environment. Servant girls were told not to "blush for earning an
honest living." It was assumed that women worked outside of their
own homes only out of necessity. "That you are dependent on your
labor," Father O'Reilly explained, "is not a shame nor a disgrace, nor a
sin; your poverty is honorable." Advice books such as Xavier Sutton's
Crumbs of Comfort for Young Women Living in the World told working
women to perform their work to please Jesus, and "if but feeble rays
of joy and comfort come to you in this life" they should look to heaven
"where in the bosom of God, you will rest your weary limbs and drink
the eternal delights of Heaven." Novelists saw domestic service as a
type of preliminary preparation for housewifery. Work outside of
someone's home—factory work, teaching, sales work—had no connection with the sacred quality of the home and thus was looked upon
with suspicion. Women who sought more adventurous careers should
become teaching or nursing sisters.[24]

The ambiguous attitude toward the relationship between work and
home can also be seen with regard to men's activities. Hard work
certainly was valued, but domestic writers feared that men who tried
to move up in American society would lose their virtuousness. Mary
Sadlier condemned her Blake family because the father was "more
anxious for making money than anything else . . . religion was, with
them, only a secondary object . . . so that it did not engross too much
time or attention." Work which had strong family connections was
valued: the virtuous Mr. Flanagan ran a family business where "all
three worked into each other's hands," and so nothing was "paid out
to strangers." Other male characters either eventually owned their
own businesses or went into farming. The best families mastered the
difficult process of connecting work to the home, while still keeping it
as a place of rest.[25]

The fiction writers' fondness for the Catholic aristocratic family
could have presented a problem. How could a family be wealthy and
still not transgress the rules of domesticity and religion? Writers
solved this problem conveniently by eliminating the father, who might
have been tainted through acquisition of wealth, and leaving a virtuous widow in his stead. Mary Sadlier described the head of the
Rheinfeldt House, an Irish woman who married a German nobleman,
as "a picture of reverend age, venerable but not decrepit." In wonder-
fully gothic fashion she was "stately even in decay" like a "well pre-

served ruin." Real wealth was not earned, but in true European style was inherited.[26]

Writers saw *social mobility* as a danger to domestic and religious sentiments. Virtue was to be exhibited and could not be obtained through changes in social status. The less-than-virtuous Blake family sent their children to public school because the father believed this would give them a better chance in their new country. The son, Harry, eventually went on to law school at Columbia and became a lawyer. All this was seen as problematic to their creator, Mary Sadlier, who wove nothing but sorrow for the Blake family. They had exchanged religion, family, and national (Irish) identity for the superficial luxuries of America. In another Sadlier book, *Confessions of an Apostate*, the main character who married into a wealthy Protestant family later found himself old, friendless, and without family. He eventually saw the error of his ways, returned to Ireland, but still had to face a lonely existence. In the words of Anna Dorsey's Nora Brady, "let everybody mate with their equals, high as well as low." Families should strive for virtue and not wealth.[27]

A popular convention used by writers to symbolize this attitude was the changing of names. Characters who tried to blend in to a Protestant America often changed their names or added new Americanized names. Maurice Egan's protagonist Patrick Mahaffy changed his name to Perseus because it gave "an air of 'Americanism.' " His life eventually became "wretchedly unhappy—but it was growing in riches in this world's goods every day." Nelly of *The Lost Rosary* changed her name to Helen. Charly O'Grady became Charles Graham. The Gallagher daughters all added "elite" first names to their own to signal their change in status. Although such name changes always had a humorous quality to them, they showed how movement from one class to another was understood as necessitating the loss of family, social, and religious ties.[28]

Changes in social status threatened the stability of the family because it called for the reorganization of the lines of *authority*. Authority as an important domestic virtue permitted the continued assertion of order. European writers on the family were rigid in their description of the hierarchical organization of the family authority structure. This structure could be seen in the relationship between God and his people, and in the Church, where a Pope heads a procession of cardinals, bishops, and clergy. As in heaven and in the Church, the family "should work with precision and harmony . . . each of the parts of which it is composed should remain in its own place."[29]

In the introduction to *The Christian Father: What He Should Be and*

What He Should Do, the Bishop of Buffalo stated that "the father actually holds the place of God, and exercises an authority subordinate only to that of God, over his children." In return, he should receive respect and honor "approximating the honor paid to God himself." Children, and wives to some extent, were under the direct authority of the father. Sex and age roles strengthened the ties of authority which were seen as natural and God-given. "Nothing in the life of the Christian family," explained Monsignor d'Hulst, "has been left to mere chance."[30]

Catholic writers felt impelled to counter what they saw as the American tendency to promote independence of children over the authority of the family. The American fascination with "freedom" had spread dangerously to their children. Mrs. Hughs has one of her characters in *The Two Schools* comment with an air of disappointment that "the young people here are not kept children half their lives, as they are in England. You know this is a free country, and the children, of course, are free as well as their parents." The dutiful daughters in *Lost Rosary* remain in Ireland at the command of their father, rather than follow their boyfriends to America. Breaking away from the family, by men or women, was looked upon as a fundamental domestic sin. Those children who respected and obeyed their parents eventually would "succeed" in their lives, but only after first fulfilling family obligations.[31]

The cornerstone of the Catholic family was its commitment to *religion.* Sectarian religious commitments were crucial in defining the Catholic family over-and-against the moral but erring Protestant families. The inclusion of a good Protestant in a novel or short story usually meant he or she was targeted for conversion. As will be described in the next chapter, Catholics did not stress family worship. Religious sentiments were expressed visually, in a private home chapel or in the display of religious articles throughout the house. Changes in the expression of religious commitment occurred during the nineteenth century in both Ireland and America and colored the ways families displayed their religious character.[32]

The pre-famine Irish were not particularly "religious" by orthodox Catholic standards. They had low church attendance, did not understand the basic tenets of their religion, and carried on religious practices that their more educated clergy termed "superstitious." Although reasons for this varied, one cause was the severe oppression of Catholics by the British during the seventeenth and eighteenth centuries. Even after the full reestablishment of Catholicism, poverty and lack of education prevented understanding of the "universal" aspects of the Church. Years of saying Mass in the fields, a low priest-to-people ratio, and weak episcopal leadership had weakened Irish Catholicism.[33]

To remedy this situation Irish bishops conducted a "devotional revolution" to reorient Catholics to more legitimate (i.e., Roman) practices. They condemned conducting religious ceremonies such as mass and confession in the home and encouraged the development of parish-centered activities. Traditional wakes and pilgrimages to holy wells were criticized, and Catholics were urged to attend Sunday mass, receive communion, and join religious societies. Wealthy churches decorated their altars with enthusiasm and strove for greater "mystery" in their rituals. Medals, scapulars, prayer books, and holy pictures were given to the people in the hopes of heightening their religious sentiments and transferring their "paganisms" to orthodox Catholic sacramentals.[34]

The Irish priests who followed their people to England and America brought this devotionalism with them. In London Catholic priests sought to create a Catholic culture as an alternative to English working-class life. By modifying social and religious behavior the Irish immigrants could more easily fit into an increasingly centralized, Roman, Catholicism. American Catholicism underwent similar changes. The parish structure helped the Irish to assimilate into mainstream American society by providing social and economic services and by creating a regularized Catholic culture. By the 1880s Catholics were told to send their children to Catholic schools, to join religious societies like the Sodality of the Blessed Virgin Mary or the Rosary Society, to attend Forty Hours devotions, and to take temperance pledges. The parish acted as a social, political, educational, and religious center.[35]

Where did this parish focus leave the Catholic home? The strong parish life of American Catholicism lessened the home's function as a religious center. Performing religious rituals such as Mass or even weddings in the home was seen by the clergy as inappropriate. Now that Catholics practiced their religion in public and supported the church financially they turned away from the private space of the home. Home worship was tainted by a past of secrecy, poverty, and oppression. During the latter part of the nineteenth century, the "bricks and mortar" period, Catholics constructed monuments—churches, hospitals, orphanages, schools—to their newfound religious freedom. The myriad of private devotions so popular after the 1850s could now be said in the presence of God in his sanctuary.[36]

On the other hand, the home itself had so many connections with religion, virtue, and morality that it could not be stripped of all of its sacred aspects: middle-class perspective held that the family, not the parish, was the foundation of society. How then should the home demonstrate its sacred function?

Catholics attempted to resolve the tensions between home and church by visually sacralizing the space within their houses. Rituals might be performed only in the church, but a religious atmosphere could, and should, be created in the home. To accomplish the transformation they turned from the more traditional Irish simplicity of a sparsely decorated cottage, with its proverbial St. Bridget's cross, and toward the Victorian fascination with things. Combining the traditional Catholic preference for the visual with a Victorian concern for material goods, affluent Catholics could afford to purchase religious articles which demonstrated their spirituality. Unlike Protestants who decorated their homes with "the Word" and pseudo-Gothic embellishments, wealthy Catholics could have the "real thing."[37]

The "better" Catholic families in novels had their own oratories or private chapels in their homes. Mrs. Clavering's secret oratory has blazing "tapers," a finely wrought ivory crucifix, a statue of the madonna and child, crimson draperies, "two or three superb paintings in oil," and vases of flowers. The flowers in the oratory at the Von Weigels were "artificially forced into bloom by horticultural skill, even under the icy reign of winter." In true Gothic style the Von Weigels' oratory "had but one . . . arched window of stained glass, whose somber tints cast a quiet subdued light into the little room." Even at noon the light was "soft and dreamy as the evening twilight." The Botelar's oratory had an organ which accompanied their evening devotions. Companies like J. R. Lamb in New York sold "fittings for oratories," and a prie-dieu could be purchased for twelve dollars.[38]

Oratories, miniature churches built into the house, provided an extreme example of how religious sentiment could be heightened within the home. "If you cannot set apart a room 'for God,'" explained the *Sacred Heart Review,* "then at least have a corner of some room for Him. Let it be your oratory." Catholics collected religious articles and displayed them throughout the house. Since most devotions were private and not done by the whole family, bedrooms often contained impromptu altars. When the door to the Kiely's "peasant" bedroom stood ajar one could see "a statue of the Sacred heart on a little altar with gauze curtains and a red lamp lighting [it]."[39]

Home altars were often created when a family member fell ill. Little Susie Flanagan's brother built her an altar in her bedroom with a crucifix, a statue of the Blessed Virgin, marble candlesticks, and wax tapers. Each family member donated part of the altar and they assembled there to say the rosary. When someone became so sick that the priest came to administer the last rites or give communion, special arrangements had to be made. The house was thoroughly cleaned and a small table covered with a clean white napkin set up. On this table sat a vessel with pure water, a crucifix, and two candles. The priest would bring his own anointing oils, but families sometimes kept emergency supplies.[40]

Middle-class families imitated the paintings of churches and oratories by purchasing religious engravings and lithographs. The cheaper versions cost a quarter, but for $1.25 one could buy a chromo of the Sacred Heart "mounted on handsome tinted and pebbled mat, lined in gold and colors, with glass over its whole surface and rings to hang it up." The *Boston Pilot* advertised pictures of Pope Pius IX, Cardinal

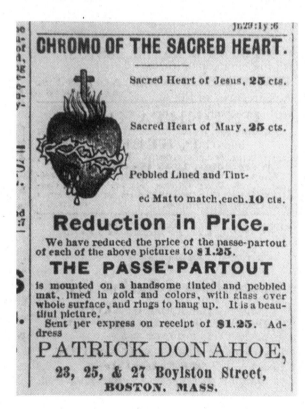

Advertisement for chromolithographs. *Boston Pilot*, several issues, 1876.

McCloskey, and Bishop James Healy, as well as a two-dollar marble bust of Daniel O'Connell ($4.00 bronze). In Philadelphia Catholics could even buy sacred pictures made out of lace as "Downing's" had "a splendid variety, suitable for bookmarks—plain, colored, and spangled." Religious prints and reproductions of the "masters" would be hung throughout the house with the best prints reserved for the parlor.[41]

After the development of photography, entrepreneurs sought to sell pictures of favorite actors and actresses, local politicians, or family members. These photographs were assembled in carte-de-visite albums and shown to guests. The more religiously inclined collected pictures of their favorite ministers, or in the case of Catholics, priests. Just like other middle-class Americans, Catholics displayed their carte-de-visite albums in the parlor. In 1866 John R. Downing of Philadelphia advertised the "only complete collection of the carte-de-visite of the clergy of this and other dioceses." He bragged that his "portraits are mostly from life, are faithful likenesses, and fine specimens of the Photographic Art." He listed the names of five cardinals, eight archbishops, eighteen bishops, and eighty-one lesser clergy all of whose photographs could be collected.[42]

Toward the latter part of the nineteenth century, Catholic popular preachers in Europe began to encourage the devotion to the Sacred Heart among families. The devotion usually involved a representation of Christ pointing to his wounded heart, which was pierced with a crown of thorns, ablaze with divine love, and topped with a small cross. Displaying a picture of the Sacred Heart in the living room, often surrounded with flowers and candles, became a hallmark of the Irish Catholic family. Demonstration of religious sentiments in the public space of the parlor, however, was a relatively late development. The "Enthronement of the Sacred Heart" (installation of the picture in the home by a priest) originated in France and was propagated by Father Mateo Crawley-Bowvey in 1914. Pope Benedict XV granted special indulgences to those who consecrated their homes to the Sacred Heart in 1915. Although house blessings by priests had a long Catholic tradition, this specific visual reminder of the sanctity of the home belongs to the twentieth century.[43]

Families distributed crucifixes, statues with vases of flowers, and blessed candles throughout the house. Holy water fonts with blessed water might be placed near the doorways. The traditional blessing of the water explained that holy water "may be efficacious in driving away devils and curing diseases," and whatever it was sprinkled on was "freed from all uncleanness and delivered from all guile." Holy water in a home provided for the "safety and repose of the indwellers." Those who made and recited the sign of the cross "with contrite heart" received an indulgence of one hundred days.[44]

Even the poorest Catholic would have a small statue sitting prominently in the room. Palms given out on Palm Sunday could be woven into a cross and placed over the bed. Irish Catholic families continued the ancient custom of weaving St. Bridget's crosses as a means of home protection. The *Sacred Heart Review* recalled with nostalgia the "Old Catholic homes" where Christ's image "could be seen on almost every wall, informing the stranger-guest that he was in the house of the common Parent." Likewise the article asked the readers to recall "the

Holy water font (c. 1830–1870). Ryan memorial
Library, Archives and Historical Collections,
St. Charles Seminary, Philadelphia.

narrow room of the city families, on whose bare but white walls there was no ornament but the Crucifix." Rich and poor alike marked their homes visually as Catholic and sacred.[45]

Although Catholics were sold items like carte-de-visite albums which had secular or Protestant roots, most of their religious articles were overtly Catholic. The major exception was the parlor organ. Catholic newspapers carried extensive advertisements for parlor organs which sold for as little as $75. The Beethoven organ could be purchased as "a Christmas present for mother, wife, sister, or daughter," for it was "a delight to the whole family, an ornament to the parlor, and a satisfaction to yourself." Parlor organs, of course, were not traditional Irish instruments, but soon were adopted as symbols of middle-class respectability. An 1890s play about Irish social climbing described "Maggie Murphy's Home" as having "an organ in the parlor, to give the house a tone."[46]

Since Catholics, unlike Protestants, did not normally sing hymns at home, appropriate music had to be written for the organ. It would not be proper for Catholics to join in on "What a Friend We Have in Jesus." Consequently, in 1890 the Misses Jordan and de Lande published a series of choral leaflets "composed especially for the family circle" which could be played "in every family that possesses a piano or a parlor organ." The brief note concluded that since the leaflets only cost ten cents they were "certainly within the reach of everybody."[47]

The articles which could be purchased to elicit religious sentiments in the home were seemingly endless. Catholic daily calendars (in eleven colors) with pictures of the Pope and St. Peter's in Rome listed feast, fast, and Ember days, the Holy Days of Obligation, and the devotions of the month. Marbleized pedestals and wall brackets were sold to hold statues, prayer books, and bronzes. Family "charity boxes" were made and passed around to "foster a spirit of genuine, considerate, conscientious charity." Temperance, sodality, and First Holy Communion certificates could be framed and hung. Samplers with Catholic images could be sewn. Catholics readily combined their religion's penchant for sensuality with the Victorian trend for display and surrounded themselves with symbols of their religion and culture.[48]

Notably absent from this array of religious goods was the Bible. Although Catholic publishing houses printed an authorized version of the Bible, it did not figure prominently in the household. Only in the latter part of the century was Bible reading encouraged by the clergy. In 1898 Pope Leo XIII granted a plenary indulgence to those faithful who read daily in the Bible for one month. Equally important to the distribution of family Bibles was the inclusion of approved "Holy

Catholic Bibles" in the 1897 Sears and Roebuck catalogue. The nearly 1600-page Bible contained a Bible dictionary, the life of the Virgin, narrations of "great events in Catholic history," and seventy full-page illustrations—all for $5.75.[49]

The purchase and display of religious artifacts was not done for religious reasons alone. Such displays demonstrated the *refinement* and good taste of the family. Middle-class Catholics sought to separate themselves from those immigrants who populated urban slums and gave Catholicism a bad name. Catholic writers therefore combined European refinement and gentility with the American Catholic home. The true Catholic home stood out from other American homes as the true religion stood out from the false. Mrs. Botelar's house in Baltimore "gave the undoubted evidence of the character and standing of its inmates" and stood apart from all of the other "gaudy modern buildings" with their "elaborately carved iron railings and glaring brass nobs."[50]

European refinement, which included the simple beauty of the peasant's cottage, supported the Catholic contention that old was better than new, grace better than ostentatiousness, and tradition better than change. Just like Catholic teaching, good taste was eternal. Consider this description of Mrs. Botelar's tea service which sat on a silver waiter,

> in a dignified state the ancient though elegant teapot, sugar-bowl, cream pitcher, knives and forks, all of the same costly metal. There was nothing modern about them, even the cups and saucers and plates were of an age long gone by, and though made of the finest and most transparent china, would have been banished from a fashionable board of the present days as too old timed to appear in good company.[51]

True Catholicism—preserved in a clean cottage or spacious mansion—exemplified dignity, artistic sensibility, and rarified sentiments. "Religion," in the words of the novelist Mrs. Hughs, "consists of all that is grand, sublime, and beautiful."[52]

The Catholic writers' association of refinement with Europe brings up the problem of *ethnicity*. Early Irish writers, such as Mary Sadlier, insisted on connecting family, Catholicism, and Irish nationalism. To reject one of those institutions was to reject them all. The Blakes lost their family ties when they allowed their children to go to public schools and reject their Irish heritage. When parents became an embarrassment to their children because of their love of Irish music and history, family commitments broke down. Writers understood that in the Americanization process children had to transfer their loyalties from the Old World to the New. During this process parents, who represented the Old, would lose their control. Irish ethnicity—for novelists primarily a cultural rather than a political phenomenon—served to cement the family.[53]

As would be expected, the later generation of writers would not stress this nexus of religion and ethnicity. Historian Donna Merwick saw the breakdown of religion and Irish ethnicity occurring in the 1880s when piety became separated from politics. As upwardly mobile Catholics sought to separate themselves from the struggling immigrants, they looked not to Ireland but to France as their "center" of culture. The pre-immigrant Catholic church with its French origins survived as a reminder of Catholic social acceptability. French convent schools became even more popular. Madame Marlier's religious article store in Boston advertised "a thousand dainty little French novelties" which could be given as Christmas presents. French commentaries on womanhood and manhood were translated and reprinted. Women associated the French language not only with ethnicity, but with class, and one writer even noticed that women "who are familiar with the French [language] generally like to use it in religious exercises in preference to their mother-tongue."[54]

Catholic Domesticity in Protestant America

The domestic ideology writers presented to American Catholics showed only minor variation from the Protestant or "secular" ideology seen in ladies' magazines, sentimental literature, and advertising. As Catholics became more literate, economically stable, and in control of their physical environment, they embraced middle-class domestic attitudes. The belief that the home served as the nursery of the nation and the God-given foundation of society was held in common by Protestants and Catholics, clergy and laity. As Catholics became more affluent, they too saw home owning as a desired goal, and builders catered to their need for maintaining a Catholic parish community. Looking to their European past—in peasant Ireland or aristocratic France—Catholics saw the virtues they now embraced. The cheerful, ordered, refined home demonstrated the moral worth of its inhabitants, Protestant or Catholic.

To say that Irish Catholics merely used domestic values as a means of assimilating into mainstream America would be unfair. Catholic domestic commentators insisted that those virtues were eternal and natural; they pointed to their saints and the Holy Family as exemplars of proper domestic sentiments. The old-fashioned Irish peasantry and those French untouched by revolutionary sentiments, were cited as demonstrating proper home life. Catholic authors, especially those writing before the 1880s, resisted assimilation and felt that they conveyed the "true" picture of domesticity. Even the Catholic hierarchy, following the lead of Pope Leo XIII, seemed interested in family life.

What Catholic writers refused to acknowledge was that their saints led rather unusual domestic lives, and they themselves had left Europe because of the difficulty of raising a family there. No one appeared concerned that papal statements on the family came along with general condemnations of modern society. Most of the values which the Irish middle class promoted had more in common with their Yankee neighbors than with the sacred characters they sought to emulate.

Dennis Clark in *The Irish in Philadelphia* says that the Irish embraced American Victorian values and life-style quickly because their rural peasant ways no longer functioned in an urban setting. His hypothesis is further supported by Lynn Lees and John Modell who contend that, unlike other immigrants, the Irish migrated from rural communities to urban America without going through a middle stage of semi-urban life in Ireland. Creating and living in a middle-class home became an important way for families to learn how to cope with an urban environment. Industrial life demanded order, discipline, and reliability. Gone was the sense that time was determined by nature or by village life. Middle-class domesticity supported an industrial lifestyle by promoting order, division between work and leisure, and consumerism.[55]

Women brought the sense of "industrial domesticity" into the Irish Catholic family. More than any other important group Irish domestics had the dubious privilege of maintaining the "proper" Victorian home. Irish women were workers in a household factory where order, punctuality, reliability, and discipline were stressed. Protestant mistresses exposed their young charges to the "cult of true womanhood" and demanded from them purity, piety, submissiveness, and domestic intuition. When these domestics married and started their own families, we can only assume that they sought to establish homes of similar quality. They probably never consciously believed that Victorian domesticity was a way of inching into the middle class, but rather that they were creating the "right" kind of home. It would be this home which then would make them the "right" kind of people.[56]

Catholic attitudes toward the home and domestic virtues harmonized well with those values promoted by pattern-book writers, Protestant domestic reformers, and women writers. There were, however, some exceptions. Catholic preference for European writers and a nostalgia for the "old world" promoted a more traditional view of domesticity. An emphasis on authority and hierarchy colored the relationship between parents and children. Catholic writers did not see the child as the center of the family. They condemned what they saw as spoiled and independent children who ignored parental authority. Catholic publications did not publish "dead baby poetry" which sentimentalized the tender and fleeting character of young children. The "children's corner" in diocesan newspapers and the myriad of Catholic juvenile literature gave children adult-like characteristics. Children certainly made up an important part of the family, but they, too, had their proper place.

The Catholic understanding of women's role in the family also demonstrated more conservative attitudes. Women were accorded traditional family roles even by women writers. Women worked as domestics or had other employment only in order to keep their family together. Mary Sadlier and Con O'Leary both ridiculed the women's rights movement in their novels in order to assert the traditional maternal role of women. Powerful women were portrayed frequently in novels, but they were always either widowed or single. The father, when present, was unquestionably the head of the household. Catholic writers took pride in asserting their support of the patriarchal household over and against what they perceived as an increasingly feminized Protestant culture. Their promotion of the patriarchal nature of the home came into direct conflict with the general cultural understanding of women's proper sphere.

The most significant difference between the ideal Protestant and Catholic home was the way religious sentiments were demonstrated. Both groups acknowledged the importance of the home in shaping morality and spirituality. Catholics expressed this concern visually in their display of religious articles. The more "Catholic" of these articles were often used in personal religious devotion and placed in the more private areas of the home, notably the bedrooms. Family worship, so encouraged by Protestant writers, was not common. The statue of Mary placed on a hallway landing or the lithograph of the Sacred Heart placed over a doorway were not centers of worship but private reminders to the household members.

The less "Catholic" of the religious articles, carte-de-visite albums and parlor organs, were displayed in the parlor. Eventually the family Bible would assume its place in the Catholic parlor or study. Printed house blessings, illustrated enthronement texts, and reproductions of the Holy Family, beginning to appear in the late nineteenth-century home, would become a standard Catholic domestic feature in the twentieth century. Living in a middle-class society which Catholics understood as Protestant, their placement of carte-de-visite albums in parlors and their Sacred Heart statues on bedroom dressers is not surprising.

The strong parish structure which developed in the United States also worked against the privatization of religion within the Catholic home. Unlike the Protestant church structure that appeared to be weakening its hold on the average churchgoer, the development of a middle- and upper-class Irish American Catholic culture strength-ened the parish. Funds were now available to build new churches, schools, convents, and other social and religious institutions. A myr-iad of religious activities from novenas to rosary sodality meetings competed for the attention of family members. The home could be only a secondary extension of the church, both because of the par-ishes' social functions and because of the heightened sacredness of the church. The church held the real body and blood of Christ, and so no matter how much a home was laden with religious bric-a-brac it fell short of being "God's house."

Toward the end of the century the home began to be seen more and more as a religious center. With the decision to enroll all Catholic children in parochial schools at the Baltimore Third Plenary Council of 1884, attention was moved from the church to the school. Parishes built schools before churches, and priests said Mass in gyms and auditoriums. Children received greater attention, and education was taken more seriously. Mothers, nuns, and children threatened the patriarchal control over religion. We can already see movement in this direction in popular family magazines like the *Sacred Heart Review*.[57]

The general Victorian romanticization of the family within Amer-ican culture served to promote the life of the laity within the Catholic church. Unlike Protestants who built much of their theology on the family, Catholics upheld a heritage which saw the married state as second best—after the life of the religious or single person. Religious expression in the Catholic home supported a *this-worldly* ethic which implied that salvation would be accomplished by leading a virtuous domestic life. By sanctifying the home Catholics created a significant rival to the parish. If the home could so greatly influence the individ-ual, then those who created that home life assumed a powerful reli-gious role. American Catholic culture of the nineteenth century was a lay culture, and the spiritualization of the home helped secure this important change in Catholic life.

The infusion of religious sentiment into the family can be seen best in the home rituals in which Protestants and Catholics participated. These rituals supported both sectarian religious concerns and the common belief in the spiritual position of the family. In the next chapter the differences between the Protestant and Catholic understanding of the home as a sacred place will become more apparent as we examine the nature of family worship, Sabbath activities, and reading rituals.

[4]
Rituals of The Hearth

The popular theology of both Protestants and Catholics during the nineteenth century upheld the home as the God-given cornerstone of society. Adam and Eve's home in paradise had been destroyed by sin, but a glimpse of it could still be seen in the homes of good Christians. Although Catholics might uphold the church as the locus of sacredness, some Protestants went as far as to say that the "family is as strictly a religious institution as the Church." Churches could come and go, societies would rise and fall, but if "the family remains, there may be religion." Both Catholics and Protestants saw family religious activities as crucial to the production of a strong family, nation, and church. Each religious body, though, had their own understanding of the appropriateness of home religion, the type of rituals to be performed, and the role of domestic religious instruction. As the nineteenth century moved into the twentieth the differences between the Protestant and Catholic understandings of home religion—especially as it related to education—diminished, and a more common understanding of domesticity developed.[1]

Daily Family Worship: The Protestant Model

In the "truly Christian" homes of American Protestants, the religious life of the family was seen as an extension of the religious life of the individual. Personal piety had a long Protestant history which reached its apex in Puritan New England. "Secret piety," wrote James Wood following the Reformed tradition, "stands first on the list of religious duties." Retiring to one's "closet" became a metaphor for private, individual prayer. Religious writers cited Jesus' command to "enter into thy closet and shut thy door and pray to thy Father who is in secret." (Matt. 6:6) Presbyterian publications extolled the virtues of

77

personal devotion and extemporaneous prayer. "Religion is a private and personal concern," wrote James McGill; "everyone is related to God as an individual." Each morning and evening, at fixed times, Christians should "wean out [their] thoughts when quite alone." In the privacy of the closet they would discover if the spirit felt in group prayer was truly authentic or merely emotional.[2]

Although private worship and study were important, they were not sufficient. Victorian writers also noted the social character of humankind. Private devotion might eliminate hypocritical or ostentatious worship, but it ignored two values held dear in the nineteenth century: the family and the social role of religion. For many theologians, the whole house became the private closet. "God blesses and shelters the household in which he is honored," explained Reverend Miller; "prayer weaves a roof of love over the home and builds walls of protection about it." Family prayer not only seemed natural to the home but also maintained its sacredness.[3]

Protestant writers used three sources to legitimate the primacy of family worship. First, they returned to the Old Testament and gathered evidence of households worshiping God. Adam and Eve, Moses, Joshua, David, and all of the patriarchal families of the Bible attested to the need for family worship. Although Thomas Moore noticed that "there is no specific command in the Bible to worship God in the family," he quickly pointed out that "the first family altar was erected in the very sight of Eden." The New Testament, as the second source of legitimation, provided encouragement from the epistles but not from the Gospels. Christ's peripatetic life-style and his bachelorhood worked against family ties, so writers depended on stories of the disciples praying in homes. If the Holy Spirit could descend on the disciples in an upper room of a house, surely God would visit the prayerful nineteenth-century family.[4]

The third way authors legitimized family devotions was to call upon the mythical power of the peasant past. Writers, including Sarah Hale, used Robert Burns's poem "Cotter's Saturday Night" as a means of tapping into what they conceived of as an ordered, meaningful past. In colloquial Scottish-English, Burns sang the praises of the rural peasant family who when "The cheerfu' supper done, wi' serious face, / They round the ingle [hearth fire] form a circle wide," and worshiped God. James Alexander, who cited the poem in his 1847 essay *Thoughts on Family Worship*, concluded that such scenes "are presented week after week among the Scottish peasantry." His attitude, and that of many writers, was that if family worship existed in "the old days" or in the "old country" it should be continued in America. Thus the simple history of the past was drawn upon, along with the Old and New Testaments, as reasons for domestic worship.[5]

Protestant ministers and writers encouraged families to organize family worship twice a day. Morning worship began before breakfast ("food for the soul before we seek food for the body") and the day's activities. The time for worship should be fixed so that it could not be changed by business or other activities. This regularity promoted "method and punctuality in domestic affairs, which is the chief ornament of a Christian house." The father gathered all of the household, including servants and apprentices, together for prayer, hymn singing and scriptural reading. Meeting in the parlor the household started the day "bowing before the God of mercies."[6] Sarah Hale poetically described the results of morning devotions in 1842:

> What fount of strength, what draught of joy
>   That morn's devotion yields!
> It girds the soul with righteousness,

Family worship. Nineteenth-century magazine engraving, Logan Library, Picture Collection, Philadelphia.

Or from temptation shields;
It adds the pearl of priceless worth
Where life's rich gifts abound
And scatters flowers of Paradise
The lowliest home around.[7]

Morning devotions. The Athenaeum of Philadelphia. *Godey's Lady's Book* 24 (1842), p. 241.

The more liturgically minded denominations, such as the Episcopalians, outlined specific prayers for the family. After an opening prayer the household would kneel for a general confession. The father conducted a responsorial prayer with his family answering "Amen." A psalm would be recited as well as a verse from the Old Testament. Then all joined together for the Apostle's or Nicene Creed, the Collect from the *Book of Common Prayer,* petitions, and a concluding thanksgiving. If this liturgy was too formal for the family, they could begin with the Lord's Prayer, thank God for preserving them through the night, mention any upcoming family events, and then dedicate the day to the Lord. The service would be concluded with a prayer to keep them from sin, perform the day's duties, and deliver divine guidance.[8]

While Episcopalians felt free to sprinkle their services with "Collects for Grace" and the prayer of St. John Chrysostom, lower church Protestants strove for simplicity in worship. The day's obligations limited morning worship, making evening worship of greater concern. Writers on family religion took care to explain that evening devotions should be conducted before everyone was too tired to worship God appropriately. Small children were a particular problem. Methodist Charles Deems encouraged families to say prayers early before "others in the family became engaged in study or in work, [and] the children are soon sleepy." This more informal Methodist felt that the dining room would be the appropriate place for such prayers. It was the "room in which we are daily fed by His hand," and family worship should be considered "but a part of the daily meal . . . the first and the last strength of the day."[9]

Once the household assembled, the father recited family prayers. Family prayers could be read from denominational prayer books such as the *Book of Common Prayer;* contemporary manuals like Samuel Fisher's *The Family Assistant; or, Book of Prayers for the Use of Families;* or traditional books like *Prayers and Offices of Devotion for Families* written by Benjamin Jenks in 1697. Prayer book writers devised prayers which addressed the family troubles of illness and death. Of a more individual nature, Louise Houghton's 1879 prayer book, *The Sabbath Month,* contained a series of prayers which allowed a pregnant woman to meditate on the upcoming birth, the birth process, and the following "weeks of retirement." Other prayer books petitioned for good harvests, safe return from journeys, fair weather after excessive rain, or rain after drought. Depending on how aware of the liturgical calendar the denomination was, prayers could change with the holiday seasons.[10]

Authors warned against over-zealous fathers who burdened their families with long-winded prayers and sermons. The writers of prayer books, such as James Weir in 1879, hoped his prayers would "supply helps to this duty of social prayer, and, without inducing any slavish imitation in language." Even at an earlier date James Alexander in 1847 believed that the length of domestic services was worthy of attention, noting it "was the fault of our forefathers to make it sufferably long." In spite of his sensitivity to the length of service, Alexander insisted that "every secular task or amusement will be suspended, and absolute silence and quiet will be enforced, even in the case of the youngest children."[11]

Although Alexander quoted the British Anglican Richard Cecil who stated that gloomy and austere prayers were unnecessary, he maintained that worship was for God and not children. "The solemn service of God," he later concluded, "should not be made a school-lesson." This attitude came under attack by women writers like Lydia Maria Child who early in 1831 insisted that "it is the first duty of a mother to make the Bible precious and delightful to her family." Women, whose task it usually was to quiet baby during daddy's prayers, rejected domestic worship as a solemn service to God early on. They emphasized the teaching aspect of domestic religion over the worshiping dimension.[12]

Protestant ministers accepted the early warnings of women writers only at a much later date. In 1882, the Presbyterian Board of Publication issued James Miller's *Home-Making,* which acknowledged the "irksome and wearisome" quality of much of family devotion. He responded to what he perceived as a common misunderstanding—that it "is evidence of their [children's] depravity that they fidget and wiggle on their chairs"—by emphasizing the positive nature of home worship. Worship should be simple, appropriate to the family's situation, pleasant, and topical. While forty years earlier Alexander tried to persuade his readers that only the father should read from the Bible "with all solemnity and expression, and without interruption," Miller preferred that children take turns stumbling over simplified prayers and scriptural passages.[13]

Family hymns often followed prayer. Singing enlivened worship without detracting from the serious nature of the activity. With the musical enthusiasm of a good Methodist, Charles Deems explained that "music is a blessing from God. The family where there is no song is a family indeed unblest." All agreed that lack of innate musical talent was no excuse for not praising the Lord through song. Family hymns reinforced general religious perspectives and particular denominational teachings. In B. B. Hotchkin's story *Manliness For Young Men* the family included in their worship a hymn which summed up the struggles of the preceding chapters: "When in the slippery paths of youth / With headless steps I ran / Thine arm, unseen, conveyed me safe / And led me up to [be a] man." Presbyterians gave children their own hymn books which kindled early the Reformed perspective on sin: "I know that I was born in sin / I feel much evil work within / Sins that offend my Maker's eyes, / Dwell in my heart, and often rise."[14]

Family hymns of the later nineteenth century, under the impact of liberal evangelicalism, stressed more positive values. Family hymn books included Protestant standbys like "The Old Rugged Cross" and

"What a Friend We have in Jesus," but they also contained hymns which asserted the importance of domesticity, both on earth and in heaven. J. P. Thompson in *Home Worship for Daily Use in the Family* presented several hymns which praised the family for praising God. "Lord! let us in our home agree," the family sang, "This blessed peace to gain / Unite our hearts in love to thee / And love to all will reign." If the home was a glimpse of heaven, then heaven must be the perfect home. When members of the family died they met again in heaven where they set up celestial housekeeping. The hymn "Our Home with Jesus" started with a solo voice singing, "My heavenly home is bright and fair," and the chorus responding, "We'll be gathered home." Domestic hymnody echoed the popular thought that death only temporarily separated the family and that the joys of the home comprised the joys of heaven.[15]

The center of family worship, of course, was the Bible. The Bible was "in a word . . . God talking with his creatures." In general families read the Old Testament in the morning and the New Testament at night. Many writers, like Caroline Fry in 1852, "never thought it good to read much of the Scriptures at once," but preferred to "meditate on a short portion." There was some discussion as to whether one should read only the important passages, or if it was better to start at the beginning and go chapter by chapter. To help families decide which parts of the Bible to read, Charles Deems included in his book *Home Altar; An Appeal in Behalf of Family Worship* a table of lessons "which embrace, perhaps, those portions of the sacred Scriptures likely to be most profitable when read aloud."[16]

As the focus of domestic worship, the family Bible was accorded special reverence. Unlike other books which might be placed in the library or father's study, families displayed the Bible prominently in the parlor. Decorative arts books contained patterns for constructing special tables where the Bible sat. Table cloths with the gold-embroidered letters "I. H. S." (from the Greek name for Jesus) on purple velvet gave these tables an ecclesiastical look. Other books showed women how to build parlor lecterns for more formal biblical readings. In the children's story *Jennie Prindle's Home*, the family received a small Bible-stand with a marble top along with Grandma's Bible, "the most precious earthly thing that she had."[17]

Marble and wood brackets could be built to hold the Bible or prayer book. *Household Elegancies* displayed one bracket shaped like a Gothic window, eighteen inches high, and carved out of walnut. "Its beauty of form is greatly enhanced by having the carving carefully and neatly done," explained the author, "the leaves rounded off neatly, each vein

Left: parlor lectern/reading stand; right: cross and Gothic window
bracket. The Athenaeum of Philadelphia. Williams and Jones,
Household Elegancies, pp. 126 and 97.

cut and scratched with the sharp point of the knife." Constructing
such elaborate furnishings demonstrated the spiritual quality of the
family and the piety and artistic talent of the mother who made
them.[18]

The Bible also served to connect the generations of the family.
Oversized with elaborate engravings and inscribed with the birth,
marriage, and death dates of the family, the Bible brought together
religion and the family symbolically. "When I look at the folio Bible
which was my grandfather's," explained James Alexander, "I cannot
bear the thought that it should stop with me." Religion and the family
continued forever. Two possessions hallowed the house of Catharine
Sedgwick's fictitious family the Barclays. Mother had her "rocking-
chair and Bible, and [so] I trust she will have a happy home after all."
For Sedgwick, as for most writers, the Bible was "as essential to a home
as the foundation-stone to an edifice."[19]

The Bible formed, in effect, the "home altar" which good families must construct or repair "if it has fallen into decay." Although James Wood waxed eloquent about the household of Jacob who lit "the sacred fire on their domestic altars" by carrying the coals back from the temple, Bible reading had replaced the sacrifice of the ancient Israelites. Protestantism changed the ritual from one of sacrifice to one of instruction. The altar of the Protestant home, both metaphorically and physically, contained only the Bible, hymn book, and a candle to read by.[20]

Family worship at the home altar was a teaching ritual. Although praise, thanksgiving, and petitioning were important in family worship, prayer took a backseat to instruction from the Bible, especially in the evangelical churches. Fathers could shy away from extemporaneous instruction by reading published sermons, but "the observance of a formal morning and evening service at the family altar . . . which is accompanied by no religious instruction, accomplishes little more than to remind the household that a profession of religion is made in their midst." Reading from the Bible constantly reminded the family of the religious goals which they pursued. Daily reference to that instruction, whether through scriptural readings or the telling of biblical tales, was essential to Protestant domestic worship.[21]

Religious instruction based on the Bible exceeded the boundaries of morning and evening devotion. Daily activities limited the amount of time a family could spend in formal, group worship. Home Sabbath devotions, life-cycle rituals, and informal instruction also provided ways that religious teaching entered the family.

The Catholic Model

Unlike Protestants who saw their homes as an appropriate space for worship, Catholics saw the church as the primary space for religious activities. The aristocratic European home might contain a private chapel or oratory where the family priest would say Mass. This space was distinct from the rest of the house and was specially consecrated. The devoted family would gather each morning to hear Mass. Few American Catholics would ever have such a home, but you will recall that Mary Sadlier in her novel *Old and New; or Taste versus Fashion* gave the "tasteful" Von Wiegel family a room which functioned as an oratory. Unfortunately, the paucity of priests in America prevented the Von Wiegels from having Mass said at their oratory. More importantly, the Von Wiegels lived "at too great a distance from any Church to have the privilege of hearing Mass on week-days."[22]

For the Catholic, hearing Mass functioned as a major way to work toward spiritual perfection. Domestic devotions substituted for devotions which should take place in the church. Historically, daily devotions originated in the monastic communities where the recitation of the Divine Office—a series of psalms and prayers chanted at specific times—marked the religious day. Monks and nuns returned to the chapel from the fields and libraries to worship in a prescribed manner. The lay Catholic, who pursued the spiritual life within the world, attempted to imitate this monastic model of hearing Mass and reciting the Divine Office. In "French Home Life," an article which the *Catholic World* presented to its American readers as a model of the Catholic family, Mme. Lamartine went "to Mass every morning with [her] children at seven." Mary Sadlier's orphan character Willy Burke remembered his dead mother taking him daily to Mass at the cathedral. It was these visits "to the foot of the altar" which allowed Willy to remember his mother after she "had been long mouldering in the grave."[23]

If attending Mass and reciting the Divine office were impossible, then rituals which might have taken place in church could take place in the home. Morning and evening prayers thus figured into the religious life of the Victorian Catholic family, though the Catholic hierarchy never constructed family liturgies for home worship. Morning devotions cited in Catholic fiction were individualistic and informal. Characters in the stories "say their prayers" for about half an hour. The Catholic reader needed no further explanation. If the prayers were the familiar Aves and Paters (Hail Marys and Our Fathers), then no written devotionals were needed.

The American Catholic's dependence on European models of domesticity—either the honest home of the poor or the paternalistic home of the aristocracy—shaped the descriptions of home devotions. In Sister Mary Carroll's story, "A Washerwoman's Household," the father rose at four in order to have time to say his morning prayers before starting work at five. "A simple laborer," Mr. Keane assembled his family in their simple cottage and "before retiring, all [would] kneel, thank God for his mercies, implore pardon for their faults, and recite the Rosary of Our Lady." The author then mentioned that "all of this does not occupy half an hour." On the other hand, Anna Dorsey presented the "other" Catholic family who assembled their domestics and "two old pensioners" into their private oratory where Alice Botelar first "commenced the sweet notes of a sacred melody . . . then followed the night prayers and litany of the blessed Virgin."[24]

Reports of Catholic home rituals in newspapers seemed more realistic. Writers assumed that those who felt called to the religious life entered the convent or the priesthood. Those who didn't lived in the world and had to deal with the demands of everyday life. The working-class Irish family, where everyone (not just the father) went off to work before six, could hardly be berated for not hearing morning Mass and having family prayers. In 1891 Cardinal Gibbons, in an address entitled "The Duties of Parents," quietly implored Catholic families to have at least evening devotions. "I do not wish to impose heavy obligations upon you," he explained, "but if the father and mother would gather their family together and have a short family prayer at night—I do not ask it in the morning—then will God's blessing rest on you."[25]

Only the most aristocratic American Catholic families, like the fictional Botelars or Von Wiegels, would "at nine o'clock precisely" summon by bell "Jan and Betty [the servants] to assist in the family devotions, after which they were dismissed for the night." A more probable experience was that of another of Sadlier's characters, the maid Bessy Conway. Bessy, the good Catholic, was one of the "household" who the good Protestants assembled for morning worship. In her always polite but direct manner Bessy told her mistress Mrs. Hibbard that she was a Catholic and didn't say the same prayers that Protestants did. Luckily Mrs. Hibbard chalked this up to the peculiarity of "Papists" and let the matter pass.[26]

Bessy, however, was not devoid of religious sentiments. Mrs. Hibbard might read her morning Bible verses, but Bessy and her fellow servants said their "beads." A popular devotion throughout the Catholic world, saying the rosary began in the eleventh century when the Blessed Virgin Mary appeared to St. Dominic and commanded him to "Preach the Rosary, which is a shield against the shafts of the enemy." By far the most popular of the Marian devotions, saying the rosary consisted of the recitation of Aves and Paters, one "Our Father" for each ten "Hail Marys". This series was repeated five times while one meditated on specific events in the lives of Mary and her son Jesus. Father Lambing in his book on sacramentals remarked that the rosary took the place among the laity that the Divine Office occupied for the clergy. Again, we see how the religious activities of the laity imitated in a slightly less rigorous way the life of the professional religious.[27]

Saying the rosary was an individual devotion but lent itself to communal recitation. *St. Agatha's Parish Calendar* of January 1899 suggested that "families should assemble every morning for the public recital of the Beads" in addition to the morning and evening prayer.

St. Dominic receiving the rosary. Ryan
Memorial Library, Archives and
Historical Collections, St. Charles
Seminary, Philadelphia.

One person recited the first part of the prayer while the others
responded with the remainder. In an article on family prayer in the
Sacred Heart Review the writer remarked that "one need not set it aside
for any other devotion, for it contains in one, every devotion existing
in the Church." The prayers included in it were "so simple in [their]
vocal expression that all can say it," and yet as a subject for contemplation "even the loftiest minds can never exhaust its treasures."
For the poor American Catholic, the writer concluded that reciting
the rosary was "so clear that the most illiterate can read its meaning
upon the surface."[28]

Saying the rosary was so much a part of Catholic life that few writers
stopped to describe its impact on the spiritual life of the family. One of

the more eloquent of these few came from the slums of Irish Catholic London and most likely described a common Catholic experience:

> What chance to be clean was there in a house on whose only floor bags of dusty rags and putrescent bones were spilled out to be sorted? Nevertheless, we were used to this, and before going to bed we all knelt down, after a supper of Indian meal, on the bare uneven brick floor and recited the Rosary, father leading off: one Our Father to ten Hail Marys: one of the prayers spoken fifty times by the help of a string of beads: and we arose feeling good and comforted and strengthened for the morrow's work.[29]

Like the Bible for Protestants, the rosary held special meaning for Catholics. When Willy Burke's mother died he kept her rosary as a sacred memento of her. *Catholic Anecdotes,* written in 1870, depicted the rosary as an "amulet of protection" and gave examples of situations in which the rosary fended off sharks, deflected bullets, and cured illnesses. Catholics reported saying the rosary at the bedside of the sick. Aunt Dee, in a letter to "The Children's Corner" of the *Baltimore Catholic Mirror,* recounted the last days of her little nephew Paul. Paul, "whose death was like his sweet little life," was devoted to his rosary, and "every morning and evening his mother and I used to say it kneeling by the side of his bed." Little Paul died "just as we began the third decade . . . all the pain had gone and he was happy in heaven."[30]

Daily reading from the Bible was not a common Catholic family ritual. Irish American literacy rates were rather high, but Catholics still chose not to read the Bible. Characters in Catholic novels read Bible stories and studied Bible history in school but shunned reading the Bible itself. Under pressure from their Bible-reading Protestant neighbors, some didactic writers created reasons for Catholic disinterest in the Bible. Mary Sadlier insisted in 1866 that the Bible was a very powerful book which needed interpretation by an educated clergy. In *Aunt Honor's Keepsake,* two illicit young lovers read Canticle of Canticles to one another. First pointing out the stupidity of the Protestant fixation on Bible reading Sadlier then exclaimed, "talk of sentimental novels, but I say that the Bible—at least the Old Testament—is just as unfit to place in the hands of the young of either sex, allowing them to read where and how they will."[31]

By the 1880s Catholic reading of the Bible had become more acceptable. Catholic clergymen promoted Bible reading in order to counter the influence of Protestant Bible societies and biblical criticism. In a pastoral letter following the Third Plenary Council of 1884, the bishops reminded their people "that the most highly valued treasure of every family library . . . should be the Holy Scriptures." Local Catholic newspapers, such as the *Baltimore Catholic Mirror,* carried articles such as "Read the Bible" which encouraged the reading of the New Testament. In the Protestant tradition, the article portrayed the Bible as an ethical guide "making plain what is right and wrong" and pointing out the means to perfection and heaven. While Rome condemned the new liberal biblical criticism and restricted scholarship on the Bible, the American Catholic laity appeared more ready to read the Bible on their own.[32]

The other traditional daily prayer for Catholics was the recitation of the Angelus. Three times a day the European churches would ring their bells to call their people to a moment of prayer to Mary. Catholics in the New World established this tradition of ringing church bells at six in the morning, noon, and six in the evening. Like saying the rosary, the Angelus was basically an individual recitation of Hail Marys, but the *Baltimore Catholic Mirror* in an article called "Happy Homes" urged its recitation in all good families. To facilitate its recitation in nations where one might not hear church bells, the *Boston Pilot* advertised an "Angelus Clock" for the rather high price of twelve dollars (deluxe edition $20). This clock did not chime the hours of the day but the times for reciting the Angelus, and was "finished in hard woods, handsomely gilded, faced by a beautiful chromo-lithograph of the Annunciation, and surmounted by a cross."[33]

Catholics performed other devotions at home in addition to the Angelus. Most of these devotions were abbreviated versions of church activities. Saying the "Stations of the Cross" commemorated the Passion of Christ via meditation on the fourteen "steps" to Calvary. Families bought hand-colored "Stations of the Cross" and miniature Stations painted on scrolls which could be rolled up. Home recitation of the Stations gained no indulgences unless the Catholic was unable to visit the church. Father Lambing warned that saying prayers in front of "small pictures of the fourteen stations so joined together as to fold up, but which had no crosses" would not receive the indulgences. He concluded by stating that "we must in all cases conform strictly to the conditions laid down by the Holy See . . . for nothing is left to our free choice." Although Catholics most likely continued praying the Stations of the Cross at home, the clergy emphasized that the proper place for such devotions was not the home but the church.[34]

Rome laid down rigid guidelines for the proper religious conduct of Catholics. Ever since the Counter Reformation the church attempted to teach the people a common set of liturgical practices and theology and to rid them of local devotions considered superstitious. The church restricted the activities of the individual and the family, but at the same time gave Catholics assurance that if they abided by the rules they were on the right path to salvation. Protestants, with their emphasis on the individual standing alone before God, were never sure whether they had done enough for God's glory. This difference between Protestant and Catholic attitudes can best be seen in how the two groups understood the meaning of the Sabbath.

"Remember Keep Holy the Lord's Day": *The Sabbath at Home*

The Protestant debate over the propriety of Sabbath activities centered around the meaning of the biblical injunction to "remember the Sabbath day, to keep it Holy." (KJV Ex. 20:8) By the nineteenth century the New England Calvinist Sabbath had reached almost mythical proportions and stood for all forms of unreasonable, harsh religious devotion. The Puritan, who hung his cat on Monday for killing a mouse on Sunday, became a symbol for New England rigidity and

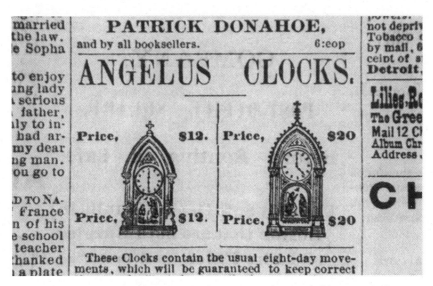

Advertisement for Angelus clocks. *Boston Pilot,* several issues, 1876.

old fashioned attitudes. Even writers within the Reformed tradition commented that previous generations had been too extreme in their demands for a sacred Sabbath. And yet, the Sabbath continued to be a day devoted to God, devoid of work, amusements, and secular activities. Few Protestant writers would challenge the Sabbath's religious nature; they did question the ways of assimilating that religion.[35]

The traditional Calvinist understanding of religion, as seen in colonial Puritanism, was that God and salvation were serious, adult matters. The Puritans expected their children to rise to the urgency of their salvation, if not with adult sophistication then with adult seriousness. Sabbath was a time for private contemplation of God and salvation, and children were expected to act with the same decorum as adults. Although religious education was important, it was not to be "watered down" for childhood consumption. Just as adults refrained from all work, visiting, and secular activities, so children should focus their attention on divine matters. Play, reading storybooks, and idle conversations distracted children from Sabbath religious study and meditation.

By the mid-nineteenth century, attitudes toward both religion and children were undergoing substantial changes. The harsh Puritan Sabbath came under criticism from writers who saw religion as a more joyful system and children as individuals, not small adults. Women writers like Catharine Sedgwick were some of the strongest critics. In her 1835 novel *Home,* Sedgwick tried to humanize the Sabbath by making it a time for religious education. Following a religious service at their local church (no mention of denomination), the Barclay family took a walk by the seaside and pondered the natural beauty of God's world. Later in the day Mrs. Barclay read the Bible to her children, showed them Bible pictures, wrote them little sermons, taught hymns, and "when she wants to read to herself, she sets us all down . . . with our slates to copy off some animal"—from the Bible of course. "Sometimes," according to the children, "we form a class,—father, mother and all, and we ask questions, in turn, from the Bible, 'what such a king did?'—'when such a prophet lived?'—trying most of all to puzzle father and mother, and get them to the foot of the class." The enthusiasm of the children for their Sabbath was enough to cause the doubting neighbor "to make me envy your pleasant Sunday evenings at home, and to inspire me with the desire, and as far as I can, to go and do likewise."[36]

Sabbath reformers, like Sedgwick, hoped to gear Sabbath activities to children. Julia Corner claimed that she had written a Sabbath book for children "no less entertaining than their every-day story-books," but which inculcated some useful moral lessons and scriptural history. Unlike the traditional Calvinist who scorned frivolity on the Sabbath, Corner (whose book was published by the Presbyterian Publishing Board) sought "to instruct, to improve and to amuse." In 1853, *Children of the Bible* compared the Bible to "the picture-gallery of a king" and sought to save children from "pointed rocks and hidden sands" by telling the stories of biblical children. Since secular reading material was suspect, most denominational publishing companies provided a variety of moral tales suitable for the home or Sunday School. Bible reading was certainly still considered important, but was often replaced by Bible stories geared for the childhood imagination.[37]

The traditional Puritan also enjoined his family to carry on only pious conversations on the Sabbath. Reformers modified this tradition to meet the changing expectations of children and parents. Lydia Sigourney encouraged mothers in 1839 not to "dismiss [the children] to Sunday school, and think no more about them," but instead to "spend as much time as you can, in religious conversation with them." Mary Hughes wrote a series of dialogues for the Evangelical Lutheran church between a widow and her children, demonstrating how informal conversations supported public worship. Before and after morning and evening services the family "placed themselves around the tea-table" and discussed religion. The children took turns paraphrasing the sermon, and long walks helped create a meditative atmosphere.[38]

The purpose of pious conversation and reading was to instruct children on religious matters. Sabbath home activities no longer were intended for the worship of God (which could be done in church), but for the education of children about God. Instruction replaced worship as the primary religious ritual of the family. The home, especially on the Sabbath, was "God's university," a "divinely appointed institute for the training of the young." Mother as teacher replaced father as priest and therefore as the director of religious rituals. Although the church might begin to direct the child, it was the conversations, the games, the walks, the cajoling before and after the public service which imparted "to the mind the desire and capacity for all that is truly great and good." Protestantism by the mid-nineteenth century had moved from being the religion of the converted adult to being the education of the innocent child.[39]

Catholic attitudes toward the Sabbath differed substantially from Protestant perspectives. In a biting 1876 essay in the *Catholic World,* an anonymous writer analyzed the inequities of imposing a Protestant religious outlook on a religiously diverse nation. The author presented the traditional Puritan Sabbath in all its stereotypical glory: children punished for whistling, breakfast eaten in silence, long incomprehensible sermons later remarked on by "the paterfamilias," and mother noticing the trimmings on Mrs. X's hat during the endless church services. Catholics could take solace, however, in the self-evident fact that children reared "by tedious Bible-reading, hymn singing, and long-winded prayer" would grow up to "loathe and abhor all religion." Protestants, in the essay, were seen as dull hypocrites who refused to work themselves but expected the Sunday labor of others.[40]

Catholics, of course, did not have to look forward to such a dreary Sabbath. The Church, the *Catholic World* explained, enjoined "her children at least to hear Mass devoutly and to abstain from servile labor on that day." Noting that the Church had to "provide . . . for all sorts and conditions of men," the author added "that reasons of necessity or transcendent charity will excuse us from either obligation." The maid Bessy Conway could work on Sunday because the church recognized the necessity of her labor for her existence. Sunday was for worship and relaxation, and since man was not "a law unto himself spiritually, he invents for himself no obligations superadded to those of the church." The good Catholic then could legitimately go to a concert, visit friends, write a business letter, or (to the horror of Protestants) take a drink at a local cafe.[41]

The church demanded that Catholics attend Mass and left returning for evening Vespers optional. Sunday was for worship; the nineteenth-century Mass left little time for instruction. Priests delivered brief sermons geared for adults. Most of the Mass was in a language which the people could not understand, and so they read their prayer books or recited the rosary. Mass was a sacred sacrifice, not an occasion for instruction. American Catholics exposed to travelling "missions" (the equivalent of Protestant revival meetings) might receive some theological instruction on Sunday evening, but this was strictly outside of the rubric of the Mass. Both clerical and lay Catholic writers never specified Sunday as the day to catechize children. The *Catholic World* article assumed Sunday was primarily a "family day" and that religious duties ended after church.[42]

The only exception to this general Catholic attitude toward Sunday might have been the use of a book called Goffine's *Explanation of the Epistles and the Gospels.* Leonhard Goffine (1648–1719) was a German priest who sought to compose a Catholic equivalent to Luther's householder's book called a *postille* (Latin for "after this [text]"). In 1690 he published in Mainz a book in Latin which contained the epistles and gospel readings for the church year followed by brief devotional commentaries and an introduction to the church calendar. It became a very important book for families in Germany and in Switzerland during the nineteenth century, taking the place of the Bible in Catholic homes.[43]

Benziger Brothers, a German-oriented Catholic press, published the first American translation of *Goffine* in 1859. By 1880 many editions had been published, and the text read more like an adult catechism than a theological treatise. Winand Wigger, the Bishop of Newark, wrote in 1884 that "if on every Sunday afternoon the Explanation of that particular Sunday's Gospel and Epistle were carefully read in every Catholic family, we would soon see a wonderful change for the better among our people." William Elder, the archbishop of Cincinnati, believed it would "bring blessings on any house in which it is kept and used."[44]

It is difficult to judge whether *Goffine* was used in non-German families, its English translation being a concession to the number of German-American families who no longer used German at home. Toward the end of the century, as home devotions and family worship were emphasized by the clergy, Goffine might have been a convenient way to encourage household Christian education, especially on Sunday. It might have served as an encyclopedia for the Catholic laity. The 1880 edition contained not only all of the gospels and epistles, but information on the rosary, heaven and hell, the sacraments, churching women, the consecration of a new church, and even illustrations of the Holy Land. It spanned almost a thousand pages and was a clear statement of current Catholic belief and practice.

What were, then, the differences between Protestant and Catholic attitudes toward the family's role in "keeping the Sabbath holy?" For many Protestants, religion was education about religion. The Sabbath, whether it was spent listening to the traditional Calvinist father drone on about hell and damnation or the enlightened mother teaching Bible games, dealt with the education of the household. Since education is an endless task and measuring its progress almost impossible, domestic instruction had no boundaries. The level of enjoyment might have changed, but the level of commitment to Sabbath instruction did not. The enthusiasm of many women for religious instruction probably increased the spiritual intensity of Sabbath home devotions. Consequently, both liberal and conservative Protestants could never be quite sure that they had honestly fulfilled their domestic religious duties.

The legalism which marked nineteenth-century Irish Catholicism released Catholics from this fear. Catholics felt comfortable with the common adage "where there is no law there is no transgression." By attending Mass and refraining from unnecessary labor they fulfilled their Sabbath obligation. Sunday's focus was a ritual which could not be performed at home and demanded professional religious leaders. For most Catholics, worshiping meant "attending" or "hearing" Mass. The emphasis was on experiencing the divine sacrifice, not on learning morality or theology. Religious education might be valued, but it stood separate from the expression of the sacred in the Mass.

Life Cycle Rituals

The Catholic understanding of the separation of the sacred and the profane can best be seen in the relationship between the home and the sacraments. The sacrament of the Eucharist typically was confined to the sacred space of the church. Only under special circumstances, such as severe illness, would one receive communion at home. In general, this was the case for the other six sacraments. Sacraments linked the human with the divine in a mysteriously powerful way. This power needed to be controlled by a priest in a consecrated area. Consequently, those sacraments which mark stages in a person's life— baptism, confirmation, matrimony, and extreme unction—normally took place inside of the church. The notable exception, extreme unction, entailed the sanctification of domestic space by the priest.

Popular writers on the sacraments in both Ireland and America discouraged the reception of the sacraments at home. Due to the restrictions placed on Catholicism by the British government, saying Mass and hearing confessions at home was common in Ireland and England. Wealthy Catholics provided home oratories for their priests. A character in Ella Dorsey's "Speculum Justitiae" received his first holy communion in the family chapel. The heroine of *Old and New* was married in the oratory of Rheinfeldt house.

The sacraments were also conducted in the homes of the Irish poor, although Catholic reformers decried hearing confessions in "wretched filthy cabins" where priests "cannot utter a word of encouragement to the sinner except in the lowest and therefore unintelligible whisper." They also condemned the common practice of asking for exorbitant "offerings" for celebrating baptism and matrimony in homes. The sacred quality of the sacrament deserved the hallowed space of the church, not the earthen floor of a cottage.[45]

The remnants of Irish traditions carried over to America. Memories of domestic rites, a sparsity of churches, and the Protestant acceptance of home rituals made Catholic educators fear for the continuation of sacramental practices at home. Priests were alerted to the improprieties of unnecessary home rituals, and the laity was chastised through the Catholic press. Evening marriages, even when held in the church, were prohibited because they tended to turn into parties, defeating the sacramental nature of matrimony. Noting that

Wedding gowns. *Godey's Lady's Book* 40 (1850), p. 127.

Protestants conducted unsacramental marriages "in any place," the *Baltimore Catholic Mirror* warned that Catholic weddings should occur only in the morning, not during Lent, and in a church. The fact that Catholics who married Protestants were forbidden to marry in a church further stigmatized home weddings.[46]

Unfortunately, Catholics spoke more about Protestant home weddings and christenings than Protestants. Each denomination had its own opinions about the appropriateness of home rituals, but most Protestant ministers felt comfortable in performing at least weddings at home. The need for space more than theological necessities moved the wedding to the church. Christening the baby often took place at home in the parlor. More formal than family worship, these rituals called for the services of the minister. The more liturgically oriented denominations still insisted on the sacred space of the church and argued against the superficial atmosphere created in home services.[47]

For the Victorians, both the middle-class Protestants and the Irish, the most important life-cycle ritual did not take place in a church, but in the home. By the mid-nineteenth century, rituals of the dead—preparing the body, sewing mourning clothes, playing games at the wake—had become elaborate and intensely meaningful. The Catholic clergy struggled against the Irish immigrant's fascination with the wake to little avail. The church controlled extreme unction, but the preparation of the body and funeral came under family control. The actual funeral Mass, if one was said at all, often took second place to the keening, drinking, smoking, mock marriages, and games which made up the wake. It was in the home that the body was washed and dressed—usually to the dismay of the clergy—in the best clothes available funds could purchase. Laid in the coffin, the corpse held "the sign of his redemption,—the crucifix," and above the head another crucifix hung between burning candles. Articles appeared in the Catholic press explaining why the room in which the body lay was a sanctuary where "no noise or unseemly conduct" should be allowed, but the waking tradition persisted. Finally with great pomp and ceremony the body was escorted to the church and then to the burial ground.[48]

Although Protestants believed that Catholics participated in outrageous funeral rites, their own death rituals were equally complex. The simple and stark rites of the Puritans had been replaced by elaborate mourning rituals, many of British origin. As with the Irish Americans, little expense was spared. The body was washed and dressed in fine clothes, usually by women, and laid out with coins on the eyes. Seamstresses quickly made special clothing for the grieving family. Rings, gloves, and woven hair memorabilia were given to the relatives and friends. Families draped volumes of black crepe over the casket and room. Flowers, both fresh and dried, added to the already "stuffed" quality of the Victorian parlor. Even after the body had been carefully put to rest in one of the newly created cemetery parks, the family would continue to observe the highly prescribed rituals of wearing mourning dress, sewing commemorative samplers, or even contributing memorial poetry to their favorite journals.[49]

The elaborate funeral customs of Victorian Americans underwent many changes during the nineteenth century; family control over the ritual allowed for the creation of a heightened domestic drama. This drama far surpassed the church funeral for eliciting emotion, creating social bonds, and making statements about the "quality" of the family. In spite of condemnation of elaborate mourning rituals by priests and pastors, families continued to invest considerable amounts of money, time, and sentiment in these ceremonies. Domestic control over this important rite of passage by both Protestants and Catholics emphasized the crucial role that the family had in defining its own religious and social priorities.

Another way that the laity controlled their own religious activities was through informal religious education. Lay writers, both men and women, created their own theology under the guise of fiction and edifying biography.

Informal Domestic Religious Instruction

For nineteenth-century Protestants, the formal presentation of denominational theology through catechism had become less common in family life. The spirit of the 1648 Massachusetts law which commanded "all masters of families do once a week (at the least) catechize their children and servants" had faded. Although more theologically minded Protestants, such as the Presbyterian John Carter, recommended parents to "familiarize their children with the distinctive doctrines and order of the Presbyterian Church," many authors assumed the nonsectarian quality of domestic instruction. Writers widened their audience by attempting to appeal to "any of the Evangelical denominations" or "any who are striving to serve the Lord."[50]

This popular understanding of "Religion of the Gospels" saw devotion as a means to achieve "cheerful and fervent piety, a contented, obedient, and grateful frame of mind, feelings of affection and kindness towards our friends, and of active benevolence towards all."

Since "true" religion molded children into respectable and useful members of society, specific denominational catechizing seemed superfluous. In 1882 J. R. Miller stated what women writers had concluded a generation before: that children's lives "are so sensitive that the slightest influences will leave imperishable impressions upon them, that a wrong touch may mar them forever." Drilling children in denominational theology seemed unduly harsh. The way to teach children, and by implication adults, was to recognize the futility of Calvinist rigidity in religion and to present it instead "in a pleasant way."[51]

What developed out of this desire to present religion "in a pleasant way" was a literature geared to inculcate religious values through fiction. This fiction, directed toward women and children, was read at home as an alternative to sectarian theology and, at times, the Bible. Reading religious fiction—anything from moral fables to the retelling of biblical adventures—functioned as a way to apprehend "true religion." While some Methodists might enthusiastically insist that their followers "exclude novels from your house as you would the poison serpents, or the angel of death!," their publishing houses produced countless moral tales for domestic consumption. By 1860 the Methodist magazine *The Lady's Repository* included fiction of a pious nature. Reading moral fables, both to children and for individual adult edification, soon became an acceptable domestic religious activity.[52]

Along with the publication of denominational moral fiction came an increase in the number of novels which had religious overtones. These dealt with the inner struggles of characters who tried to find ultimate meaning in their lives. Such fiction showed women and men overcoming personal and societal odds and achieving self-fulfillment. It also helped reinforce new perspectives on religion—that God preferred love over money, that perfection was achieved through trial and self-sacrifice, and that true religion was interior and devoid of institutional structure. Women novelists presented their readers with strategies for personal individuation, social interaction, and building a new faith on the ruins of old theologies.[53]

In the latter part of the nineteenth century the retelling of biblical tales or the setting of stories in biblical times became popular. By 1880 Lew Wallace's *Ben-Hur. A Tale of Christ* harnessed heroic action, emotional conversion, and pagan spectacle without seeming irreligious. No longer were such religious tales meant solely for women and children. As the denominations tried to "masculinize" religion in the Social Gospel movement, the effect could be seen in the informal theology of fiction. In Elizabeth and Herbert Ward's novel *Come Forth!*

(1891), Jesus walked across the water in order to rescue a woman friend of Lazarus and later raised Lazarus from the dead so that he might join her. Biblical figures could be transported to contemporary America by more imaginative authors. *If Christ Came to Chicago*, written in 1895 by William Stead, exposed the political corruption and social ills of one of America's growing urban centers. Whatever the creative setting, these novels became popular because they tapped into the long-standing Protestant need to read for religious instruction.

The readers and writers of popular fiction insisted that this literature should instruct the modern reader in religious values just as the Bible did. Moral instruction still was accomplished but in a more "pleasant" manner. As the nation became more secular and less controlled by specific theologies, insights into morality and religion appeared in more secular garb. Writers transformed religious instruction into entertainment, which in turn legitimized entertainment and revitalized religion. Through imagination the reader could act out the religious intensity, dramatic excitement, and moral righteousness of the story. Enthusiasm for moralistic novels supplanted enthusiasm for Bible reading. In both cases the need for religious instruction via private reading was preserved.

Next to fiction stood a large body of "imitative" writings meant for Protestant instruction. This literature recounted the adventures of heroic men, women, and children who stood as shining examples of religious zeal and moral strength. Writers expanded the earlier Calvinist model of ministerial "memorials" which praised virtuous parishioners. The exploits of women missionaries, pioneers, and successful entrepreneurs were presented as means for the ordinary person to evoke religious, moral, and philosophical sentiments. Pious biographies both enforced prevalent views on morality and sex roles and provided models of men and women who broke through the confines of prescribed society.[54]

The playing out of strategies for social, psychological, and spiritual development through reading fiction or biography was certainly not only a Protestant phenomenon. Although the Catholic catechism played a greater role in theological learning, home religious reading also included both imitative and fictional literature. Catholic catechisms, culminating in the famous *Baltimore Catechism* (1884) issued after the Third Plenary Council, taught the essentials of religion via memorization. Dutiful parents helped their children to memorize questions and answers but left explanations of the doctrine to the priests and nuns. Understanding the doctrine took a back seat to the ease demonstrated in repeating the correct response.

A product of official Catholic theology, the catechism was seen as a sacred document with which the laity should not tamper. The laity felt more comfortable reading the didactic novels published by Catholic presses, short stories in newspapers and journals, and traditional imitative literature. Catholic publishing houses—Benziger in Cincinnati, Sadlier's in New York, Eugene Cummiskey in Philadelphia—carried a steady supply of Catholic literature for children and adults. Although much of the literature originated in Europe, American writers added their own perspective on educating and entertaining Catholics.

As with Protestants, reading of Catholic fiction at home became an acceptable way of teaching religious truths and social strategies. This was particularly important in America where contacts with Protestants had challenged the traditional Catholic world view. In America Catholics saw that ignorance of their religious traditions encouraged Protestant criticism. Writers realized that adult Catholics had to be taught the basics of their faith and the errors of Protestantism before they could assert their religious superiority. At the same time, fiction writers created social scenarios in which immigrant Catholics triumphed over the Protestant natives. While the literature often presented realistic situations, it more often solved new social problems with old Catholic answers. Fiction succeeded in explaining Catholic theology and morality, but failed to provide creative solutions to uniquely American problems.

Catholic fiction supplemented more traditional religious reading. Histories of the lives of Christ, Mary, and the saints were popular among American and European Catholics. Many Catholics knew the lives of obscure saints better than Bible stories. Butler's *Lives of the Saints,* reprinted in condensed home versions at low cost, brought the heroic lives of the saints into every household. From the wealthy Mrs. Von Wiegel's large German edition to Tim Blake's life of St. Patrick, Mary Sadlier's characters read the lives of the saints. The stories of the saints remained an important part of American Catholic literature throughout the nineteenth century in both home reading and Catholic schools.

How the reading of the "Lives of the Saints" affected American Catholics psychologically and sociologically remains unstudied. Certainly the life of St. Patrick was held up as both a religious and national symbol of strength and ability. What, however, was the impact of reading about the life of the popular St. Aloysius of Gonzaga, who, "owing to his virginal modesty, did not know by their faces many ladies among his own relations"? Many of the lives of the martyrs and virgins illustrated the Victorian values of purity, modesty, and self-sacrifice, but they were short on domestic sentiment or work ethic (of the material kind). How did the stories, steeped in other-worldly values, function for Catholics trying to cope with an American environment? Did Catholics revere saints like Aloysius, who "in hearing Mass . . . often melted into tears, in profound sentiments of love and adoration," because he fit into contemporary notions of religiosity? Or did the appeal of the saints' disdain for the flesh—their fasting, mortifications, celibacy, and often tortured deaths—have deeper psychological meaning?[55]

The Irish American penchant for linking religion and nationalism can also be seen in domestic literature. The exploits of Irish national leaders took on spiritual overtones, and it becomes difficult to separate political from religious aspirations. Storytelling, a hallmark of traditional Irish culture, served to remind the immigrants of life in the old country as well as its political problems. The exploits and biographies of European royalty also served to link the poor American Catholic with a glorious Catholic past. Reading about the achievements of French kings could not help but encourage the Catholic whose religion in America was considered not much more than superstition.[56]

Catholics read Protestant literature, whereas Protestants most likely did not read Catholic works. The *Boston Pilot* often mentioned issues of *Godey's Lady's Book* noting that "this magazine will be found of great assistance to those ladies who try to fashion their own clothing without resorting to the dressmaker's skill." Although Anna Dorsey wrote a biblical tale called *Palms* in 1887 which was set in early Rome, Catholics probably preferred best-sellers like *Ben Hur.* By the end of the century Catholic reviewers felt comfortable enough with the nonsectarian religious character of *Ben Hur* to praise it as a "genuine and rare gem of literature" because it sought to "teach the most important of all religious tenets—the divine character and mission of Jesus Christ." The changes in the character of Protestant literature, while perhaps making it more secular and sentimental, also made it more ecumenical.[57]

The Varieties of Domestic Rituals

Protestants and Catholics moved through a daily, weekly, yearly, and lifetime cycle of religious rituals. For Protestants, much of this devotion centered around the family. The contrast between the two religious groups were substantial and accentuated their historical, social, and theological differences.

In spite of the Protestant and Catholic assertion that the family was the God-given foundation of society, their differing concepts of sacred space created distinct notions about the importance of domestic rituals. For Protestants, people created sacred space when they came together to pray, sing hymns, and read from the Bible. Proponents of family worship pictured young and old, mother and father, servants and masters, all coming together as equals in the sight of God. Class, sex, and age differences would temporarily end as all sought God's blessings. Family religion created a sacred time when the change and chaos of the profane world dissolved into the order and meaning of the eternal. The more the family was seen as a refuge in a dangerous world, the more significant domestic rituals became in renewing that sanctuary.

In contrast, space became truly sacred for Catholics when God, in the form of the Blessed Sacrament, was present. God, not people, made the space sacred. The real presence of Christ, signaled by the lit altar lamp, rendered the space powerful and mysterious. The rare domestic oratory was a separate church inside the home. Catholics, both laity and clergy, asserted the importance of the family, but the family could not sanctify space. Only the actual presence of God could translate profane space into sacred space.

This distinction in concepts of sacred space permitted Protestants to develop an involved domestic ritual, whereas Catholics could not. Since Protestantism did not demand the "real" presence of God for its rituals, the home could function as the center for devotion. The Bible defined Protestant worship, and it could be read easily in the family setting. Protestant home worship equaled the church service, and many believed it actually was more effective. Since the days of Luther, Protestant morality and spirituality originated in the home. The church acted as an extension of the family.

The Victorian Catholic viewpoint was the reverse: the family was an extension of the church. Catholicism's sacramental emphasis focused on the physical space of the church, and the home remained only a reminder of that sacredness. Consequently, Catholic domestic rituals could never substitute for church rituals. Religious obligations centered around church attendance, and Catholics understood home religion to be a secondary activity.

Prior to the 1890s Catholic devotions at home were almost exclusively performed by the individual. Prayer books and descriptions of the spiritual life were common during this period, but they never encouraged family worship. The path to perfection was to be walked by individuals, not groups. Catholics depended more on private devotions to Mary and the saints than on other family members to help them reach heaven. The popular Catholic world view set the living individual between the saints in heaven and the souls in purgatory. It was the vertical relationship between earth, heaven, and purgatory which was crucial for salvation. The family was important socially and personally, but the saints were more helpful religiously.

It was only in the last years of the century that Catholic writers promoted family worship, adopting many Protestant attitudes on home religion. Under Pope Leo XIII the family became an important institution in the battle against what Rome saw as encroaching modernism. Popular devotions, which traditionally had been conducted by individuals, were now promoted for family prayer. Religious iconography within the home increased. After the 1884 push for parochial schooling, Catholic attention focused on children. Home religious education easily paired with the perceived need for a thorough Catholic school system.

Unlike Catholics who had their saints and private devotions, Protestants had the family to help them reach salvation. Christian nurture, promoted so strongly by liberal theologians, was a way for parents to save their children. Even among more conservative Protestants who stressed the importance of conversion, it was the family who prepared the children to be open to salvation. The family cultivated the religious sensibilities of the children and maintained the emotional spirit generated in revival meetings, benevolent associations, and in the local churches. The popular evangelist Dwight Moody told his audience to go home that very night and "erect a family altar, and call your children around you . . . and so you may gather them all in, and you will have them with you when the morning of the Resurrection shall come." Historian Sandra Sizer explained that in Moody's vision "the family was not only an analogue but the actual means of salvation." In a world full of turmoil and strife, the family provided both the alternative to social disorder and the pathway to eternal peace.[58]

Home religion enabled the whole family to live together forever in heaven. Most Protestants assumed that families would meet in heaven, and woe be it for the family if some were "in the fellowship of heaven, and others in the companionship of hell." The home, especially when it was sanctified by worship, was the earthly equivalent of paradise. Paradise had become not the final joining of the individual with God, but the creation of eternal family life.[59]

Family life for middle-class Protestants, by the late nineteenth century, was thoroughly child-centered. Domestic religion encouraged this by focusing its attention on the nurture of Christian citizens. Irish-American Catholics, however, contributed the earlier idea of perceiving children as small adults. The concept was reinforced by economic conditions which placed children in the workplace and gave them adult responsibilities. Although many Catholic writers decried the condition of urban living which placed children in dangerous situations, they never assumed that children were tender flowers. This attitude toward children combined with the Catholic emphasis on the mystical and powerful nature of religion to form a particularly "adult" religion. Children were expected to memorize the catechism, not to understand it. Religious services were geared to adults, not to children.

The maintenance and promotion of religious truth also differed between the two groups. Protestantism depended on teaching and preaching as its primary religious ritual. The written word, especially as presented in the Bible but also as it appeared informally in hymns, sermons, tracts, novels, and children's stories, was sacred. Reading and teaching formed the basis of Protestant ritual. This written culture contrasted with the oral/visual culture of Catholics. Catholicism was not learned, it was "passed down" and then "experienced" through the senses of sight, smell, and hearing. Literacy was not a prerequisite. Irish Americans belonged to a culture in which oral tradition still predominated. What the Protestants did through reading, the Catholics did through seeing. Protestants sanctified their homes through utilizing the sacred word in home liturgies that emphasized Bible readings, prayers, and hymns. Catholics sanctified their homes with sacred images: the Sacred Heart picture, candles, crucifixes, and holy water fonts.

Protestants, through domestic rituals, attempted to create a concept of "Christianity" which would link them together under one common moral canopy. The evangelical vision hoped to counter the trend toward pluralism in America with the idea of a unified "Christian" nation. Domestic Protestantism, which asserted the values of hard work, purity, individual morality, and patriotism, was the foundation of this vision. The values of the home stood as eternal truths, whereas denominational theologies appeared splintered and irrelevant. Family religion arose as a means of returning to "simple Bible truths" which made good citizens.

To combat this evangelical vision, popular American Catholic writers strove to demonstrate the factionalism of Protestantism and the unifying strength of Catholicism. They refused to alter their religious outlooks to suit the Protestant concepts of Christianity. For nine-teenth-century Catholics there was only one truth. That truth resided in the organization and spirit of the Catholic church which stood unchanging in its theology. Popular writers showed the Church, in spite of attacks by the modern world, to be steadfast in its mainte-nance of a unified religious structure. Home prayer might support that truth, but it certainly did not have to act as the last stronghold of true religion. The Church—understood as the religious profession-als—maintained authentic religion.

Catholics shared with Protestants the use of informal teaching to promote religious understanding. The American situation challenged the traditional Catholic world view brought from Ireland. For the first time Irish Catholics were in direct contact with Protestant, urban life and could no longer depend on the traditions of the village to define their religious and social world. Education became more important as Catholics moved from a world based on tradition to one based on progress and change. Reading, although still not as prominent as among Protestants, became a way of educating Catholics. Popular Catholic novels, written predominately by women, began to shape the way religion was presented. With the growth of the Irish American middle class at the end of the century, the attitude toward the worth of education changed.

Changes in Catholic attitudes toward informal and formal educa-tion contributed to the increased involvement of laywomen in reli-gious activities. Since Catholics had few formal domestic rituals and Protestants placed so much importance on religious instruction, the role of the domestic patriarch was replaced by the matriarch. The image of the Old Testament father leading his household in worship faded into the picture of a New Testament mother lovingly teaching her child to read. In the following two chapters we look more closely at the evolution of paternal and maternal perspectives on domestic religious leadership.

[5]
Leaders at The Domestic Altar
The Paternal Model

If the home rivaled the church as the center of Christian nurture, then who directed its religious activities? How did the guiding actions of fathers differ from that of mothers? Domestic Christianity for Victorian Protestants and Catholics vacillated between two traditional perspectives on religion: a paternal model and a maternal model. These two models of the nature of Christianity influenced how writers perceived the roles of mothers and fathers within the home. Commentators on the religious life of the family made use of the two models in order to define appropriate leadership patterns. The maternal and paternal models are not merely stages in historical development, even though their appearance in the literature waxes and wanes with changing social conditions. Victorian Catholics and Protestants adapted these two models to fit their particular historical situation. In this chapter we focus on the paternal model—father's role in domestic religion. In the next, the maternal role is brought into view.

Paternal Protestantism

The paternal model of domestic religion, which occurs throughout Christian history, draws its strength from a particular reading of the Old Testament. God is the supreme father who rules and watches over his people. Social arrangements imitate this relationship. The human father heads his household, exercising authority over it. The household is comprised not only of parents and children, but of servants, slaves, apprentices, and their children. Fathers accomplish the ordering of this large household, as God does with his world "household," through authority, obedience, and fear. Children are expected to obey out of respect for the father, and authority precedes love.

Assuming that God heads a pyramid-structured universe, the paternal model rests on authority and dependency relationships. Within traditional medieval Christianity this hierarchy appears in the very structure of the universe, the order of the angels, and the levels of the clergy. Although Protestants tried to rework this pyramid, they constructed their own system of clergy, transferring certain pastoral obligations to the parents. The father headed his household, the mother and children were his parishioners and subjects. Family government, education, and worship were the responsibilities of the father.

In spite of the nineteenth-century assumption that women's proper place was in the home, domestic reformers upheld the father's privilege as head of the household. The longtime association of domestic order, discipline, and obedience with paternal authority was the model from which writers developed their views on domestic religious leadership. In 1840 Presbyterian S. G. Winchester described the father's role in the family as one of king, prophet, and priest. Sarah Hale, noted for her steadfast promotion of women's domestic activities, also echoed this belief that the father functioned as "prophet, priest and king" when leading family devotions. She even went so far as to italicize the word "father," making sure that all the ladies recognized the religious leadership of the male in family worship.[1]

This triple role of "prophet, priest, and king" formed the basis for the paternal model of domestic leadership. All three titles find their origin in traditional Christian theology and depend on authority and obedience as their source of power. The father's position of *prophet* to his family rested on his ability to prepare his household for conversion and salvation. The Puritan father's responsibilities to his family included both creating an atmosphere where the importance of conversion could be felt and also presenting the specific truths of religion to his household. From Cotton Mather's struggles with his daughter Katy to Francis Wayland's attempt to break the will of his fifteen-month-old son, the paternal role of exhorting his family to righteousness had been embedded in the minds of American Protestants.[2]

By the mid-nineteenth century concepts of conversion and salvation had begun to change, but paternal involvement in educating the household remained. John Carter, who insisted on the need for Christian instruction by the father, went against prevailing trends by encouraging "the parents of our beloved Zion that they familiarize their children with the distinctive doctrines and order of the Presbyterian Church." The father, as prophet to his family, was to counter the "fearful current of infidelity and atheism" and to present Calvinism as "the precious truth of God." The use of the term "prophet" by the Victorians clarified the quality of this type of domestic instruction. As prophet the father made religious pronouncements to his family and expected obedience.[3]

In order to lead his family, the father prepared himself in religion. "Oral exposition, by the father of the family," wrote James Alexander in 1847, "should not be attempted without due consideration." Fathers needed to read not only the Bible, but biblical commentaries, prepared sermons for the home, and family prayer books. Methodist John Deems recommended the "devotional parts of the Bible" and books of prayers such as "Jenks', and Jay's, and Thornton's, and Berrian's" to "enrich his mind with petitions which the Holy Ghost has inspired." Crucial to paternal participation in home religion was the association of religion with intellectual knowledge. Father as prophet spoke from his mind and not from his heart.[4]

In more liberally oriented writings, paternal prophethood appeared in subtle yet perceivable ways. T. S. Arthur, best known for his *Ten Nights in a Bar Room,* supported women's causes, usually at the price of condemning male activity. He could not, however, overlook the male role in domestic religion. The frontispiece for *Our Homes: Their Cares and Duties, Joys and Sorrows,* shows an engraving by J. D. Gross of evening devotions led by the patriarch of the household. In *Steps Towards Heaven* Arthur's character Mr. Marston gives up going to prayer meetings in order to read from the Bible and from religious books to his wife while she sewed. The continued male presence in domestic religion legitimized family worship, and most writers felt uneasy when father refused to perform his religious duties.[5]

Few evangelical Protestants challenged the father's right to function as *priest* to his household. The father acted as "the revered priest" who offered the family's "common confessions, supplications, thanksgivings and intercessions" to God. According to the *The Ladies' Repository* of 1871 the "father as the priest of the family" presented his family's prayers to God, thus becoming "the crowning glory of domestic piety and devotion." Formal family prayer should be led by the father who alone had the right to "bring his family to the throne of grace." The father thus functioned as the mediator between God and his family, just as in ancient Israel priests presented their nation's sacrifice to God.[6]

Mothers should set the stage for the priestly activities of their husbands. In 1854 John Power wrote that the mother must "put her house in order for the evening devotions, the books in their place, the lights brightly burning, the family all present and waiting" for the prayers of the father. The more liberal Davis Newton in 1869 told men that it was an easy task to lead family prayer. "The loving wife lights the lamp," he recalled, "lays the Bible by your side, and tells the little children to 'sit down and be still, while papa prays.'" Formal family prayer, like formal church worship, employed women as domestic acolytes—to prepare, but not to direct.[7]

If a father was reluctant to pray, the mother's preparatory acts were the means by which she lured him into performing his religious duties. By quieting the children and setting the books on the table the wife "affectionately requested her husband to pray with the family before they retired." If the shy father only began to read from the Bible, J. P. Thompson believed, soon "God will give you the grace that will inspire you for, and carry you through, prayer also." Annie Wilson acknowledged that at first mother may need to encourage

Family devotions. T. S. Arthur, *Our Homes,* frontispiece. Van Pelt Library, Special Collections, University of Pennsylvania.

home devotions, but eventually father would start one sentence prayers, "followed by each young son in succession in a single sentence or petition." Leading family prayer was the father's duty, and writers insisted that it should not be shirked. Even Horace Bushnell, who encouraged mothers to teach their children the basics of prayer, assumed that this early training eventually would allow the "child" to take the father's place at family prayer if he was absent or "taken away by death." "He will be ready," explained Bushnell, "at a very early period on his way to manhood, to take his father's place."[8]

When father was absent, "sleeping in the tomb," or absolute in his refusal to lead home worship, then mother out of necessity could conduct the service. Widows led family worship until their sons grew up and "could relieve them of that duty." Domestic writers told stories of devoted mothers and children who took on this religious burden themselves and eventually led their negligent fathers back into directing home worship. Presbyterian James Alexander, seemingly unaware of the "feminization" of Victorian Protestantism, wrote in 1847 that although leading prayers brought "a keen trial to diffidence and feminine reserve," widows needed to see it as "eminently amiable and touching." He encouraged dutiful sons to "make every sacrifice in order to lessen the burdens of the maternal heart, when engaged in such a duty." For the most part, women were asked to preside over formal worship only when the head of the family was unavailable.[9]

The father's roles as domestic priest and prophet were outgrowths of his position as *king* in the family. Ministers drew from their understanding of early societies where "the father became the patriarch, the chief or sheik." The familiar Pauline dictum "for the husband is the head of the wife, as Christ is head of the church," (Eph. 5:22) became their motto. Even if the wife was a more capable ruler, Thomas Moore insisted that for her "to refuse obedience for this reason . . . would be an absurdity." The father's authority in the family reflected the authority of God over humanity. In 1871 *The Ladies' Repository* explained that authority over the family "is an unquestionable prerogative of the husband. It is given to him by the appointment of God." The father in the family mirrored God in the world. "Every body must have a head, and every society must have subordination," wrote the *Repository*, "domestic misrule and anarchy, if universal, would be social chaos."[10]

Domestic writers never intended families to go back to the "past" when fathers were tyrants in their families. Samuel Phillips explained in 1865 that "the father's authority is not that of the despot" and the child's obedience "not that of a trembling subject." Even the more conservative Thomas Moore, who did not believe that undue severity was a common error in that day (except with the brutally ignorant or intemperate), could say that "the grand agent in executing family laws is love." Without love the parent only succeeded in "building a wall of ice between himself and his offspring." Paternal authority had to be undergirded by love or else it did not reflect God's love for his people.[11]

On the other hand, James Wood knew a woman who, when she failed at "kissing her children into submission . . . resorted to the rod, or some other mode of punishment." Disciplining children was considered a religious duty, and this woman offered a prayer that the "Lord would subdue their wills and give them new hearts." No writer, even those far from a Reformed perspective on child rearing, permitted a child to be spoiled. The parent who did not guide his child, a task which included demanding obedience, allowed the child to wander into sin. Since the home was the nursery of nation and church, the parent (notably the father) who permitted children to do as they pleased "brutalizes human nature, dishonors God, subverts the principles of constitutional society . . . and overthrows both church and state." Maintaining domestic order was linked to maintaining a transcendent order and was crucial for Victorian Protestantism.[12]

Throughout the century, writers on domestic religion feared that families neglected their religious duties. Fathers especially were accused either of making the services too formal and not personal enough or of being too busy to take time for religion. In his advice to newlyweds, William Thayer explained in 1854 that men are not satisfied with merely attaining wealth, wisdom, and stature but they must jump into these very quickly. "The notions and habits of past generations," he mused, "are too staid and too slow to suit the fiery spirit of the present day." Fathers, too busy trying to create the ideal home, ignored the spiritual needs of their actual home. According to William Alcott, these men never read the Bible; the only book they read at night was their ledger.[13]

Writers adapted to the flight of men from religion, but they were not pleased when society sought to "wean the *husband* especially from this little realm." Nostalgically Sarah Hale recalled the "might, the majesty of man" who was not seduced by the glory of the hero's battle field or the "monarch's gorgeous show" but was content to lead "on his household band, in love and faith, to heaven." Male participation in household religion legitimized the role of religion not only within the home, but within the greater society. It was not enough that mother lead the prayers; father should take his religious position seriously and direct his household.[14]

Greater masculine disinterest in traditional home religion promoted adjustments in family worship. By the 1880s domestic writers
still asked fathers to lead family prayer, but they assumed that male
religious study would not make family worship more erudite, but
more "bright, interesting, and profitable." Annie Wilson in her 1898
Presbyterian publication offered families the choice either of having
the head of the family read the scripture or of having each family
member read in turn. In 1900 J. S. Mills encouraged father to read
the Bible, but "mother or one of the children should play the organ,
and all unite in singing a sacred song." Father could lead the prayers,
but mother and the children also had their responsibilities.[15]

Domestic writers seemed willing to adapt formal worship to changing views on the role of women and children in the family. What they
found difficult was integrating father's role into more informal modes
of religious instruction. Fathers could lead family prayer, but they
could not teach children how to pray. Only mothers were presented as
able to deal with children on an individual basis. In 1850 the *Ladies
Garland and Family Wreath* contained an anonymous story about a
father and son praying together in a ship's cabin. The observer, who
intimates the pair might be German Catholics, was quite taken by the
scene, but could not credit the father with teaching his child to pray.
"This was the training of some pious mother," the author assumed.
"Where is she now? How many times had her kind hand been laid on
those sunny locks, as she had taught him to lisp his prayers?"[16]

Likewise, even in illustrations from the 1840s and 1850s, children
are always being read to from the Bible by their mothers. Fathers are
pictured surrounded by their household. T. S. Arthur, who tried to
include men in religion, revealed deeper sentiments in his frontispiece illustration for *The Home Mission*. Titled "Our Father," it shows
a heavenly angel looking down over individual children at prayer.
The mother dominates the illustration with her hand upraised in a
teaching gesture. The father looks on benignly, almost hidden behind
the mother. His involvement is one of passive admiration.[17]

Writers who felt most comfortable with a paternal perspective on
home religion focused more on formal worship and less on informal
devotion. Writers critical of that tradition, and especially women,
focused on the informal dimension of home religion. Catharine
Beecher, who never mentioned family rituals in her writing, rejected
the Calvinist mode of private paternal religious instruction. In the
Religious Training of Children Beecher spent four chapters illustrating
"Puritan Church Training" and then took the remainder of the book
condemning it. The bulk of the chapters contained the struggles

between Dr. Payson and his daughter Maria. The tears, traumas, and anxieties produced in the child thoroughly convinced Beecher that emotional father-child conversations geared to induce conversion were contrary both to common sense and the Bible. Although she never directly accused fathers of being unable to nurture their children, she questioned the traditional paternal duty of inculcating the fear of God and of damnation into children.[18]

Informal maternal patterns of domestic religion achieved what some scholars have called "feminization" of American Protestantism. The paternal model adjusted and adapted to accompanying the ma-

'"Our father." T. S. Arthur, *The Home Mission,*
frontispiece. Van Pelt Library, Special
Collections, University of Pennsylvania.

ternal model. Attempts to revitalize the role of the father in the family in the latter part of the century occurred as a reaction against an increasingly feminized Protestantism. As the Social Gospel movement reinvigorated Protestant commitment to social issues, new attention was given to the relationship between the world of men and the world of religion.[19]

Speakers for the Social Gospel movement, including Washington Gladden and Lyman Abbott, tried to reemphasize the paternal perspective on religion by directing attention to the Fatherhood of God. They presented God as both the creator of the world and the ever-forgiving father of the prodigal son. Both images attributed feminine characteristics to God and to fathers. As popular preachers, Gladden and Abbott tried to align a comforting maternal Father God with a society that increasingly demanded men to be strong, athletic, and worldly. God was neither the frightening Puritan father nor the detached Victorian father. Instead he was a protecting, loving God involved with human cares and woes.[20]

Late Victorian preachers, theologians, and popular writers sought to make Protestantism more applicable to men's lives. On the one hand they refused to give up the idea of a loving and forgiving God, but on the other hand they wanted a religion that could speak to the public, male world of business, adventure, and power. "Muscular" Christianity sought to recapture the chivalry of the past, when knights were powerful and yet devoted to their God and home. Such attempts flourished in the late nineteenth century, but succeed more in producing an accommodating Christian symbol system for a male world, than an integration of paternal and maternal perspectives on religion. By the 1920s Jesus would be transformed into the "founder of modern business" within the Gospel of Success serving as a way of legitimating American capitalism.[21]

Paternal Catholicism

The idealization of paternal domestic authority within the Catholic home changed more by type of literature than by historical period. European writers, primarily the French, expressed a harshly patriarchal understanding of the family, which supported the political and social aspirations of middle- and upper-class Catholics in Europe. Following the French revolution the church allied itself with those who felt displaced by republican sentiments. Fears of socialism fueled their insecurities. During the Second Empire period when royalty came back into style, the church cemented its newly found power by reinforcing hierarchical and authoritarian values. With the fall of both the French Second Empire and the Papal States to more secular interests, the church sought even more aggressively to present images of strength and spiritual authority.

Although removed from European politics, American Catholics experienced these trends via formal papal proclamations such as the 1864 *Syllabus of Errors* and through more informal publishing networks. Catholic publishing houses translated works from European writers and advertised them for American consumption. The conservative attitude of these writers appeared side by side with the more liberal viewpoints of American or Irish-American writers. By the 1880s Catholic publishing achieved a greater degree of independence from European concerns, manifested by an easing of preoccupation with Ireland and a rejection of European ideologies. Turning away from Europe weakened the emphasis on the paternal nature of religion and strengthened local American Catholic sentiments.

As with the Protestants, the Catholic understanding of paternal religiosity rested on concepts of authority and hierarchical arrangement. Catholics did not turn to the Old Testament for justification but found such arrangements in Catholic theology and ecclesiastical structure. Just as the Christ is the head of the church and the church reflects Christ's glory, so the father "is the ruler of the home; her [the mother's] duty it is to reflect his majesty, and see that his orders are carried out in the family circle." This relationship manifested itself not only in papal authority but also in the parish as the domain of the priest and in the home as the domain of the husband.[22]

European writers embellished paternal activities in the family by endowing the father with priestly powers. "Now this lay priesthood," explained Father Hyacinthe in 1869, "reaches its perfect fullness only in the Christian who has become a husband and father." For Père Matignon, the father's character "with which he is vested is a priesthood, and to this priesthood is given the charge of souls." Father Hyacinthe, who addressed his Lenten talks on the family only to "Gentlemen," linked priesthood, teaching, and kingship together. The father not only taught the children but also the wife who, "in the early stages, at least, of wedded life is as much of a child as of a companion, with respect to her husband."[23]

The major American Catholic voice supporting a strong paternal perspective on religion and culture was Orestes Brownson. A New England convert, Brownson condemned the popular notion that "ascribes all the noble qualities and virtues of the son to the mother" and asserted that "the paternal influence counts for something . . . in the formation of character." Women writers tended to "emasculate thought," to "enervate the mind," and thus fostered "a weak and watery sentimentalism" which ruined masculine culture. Brownson longed for the age when man "was the head of the woman, and the father was the head of the family." The influential Brownson fled from a Protestantism he characterized as "religion of gush" to a Catholicism he believed to be based on truly patriarchal principles.[24]

Both French and American writers based their insights on the authority of the husband not only on Scripture, but also on the Catholic catechism. The *Catechism of the Council of Trent*, used by priests up until the more lay-oriented *Baltimore Catechism* (1885), stated this paternal perspective. In explaining the fourth commandment, the Tridentine catechism noted it was the father's duty to "keep his family in order; correct their morals, and fix their respective employments." The mother was to "be subject to her husband," train her children, "cheerfully" maintain her home, and never leave it "without the permission of her husband." In Joseph Curr's *Familiar Instructions* based on the Tridentine catechism, he admonished the woman never to "refuse obedience to her husband" nor to "run him into debt without his knowledge or consent." He also warned the husband not to "be guilty of overbearing or unbecoming treatment towards his wife."[25]

The *Baltimore Catechism*, which actually was a series of catechisms graded for children of various ages, did not include detailed descriptions of parental roles within the family. A result of the 1884 Third Plenary Council, the *Baltimore Catechism* sought not to educate priests as the Tridentine did, but to educate children. Consequently, the stress in the fourth commandment is on children's responsibility toward their parents, and vice versa. The obedience of children, rather than the obedience of wives, is the important issue. This change indicates both the different attitude of the American hierarchy, and the shift away from paternal authority by the 1880s.

Although the catechisms stressed parents' responsibility for the religious education of children, they did not prescribe formal home devotions. The lack of established family worship posed a significant problem for the exercise of paternal priestly duties within the home. Father Hyacinthe tried to remedy this by preaching the importance of family prayers, specifically mentioning that "it is not the mother, but the father who presides, who is the high priest." Writers like Father Hyacinthe who promoted father-led family prayer found it difficult to support their ideas with traditional Catholic thought. An article in the *Catholic World* went back to the English Renaissance for evidence of

Catholic family religion. In 1530 Richard Whytford wrote a devotional for home use which encouraged both the mother and the father to nightly bless their children: it omitted any reference to family prayer or to paternal leadership in home religion. Victorian Catholics found few applicable references to justify their promotion of the father within the home from a Catholicism which historically focused on the celibate male.[26]

By the 1880s, when family prayers were being promoted in local and international sources, the role of the father was becoming ignored. Papal encyclicals, such as *Supremi apostolatus officio* (1883) and *Fidentem piumque animum* (1896), encouraged saying the family rosary, but never mentioned the father's leadership. A general exhortation contained in *Sapientiae christianae* (1890) asked fathers to "regulate the government of their households and the first education of their children," but was silent on family devotions. Cardinal James Gibbons pleaded for family prayer in 1891; however, he called on both the mother and the father to gather their children in the evening for devotions.[27]

American literary evidence throughout the century supports the position that the father functioned as priest of the family but not in the patriarchal French way. The presentation of the father as patriarch appeared in Mary Sadlier's novel, *The Blakes and the Flanagans, a Tale Illustrative of Irish Life in the United States*. The virtuous Tim Flanagan read night prayers and Gobinet's *Instructions for Youth* aloud to his family. His son Tom read the *History of the Bible*. Less-than-virtuous Mrs. Blake tried to read to her children, but to no avail. Mr. Blake, although a trustee of the church ("it's not one trustee in fifty that has a spark of religion"), took no interest in family religion. Sadlier emphasized not that Mr. Blake failed to read family prayers but that he neglected to send his children to a Catholic school. Public religious involvement, more than private activities, was the key to producing good family life. Family religion reinforced the greater commitment to parish, school, and God.[28]

Sadlier's men are far from the God-like characters in French advice books. Their patience, sincerity, and sensitivity mark them not as patriarchs but as men concerned with both family and community. The fathers in *Old and New; or, Taste Versus Fashion* wait for the wives and daughters to leave their foolish feminine ways. These men are neither sentimentalized and weak nor overbearing and evil. They do, however, possess the ability to see through female faults. Their religious activities, in contrast to those of their wives and daughters, are modest and sincere.[29]

Novelists liked to contrast understanding and sensitive Catholic men to extremes they saw in Protestant men. Catholic priests were models of masculinity and intelligence—not too rational but certainly not too emotional. In contrast, the Protestant preacher of *The Lost Rosary,* the Reverend Ebenezer Sookes, illustrated the Catholic image of the effeminate minister:

> He was a Methodist, a Revivalist, a Baptist, an advocate of women's rights, an earnest worker in the field of missionary labor, provided said field consisted in gliding here and there to nice little evening parties, shaking hands—or, more properly speaking, finger tips—with ladies whose age forbade the custom of whole-hand shaking . . . Mild tea drinking, a little sherry, claret occasionally, and other helps of spiritous kind, did go some length in elevating whatever there was of mankind in his composition to thoughts of heroic work and conversion of sinners.[30]

The other type of Protestant male was also a caricature of another extreme in masculine behavior: the harsh, patriarchal Puritan father who sent terror into the hearts of his family. Mr. Leonard in "Franklin, the Heir of Elm Grove" was such a man. He "was a tall, gaunt man, with a very sallow complexion, scanty black hair, heavy, beetling brows." Although polite and "rather stiff," he "was totally incapable of sympathizing in the sufferings of others." Mr. Leonard ruled his "household and other dependencies with a rod of iron" and showed no mercy for anyone outside of "the charmed circle which enclosed himself and his 'elect' brethren." For Sister Carroll, Mr. Leonard was a "true Pharisee" who beat his son for forgetting three chapters of Isaiah, daily locked him in a closet to help him memorize the Bible, "while he [Mr. Leonard] himself boasted that he stood secure in the blessedness of election." In the end, however, good triumphs. The son eventually realized that "if he is an elect, I don't want to be one" and became a Catholic.[31]

Unlike European writers who hoped to strengthen public lines of authority by strengthening private ones, American sources set less grand goals. Irish priests who were acquainted with French standards of spirituality tried to replace traditional Irish expressions of paternal religiosity with activities more in tune with Counter Reformation Catholicism. Irish American men were asked to alter their behavior at home and in church to conform to the prevailing ideals of domesticity and theology.

As newspapers more and more spoke to domestic and middle-class concerns, they attacked traditional Irish codes of masculinity. In 1889 the *Sacred Heart Review,* quoting Maurice Egan in *Ave Maria,* presented a "wretched and utterly vile tradition" found more commonly "among people of Irish birth and descent than among others." This wretched tradition was that "children should be brought up principally by their mothers," a practice which "works well with animals but not among men." Parish calendars clearly displayed the admonition that "respect for the Sacrament and for his own child, demands the presence of the father" at baptismal ceremonies. Men were condemned for hanging around at the back of the church during Mass instead of sitting with their families. The Irish masculine preference for the tavern over the parlor continually aggravated writers who asked, "What is there that should more interest you than your home?"[32] Few men were permitted a rebuttal, but as Tom Barclay explained:

> We males can revert to paganism and forget for an hour or two, in revel and song, the Man of Sorrows—the poor gibbetted God: where now, while we are carousing, are Gethsemane and Calvary? We are lapping in the Elysium of ale and skittles and cards. We are no Christians tonight, we, but Bacchanals.[33]

Catholic writers thus fought a two-pronged battle. On the one hand, they opposed the Irish male's preference for the company of men, a good stout, and their general ignorance of acceptable ways of displaying religious sentiment and education. On the other hand, they supported a patriarchal model of domesticity which condemned the female encroachment into family rule. Mothers should not head the family because that disturbed the order of the domestic world which mirrored the sacred and natural worlds. The large percentage of single Irish men and women, female headed households, and the instability of poverty worked against the ideals presented by Catholic writers, especially for the first generation of immigrants.

Crucial to the understanding of the ambiguous male role in domestic Catholicism was the attention paid to St. Joseph and the Holy Family in advice literature. The traditional Catholic assertion of the superiority of celibacy over married life left few role models among the saints for fathers to imitate. Until the fifteenth century St. Joseph had no special feast day in the Latin calendar and took a backseat to Mary's prominence. After the Counter Reformation Catholic writers reinvigorated the Holy Family, and St. Joseph became a central figure in their writings. St. Teresa of Avila adopted Joseph as her personal patron, and by the eighteenth century he presided over two hundred Carmelite convents.[34]

Popular nineteenth-century Catholicism portrayed Joseph as an honest workman who supported and loved his family. In order to temper the powerful image that Mary had garnered over the ages, writers referred to Joseph's position as head of the family. "The Blessed Virgin," explained an 1887 article in the *Catholic Home*, "was beyond all measure superior in dignity to St. Joseph." While Mary was the mother of God, Joseph was merely the foster-father. "But," the article goes on to say, "it is not she who guides and rules in this model family." The paragraph finished with the Pauline quotation: "Let women be subject to their husbands as to the Lord."[35]

In the *Catholic Girl's Guide* of 1905 Mary acted as a model house-keeper. She made her home inviting and comfortable for St. Joseph when he came "back at eventide tired from his day's work." Joseph was pleased to see "his evening meal ready and everything as orderly as possible." Father O'Reilly in *True Men as We Need Them* saw Joseph as the "high-souled Carpenter" who performed "deeds of unhesitating devotion and self-sacrifice to protect both Mother and Babe from the manifold perils which beset them." The presence of Joseph human-ized the Holy Family since it diminished the power of Mary and Jesus by requiring their reliance on Joseph's paternal protection and sup-port.[36]

To create this vision of the bourgeois Nazareth family in more formal Catholic devotions was difficult. In 1889 Pope Leo XIII circu-lated his encyclical *Quamquam pluries* which granted seven years in-dulgence to those who said a special prayer to St. Joseph after reciting the rosary. Although the pope extolled Joseph in the encyclical, the prayer needed to be said after the Marian devotion of the rosary. An even clearer indication of Joseph's role appeared in a prayer dating from 1893. This prayer to the Holy Family called Joseph a "glorious Patriarch," but went on to ask for assistance "by thy powerful media-tion, [to] offer, by the hands of Mary, our prayer to Jesus." Joseph might be the patriarch, but petitions made to Joseph went to Mary before going to God.[37]

This short prayer contained a succinct statement of the dichotomy of Catholic patriarchal consciousness. While Joseph might be the ruler of the family, the direct line to God was through the woman Mary. In spite of the social convenience of promoting Joseph's headship of the family of Nazareth, Catholics seemed incapable of breaking the tradi-tional power of Mary. Nineteenth-century fathers were told to take St. Joseph for their patron and thus to make their homes "like a second Nazareth." Contradictions within the tradition obfuscated that com-mand. Mary, not Joseph, linked heaven and earth. Mary, not Joseph, was born free from original sin, had conceived virginally, was assumed bodily into heaven, and was crowned Queen of Heaven. While the Scriptures told of her obedience to the will of God, they were silent on Joseph's exercise of his patriarchal authority.[38]

Paternal Domestic Leadership

The insistence by which Protestant domestic writers crowned the father prophet, priest, and king implies that paternal leadership in domestic religion was eroding. Such a model reflected a particular understanding of the social and religious worlds. Comments on the father's princely duties seemed out of place in an increasingly democratic American society. Expecting him to direct a household increasingly diminishing in size underlined his limited domestic power and responsibility. As men looked to the world outside of their families for fulfillment, challenge, and edification, their role as domestic patriarch became shallow.

At the same time Protestant writers felt compelled to maintain the paternal perspective in religion. A hierarchical order in the family reflected the order in society and in the cosmos. The father in the family was like the Father in heaven. According to Catharine Beecher, both were "unseen" but "ever present." Like God the real father was usually absent from the family, but when with the child he "loves him, cherishes him, governs him, pities him, comforts him, and sympathizes in all his pleasures." The child could then be taught that likewise the "heavenly Father, who though unseen, is ever present, and who not only hears and sees all he says and does, but knows his very thoughts." For Beecher having a good earthly father served as model for teaching the child about the good Heavenly Father.[39]

Since the family was a miniature society and even a small universe, to remove the father would be to take the head away from the ordered cosmos. From the paternal perspective the father presented the family's needs to God. If he was gone who would negotiate the relationship between the divine and the human? To assume that the father was too busy and involved with the business world to attend to his domestic religious duties was to assume that humanity could get along without the divine.

The paternal model, then, did not disappear. Instead it was tempered by mid-nineteenth-century writers and altered by late-nineteenth-century writers. Understandably, women did much of the altering. For Catharine Beecher, the father exemplified divine charac-

teristics if he was a "good" father. A good father was one who understood love, self-sacrifice, charity, and other maternal characteristics.
For many Protestants authority had to be based on love and should
not be wielded callously. T. S. Arthur warned men not to mistreat
their tender wives and to be understanding of their domestic situation. In *Home,* written by Catharine Sedgwick, father's Sabbath-day
activities balanced his wife's. Mutuality became more common, and
even Presbyterian Erastus Hopkins felt compelled to add a footnote
mentioning his use of the term "father" to signify the united parents.[40]

Protestant writers on domestic religion had to make accommoda-
tions for male involvement because traditional Protestantism emphasized the sacred quality of the home. After the Reformation the home
was considered a "school of character," and the father was the religious priest of his household. The situation for Irish Catholics was
vastly different. They were faced with a religious tradition which
separated the sacred space of the church from that of the home. Social
and economic traditions in Ireland differed from those in the United
States and demanded a different male response. Whereas Protestant
writers had to cope with men moving away from the home, Catholic
authors had to create a home to drive men toward. Both faiths
underwent changes which would demand a different perspective on
male involvement.

The Irish who came to the United States after the 1840 famine
brought with them a weak connection to Catholicism as defined by
mass attendance and reception of the sacraments. Rural Irish Catholicism had taken on unique folk traits particular to its cultural situation.
Irish Catholics depended on the land for their survival, and they
developed traditions which focused attention on nature. The Catholic
calendar was adapted to agricultural festivals. Pilgrimages to holy
wells secured fertility, good health, and protection. Nature and religious observations were closely connected. As farmers, Irish men
could relate to the combination of pre-Christian folk religion and
Catholicism. A curse on their fields could bring about illness in their
family, and a visit to the local priest to break the curse had real
significance. Celebrations of the change of seasons connected the
farmer to his work, giving it sacred status. Men's involvement in pre-
famine Catholicism empowered them by joining their working lives to
a larger, cosmic order.[41]

Pre-famine popular Catholicism also had strong communal associations. The important rituals were not the Mass and the Eucharist but
rites of passage. Baptisms, marriages, and funerals brought the com-

munity and kin together to acknowledge and celebrate changes in the society and in individuals. In rural situations, aggravated by British prohibitions against Catholicism, such rites of passage may have been the primary connection people had with the priest and the church. Community celebrations accompanied the sacraments. Since such celebrations were public affairs, men most likely organized them. Finding funds for the purchase of food and drink, communicating with distant relatives, negotiating with the priest for his fee—these would have been directed by men (if carried out by women). As with rites focusing on nature, such activities linked men with the supernatural and with the community.[42]

Sean Connolly speculates that real changes in Irish folk Catholicism probably did not occur until two or three decades after the famine. These changes took place more rapidly in the United States where urban life and industrialization broke down the folkways of rural Ireland. Such social changes combined with the push by the Catholic clergy to rid their congregations of lingering Irish "superstitions." By doing this the society and the clergy worked against male involvement in the church. The connection that religion once had with farming did not carry over to industry. Irish American Catholicism increasingly measured piety by involvement in weekly religious activities: mass, communion, parish groups. Spurts of religious commitment which men might have shown in organizing a wake were considered hypocritical. Piety was a daily expression, not something demonstrated only during times of crisis.[43]

By the second and third generations Irish Americans adapted more readily to an urban, industrial environment. Although many Irish still carried on traditions from Ireland, even in Ireland the folkways were dying. In adapting to a middle-class, urban environment, the Irish learned to separate public and private spheres of influence. Men were asked to do their socializing in acceptable religious fraternities, ethnic associations, or benevolent societies. They were asked to give up their control of rites of passage to the clergy. More importantly for this study, they were asked to take seriously the home as a center for education, fulfillment, and rejuvenation.

French advice manuals presented an impractical image of masculinity to the Irish Catholic layman. These books stated goals applicable for French gentlemen of the elite classes, not for Irish working men. It is fairly probable that such advice books were not read by laymen, but by priests who sought to adapt Irish behavior to more acceptable European standards. The Catholic French home served as a model of taste, organization, and religious zeal. Given the distrust

Catholics felt for Protestants, French models of proper domestic life seemed appropriate theologically if not practically. Protestants, who generally saw Irish culture as semi-barbaric, could admire French culture and thus lend support to those Catholics who aspired to a refined home life.

At the same time, general trends in America successfully defined the home as the sphere of women. Women, who had also lost their rural folkways when moving to America, still had some links with the old ways through raising families. Domestic writers assumed that eventually working girls would become mothers and establish their own homes based on a Victorian set of standards. They were told to educate their children in religion and to "save" their husbands. These, of course, were the same husbands who were told to take command in the household and to curb the frivolities of their wives and daughters.

Consequently, because Catholic domestic instruction and ritual during the Victorian period was basically private and informal, men were never properly socialized into taking a leadership position within the home. It was more important for American Catholic leaders to try to provide men with basic religious education and to get them involved in parish activities. To try to counter both a traditional lack of family devotions in Catholicism and the association of domesticity with women would have been impossible. As formal domestic rituals became more encouraged, their leadership fell to women by default.

The traditional role men played within Christianity defined the rising involvement of women in both American Protestantism and Catholicism. Protestantism had a strong tradition of paternal involvement in domestic religion which adapted to theological and social changes. Women found a place within the tradition because men had relinquished their domestic religious duties. Catholicism had a weak tradition of paternal involvement in home worship, a strong involvement in Irish folk Catholicism, and a theological structure which encouraged an authoritarian, hierarchical perspective. Once Irish folk Catholicism had been reduced to nostalgia, men were promised domestic authority, but women assumed religious leadership.

[6]

Leaders at the Domestic Altar

The Maternal Model

A maternal model of domestic religion exists alongside the paternal model. The maternal model depends on the popular notion that the New Testament asserted love over authority. Gone is the idea that the extended household is the basis of society, and in its place is the image of the virgin mother with the sacred infant. In the maternal model of religion the significant relationship is the mother-child bond. God the father is replaced by the image of Jesus crowning his mother, Mary, Queen of Heaven. This model calls on love and not authority to define both religion and earthly society. Love is achieved through an intimate relationship with God or with fellow human beings.

A strong notion of the group or the community is lacking in the maternal model. Religion is regarded as an individual activity standing apart from a hierarchical, social, or theological structure. Formal group worship takes a backseat to private devotion and informal moral influence. God speaks individually, as a mother does to her children, rather than as a father to his household. Consequently, individuality is valued, and a more democratic and egalitarian spirit prevails. Order is achieved through mutual cooperation (on the positive side) or subtle manipulation (on the negative). The nuclear family rather than the extended family supports this model. Women and children now become the focus of the family, and men and their activities exist on the periphery.

Maternal Protestantism

The ambiguities of the paternal perspective on domestic religion can be resolved partially by examining the maternal model. Within the Victorian evangelical churches the involvement of the father in domestic spirituality centered around formal family devotions and exercise of paternal authority in guiding the family to salvation. Nineteenth-century women writers, however, not only challenged traditional notions of sin and salvation, but they presented an alternative to paternal domestic religion. They accomplished this not through the male-controlled seminaries and churches, but through the informal network of fiction and advice literature. Horace Bushnell's presentation of the importance of "Christian nurture" only lent theological legitimation to creeds which women writers established earlier.[1]

The theology presented by Victorian women like Catharine Beecher, Harriet Beecher Stowe, Sarah Hale, Lydia Sigourney, Elizabeth Stuart Phelps—as well as many lesser known writers—supported a maternal attitude toward religion. God's loving mercy and kindness surpassed his fearsome characteristics. Intuition, emotion, and sentiment were the prerequisites for salvation. Salvation was demonstrated not by a violent submission to the will of God, but through acting out, in daily life, Christian virtues. Self-sacrifice, love, and interior devotion combined with an other-worldly orientation to create a Protestantism in which women felt comfortable. The mediation of the clergy and the institution of the church took second place to the natural connection that women perceived they had with God.

Those working within a maternal model of religion saw the preparation of the home itself as a religious activity. Catharine Beecher welded the life of the nursery and kitchen to divine intention. Believing that "this life is but the beginning of an eternal career," Beecher stressed that the formation of "tastes, habits, and character" under a mother's care would "bring forth fruits of good or ill not only through earthly generations, but through everlasting ages." Woman created a "religion of love" by securing a home "in which love reigns." In a true domestic sanctuary, according to Presbyterian James Miller, members demonstrated the love of Christ to each other in "self-forgetful ministries." Women, in the very pursuit of proper child rearing and housekeeping, engaged in domestic rituals. The family existed as "the aptest earthly illustration of the heavenly kingdom," and within that domain the woman presided as its "chief minister."[2]

Women's domestic ministerial duties differed radically from the priestly duties of men. As ministers they specialized in informal education and nurture. The power of maternal influence far exceeded the power exerted by the domestic priest. "The influence of mothers," explained John Power, "is almost resistless." God has given them a moral control "that he has not entrusted even to the angels." Protestants like Lydia Sigourney did not hesitate to refer to the "maternal influence of Monica over Augustine" as an example for New England mothers. Methodist John Newton, after asking rhetorically who influenced St. Augustine, St. Chrysostom, St. Basil, and St. Louis, used colorful imagery to describe maternal religious influence. Those Christian mothers, he wrote, "left neither the cradle nor the bed, until they had poured, drop by drop, into its half-open mouth the pure milk of the gospel." Maternal influence was as natural to women as breast milk.[3]

Mothers were the saviors of their sons and husbands. Father might "lead on his household band," but God "constituted" mother "the first teacher of every human being." Jesus commanded women to save youthful souls from sin, to lead them in the divine faith, and to teach them "triumph o'er the grave." This charge by Christ, combined with woman's angelic nature, gave women "the courage to establish a family altar in the home," thus guiding their husbands into heaven or at least to "earnest Christian service on the earth." The destiny of the immortal soul of the child was placed in the hands of mothers. "Look at the innocent!" commanded Samuel Goodrich, "Tell me again, will you save it?"[4]

The same story was told over and over. "When I was a little child," the saved male related, "my mother used to bid me kneel beside her, and she placed her hand upon my head while she prayed." Eventually mother died and left her son to the vagaries of a cruel world. Exposed to many temptations the son either yielded and then heard his mother, or "when I would have yielded, the same hand was upon my head, and I was saved." The voices of countless dead mothers called their sons back to childhood piety, thus preserving them from destruction. "Never will he hear," elegized Sarah Hale, "another word of human origin,/ which has power, like this mother,/ to restrain his soul from sin."[5]

Daughters, who by virtue of their female character were less prone to sin then their brothers, figured less prominently in conversion stories. Rather than being pulled from the brink of sin by the memory of a holy mother, they often had women mentors (usually not their natural mothers) to instruct them. In Elizabeth Stuart Phelps's *Gates Ajar,* the grieving Mary, whose brother died in the Civil War, received religious education from her Aunt Winifred. Mary, as a true woman, was not leading a life of sin, but was merely confused by current theological disputes. She needed clarification, not conversion. Illustrators frequently portrayed a woman teaching her daughter to read the Bible. Daughters, who never left the safety of the home for the temptations of the world, easily responded to the goals of Christian nurture.[6]

A mother's saving capabilities resulted equally from both her natural godly character and her conscious religious activities. In 1856 T. S. Arthur poetically told his "brothers" that a womanly angel appeared to his wrecked soul, and "with a finger upward pointing/ She turned me with a tear." Likewise, Frank Walters wrote for *Godey's* that woman was a "soul allied to heaven." Women writers agreed with these sentiments. Sarah Hale stated that women were "moulded [to] an angel stature." "Amy" in her 1855 poem "The Christian Woman" explained that standing in our midst was "a pure soul, unalloyed." The true woman was "fresh from the bending skies," an "angel-messenger" sent to redeem her family. Women's spiritual nature permitted them to mediate between heaven and earth.[7]

Not only were women angelic messengers, they also possessed important Christ-like characteristics. Catharine Beecher saw the self-sacrificing qualities of women as a model for all Christian believers. "Christ was made of woman," went an anonymous poem printed in *Godey's,* and by the end of the poem it was unclear whether Christ redeemed them or their mothers. Sarah Hale made it quite clear. When Eve fell, "'twas Wisdom tempted" and so "thus of her was promise given,/ And by her the Saviour came." As Madonna the Victorian woman not only fed the Christ; she was the Christ. In 1850 *Godey's* printed a copy of Murillo's (1618–1682) "Madonna and Child" and titled it "The Christian Mother." The accompanying poem by Alice B. Neal echoed the familiar concept that a mother's prayers and love "may bring thee blessings when thy heart is faint," saving her son from sin. God worked through women.[8]

On a less metaphysical level women saved souls through specific religious strategies. The most important of these strategies was the recognition of the individual character of the soul, especially the souls of children. Unlike the paternal model of domestic religion which sought to bring together the household for group worship, maternal religion was oriented toward individuals. Catharine Beecher in her *Religious Training of Children* encouraged mothers to adapt their styles of religious education to the personality of the child. Anna, a highly nervous child with an "active intellect and strong will," was allowed to be a tomboy playing outside without "ornamented pantalettes to be taken care of." Her outdoor activities tempered her will and naturally opened her to the Christian spirit.[9]

"M. T. R" in the *Mother's Journal and Family Visitant* upheld a similar view. In 1852 the author wrote that it was "of paramount importance that every mother should diligently study the individual character of her children." By doing this she could "ascertain what are the incentives and supports which each requires." True religion required "perfect freedom of mental action," "deliberate choices," and a will not broken but "calmly surrendered." The will was a "faculty to be trained," necessitating motherly intelligence as well as affection. Lydia

"Search the Scriptures." *Godey's Lady's Book* (1851), p. 206.
The Anthenaeum of Philadelphia.

Sigourney hoped that mothers would carefully choose their childrens' religious reading matter, keeping in view "some adaptation to individual character, or train of thought."[10]

Education became a crucial strategy for mothers to accomplish religious nurture on an individual level. The push for female education was first seen as a way in which women became better prepared for the complexities of motherhood. Educational reformers noticed that "the mass of mankind are very ignorant and very wicked." Reformers attributed this to woman's being "denied those privileges of education which only can enable her to discharge her duty to her children with discretion and effect." When women were accorded "half the effort and expense . . . which have been lavished on the other sex" then "we should now have a different state of society." Teaching children was not a purely emotional, intuitive activity; it demanded a level of intellectual competence.[11]

To qualify as the religious teacher of their children, mothers were urged to "study the great doctrines of the Bible." A mother's success as a teacher "will depend greatly on the extent and clearness of her own knowledge." The Bible was "mother's grand text-book" for the instruction of her children, and she needed to be acquainted with history, geography, and chronology in order to "elucidate its truths," and thus "convey an extensive and available fund of knowledge."[12]

The emphasis on individuality manifested itself in the way mothers were told to teach from the Bible. Unlike the paternal model which pictured the father reading to a group, the maternal perspective presented a mother reading to a single child. Victorian illustrators delighted in showing the patient mother guiding her child through the intricacies of the Bible. Visually the style of these drawings showed little distinction between mother reading bedtime stories to her child or reading from the Bible. Writers such as Samuel Goodrich believed that women naturally made the Bible as alive to their children as a storybook. "Let this [reading the Scriptures] be the special care of the mother," Goodrich wrote, "for she has that nice skill which enables her to do all this in a pleasant way."[13]

As a focus for her own education the Bible provided mothers "the first and most sublime specimens of poetry," the "earliest history," and "tales of tender and thrilling interest." The best way to learn a foreign language, according to *Godey's Lady's Book,* was to read the New Testament in that language. With the help of a grammar and dictionary, in a short time a woman could "understand the sense, and also learn and remember the words far better than when merely studying the rules and committing phrases to memory." Such intellectual activities saved women from being a "doll or a slave" and allowed instead their "genius to burn bright."[14]

Tensions occurred when it became unclear how far women could go in pursuit of the proper education for their eventual domestic religious duties. Many echoed Samuel Goodrich's statement that the "mother sways the dominion of the heart, the father that of the intellect." And yet they still agreed with Mrs. Sigourney who believed "it is the profession of our sex to teach, we perceive the mother to be first in point of precedence, in degree of power, in the faculty of teaching." What many ministers and writers agreed on was that women's intellectual activities should be confined to the home. Their

"Teaching the Scriptures." L. Sigourney,
Religious Souvenir of 1840, p. 155. Van Pelt
Library, Special Collections, University of
Pennsylvania.

approval of mother's teaching role inevitably led to the efforts of women like Catharine Beecher to place women teachers in the schools, resulting in the feminization of education by the turn of the century.[15]

Within the home mothers were encouraged to educate their families not only through direct maternal instruction, but through the artistic display of religious articles. Women made, purchased, and displayed a variety of religious goods, from simple samplers with biblical quotations to elaborate seasonal crosses. The embellishment of scripture through art linked the Protestant admiration for the sacred word with the Victorian notion of the accomplished woman. Femininity, creativity, and piety came together as mothers created religious works of art for their families' edification.

Protestant women also linked their musical talents with religious sentiments when they assembled the family around the parlor organ or piano for hymn singing. Mother or daughter demonstrated both her command of musical artistry and her pious sentiments by unifying religion and entertainment. As with the creation of religious handicrafts, domestic hymn singing functioned to instruct the family through familiar, enjoyable means. Art, music, and education were suitable activities for the Victorian woman when she produced them for the spiritual nurture of her family.[16]

By mid-century, teaching children how to pray fell within the domain of the mother. Victorian mothers were reluctant to induce the fear of eternal damnation that typified Calvinist prayer and preferred to present prayer as a comforting activity. In 1853 the Presbyterian Board of Publication printed a narrative of the "Conversion and Happy Death of J. P. B." which reflected the changing response of women to conversion and prayer. At the age of six John lay awake in his bed with terrible fears that he was sinking into hell. His mother tried to quiet his alarm, "pressing him to my heart," but with no success. For the next few pages the scene was of mother trying to love and reassure her son against the son's insistence on his depravity. The mother finally calmed the child by reciting freely from the Scriptures, but it was evident that she herself was left "deeply affected" from the conversation. John's mother used prayer not to accept the fear of God but to defend against a fearsome God.[17]

Like a mother's loving reassurance, prayers at home were personal, individual, and founded on affection. Children were not to be frightened by God's wrath. They were taught to say a prayer to Jesus before going to bed at night. T. S. Arthur portrayed a mother leading her children in responsorial prayer. The scene was so heavenly that the family "can almost hear the rustle of their [angels'] garments as they gather around their sleeping babes." In 1839 Lydia Sigourney detailed for mothers how to teach their child to "bring its humble wants, thanks, and sorrows, in its own lisping language, to the ear of its Heavenly Father." By 1900, although father should still lead family devotions it was at the knees of mother that J. S. Mills recommended the child "pray every evening before going to sleep." The bedtime prayer slowly replaced evening worship.[18]

In the maternal understanding of religion, mothers and children had direct access to God. They did not need the mediation of the priest-father or the minister. Lydia Sigourney explained that between the child and God there were "no deep descents into vice, no long continued clouds of alienation." God heard the prayers of little children. For T. S. Arthur childhood prayers were so effective that they "came back again and rested on their earthly parents." This in turn stirred the parents until "a warmer love came gushing from their hearts." Jesus' playing with little children was a popular scene for artists to illustrate. In 1872 M. R. LeWahl composed a poem for *Godey's* which cleverly combined a mother's prayer with her child's. The mother and child, saying the familiar "Now I lay me down to sleep," are heard by "listening angels" who "raise the prayer aloft."[19]

Protestant children and mothers had many interchangeable characteristics. Both could act as saviors to their fathers. Both could take over family devotions if fathers absolutely refused this duty or had died. Both were thought of as "buds of heaven" or "beings of celestial nature" whose delicate constitutions destined them to early death and life in paradise. Children and women were too good for this world, and death freed them from a life of suffering. Davis Newton could have easily been describing the "true woman" when he wrote that happy children are "courteous, cheerful, sweet, heavenly, 'olive-plants,' kind, obedient, God-fearing. They eat whatever is set before them thankfully, asking no questions, exhibiting whatever is true, honest, just, pure, lovely, and of good report." The eventual reunion of mother and child in heavenly bliss was the poetic reverie of many Victorian writers.[20]

The changing nature of home Sabbath activities justly epitomizes the maternal dimension of Victorian domestic religion. The Sabbath, which had once been a time of contemplation of the divine, became child-oriented and mother-directed. Sabbath activities—prayer, Bible reading, pious conversation—were geared to educate children as individuals. "The truth," explained Hiram Orcutt in 1874, "must be opened to their minds through their own channels of thought and action." Who would be better skilled at creating religious activities individually geared for her children's education than the mother? "Childhood must be *amused*," continued Orcutt, because "the Divine Master delights to see 'little children' happy on the Sabbath." The original dictum that "the Sabbath was made for man, not man for the Sabbath" (Mk. 2:27) had been altered. Now Orcutt could justly say, "the sabbath was made for children as well as for men and women."[21]

Maternal Catholicism

The presence of the maternal model of domestic religion in Victorian Catholicism differs from its appearance in evangelical Protestantism. Unlike Protestants who eliminated the supernatural influence of Mary and the female saints but found it again in the being of human mothers, Catholicism maintained devotions to special women. The issues of infant damnation and the depravity of the human character were nonquestions for Catholics. Christian nurture, as an alternative to emotional conversion, had been assumed in Catholicism. Ethnicity and class separated Catholic women from the leisured life of their middle-class Protestant neighbors. Catholicism, centralized and hierarchical, left little room for local variations instigated by women.

Unlike Protestant women, who published their own magazines, Catholic women had no such outlet for their views on the world and religion. In Philadelphia, the home of *Godey's* and of a large Catholic population, only two women's journals were issued by Catholic presses in the nineteenth century. Both were short-lived, *The Home* existing from 1892 to 1893 and *Our Own* surviving a mere five months in 1869. Catholic women, who until the end of the century were not a part of the middle class, either had no interest in starting their own magazines, had no capital, or felt satisfied reading "Protestant" magazines such as *Godey's*. Consequently, it is more difficult to delineate the Catholic maternal perspective because women (and like-minded men) had no strong voice of their own to present their views.[22]

Home journals, such as Chicago's *Catholic Home* and the *Sacred Heart Review*, often had women writers but were edited by men. Their concerns were broadly based and geared for men as well as women. Whereas few self-respecting males would have read *Godey's* or *The Lady's Repository*, the *Catholic Home* featured a masthead on which father read the newspaper and mother played with the babies. Lay Catholic women wrote for journals such as *Ave Maria* and the *Catholic World*, but their writings dealt infrequently with women's issues. *Ave*

Maria was primarily a devotional journal. The intellectual *Catholic World* only rarely commented on the "woman's question." Catholic women, although they produced devotional poetry, analytical articles, and domestic fiction, rarely presented their own religious attitudes.

Priests commented more directly on domestic affairs. Departing from their role as ritualists they attempted to educate men and women in their proper duties as husbands and wives. Spiritual direction, beginning in the seventeenth century, functioned as an important priestly duty in Counter Reformation Europe. The model for this was the friendship of François de Sales and Jeanne de Chantal. De Sales counselled the young widow to live a spiritual life in the world but not of it. American priests had no time for such involved relationships. Their counselling had to be limited to well-distributed books or sermons. The French model of a priest counselling individual ladies at home was totally infeasible in America.[23]

Catholic advice book writers combined spiritual direction with their insights into domesticity. They told women that just because they were wives and mothers they were not barred from religious life. An 1886 article in the *Catholic Home Journal* called mothers "home heroes" because they were modestly secluded from "men's praises" and devoted their energies to "the little ones," activities which the "outer world does not know." The mother was "retired" and "secluded," "cloistered in her home." Her martyrdom went unknown and unacknowledged. Women attained the interior quiet of the nun when they accepted their home as a cloister and their children as souls to be trained in religion.[24]

As late as the 1890s when many women were establishing themselves in the public world Catholic writers supported not only the doctrine of separate spheres but the invisibility of women within those spheres. *Ave Maria* quoted Frederic Ozanam's perspective that women were "similar to . . . the Guardian Angels—they might lead the world, but while remaining invisible themselves." Only at certain times did angels become visible, and so likewise only infrequently "does the empire of women become visible, and that we behold these angels, who were the saviors of Christian society, manifesting themselves under the name of Blanche of Castille and Joan of Arc." Catholic writers placed the exceptional woman out of reach of the average woman.[25]

Even Mary Sadlier, who included many independent women in her novels, saw the true woman as one retired from the world. Servant girls might be virtuous, but eventually they would marry and step out of the working world. There were no Sadlier women who worked outside the home for reasons other than poverty. Leisured women, such as the Von Wiegel women, confined themselves like medieval abbesses to ruling their small estate and did not venture outside of its walls. Characters like Eleanor Donnelly's Marguerite, who sought fame on the stage as a singer, faced professional tragedy. Eventually she settled down to housekeeping, telling her new husband, "my pride is justly punished."[26]

Sadlier assumed that this Catholic view of women differed from a Protestant perspective. Writing about a Catholic teaching sister, she explained that "had she been a Protestant she would have been 'a strong-minded women,' beyond all doubt; she might have taken the lead at public meetings, edited a daily newspaper in some of our great cities, delivered public lectures, and written huge volumes on metaphysics or philosophy." This woman, "being a Catholic . . . and born in Ireland" chose the better path of feminine modesty and Christian humility. She was "taught to consider human learning as a mere accessory to the grand science of salvation." The true woman chose the higher calling, "the unworldly step of retiring from the world . . . to live a life of seclusion and of mortification." In the convent or in the home, a woman's natural talents should be hidden in "the bosom of her God."[27]

The wife's activities, like the nun's, were geared to serving. While the nun gained God's favor by serving her divine spouse, the wife gained favor by serving her husband. "A wife," wrote Archbishop Landriot, "beautifies and adorns her husband's life. Like a lovely tree she bears for him the refreshing fruits of a loving heart. She dries his tears, she compensates him for all his toils and labors; she pours into his veins the oil of peace and happiness." In order to accomplish this the mother must rule over her house.[28]

Since Catholicism lacked a strong tradition of family devotions, when writers called men "domestic priests" they exaggerated their role as head of the household. On the other hand, when they called women priests they referred to woman's devotion to her family. Cardinal James Gibbons, quoted in an 1886 article, explained that women could not become "real" priests, but instead were "priests in the broader sense of the term." Women offered "in the sanctuary of their homes and the altar of their hearts the acceptable sacrifice of supplication, praise, and thanksgiving to God." Gibbons felt quite comfortable with these sentiments, and in a sermon delivered for the feast of St. Agnes he told women they were "consecrated as priests in . . . baptism."[29]

The Catholic mother presided as "priestess of the domestic shrine" not only because she kept a neat house, but because she "cultivates religion in her family, and instructs her children in its truths." In the maternal model the woman directed home religion. In 1868 Sister Mary Carroll described a scene in her *Pleasant Homes* which she "wished was more common." Before evening prayers mother gathered her children and listened to them recite the catechism. Mother did not expect only rote memorization, but "encouraged them to ask questions about anything they did not understand, that she might be able to instruct them correctly." She also read from a book for twenty minutes, explaining the evening chapter (from the Bible?), told stories about the saints to "enliven the lesson," and corrected the children's pronunciation of theological terms.[30]

Even if father actively directed his household, mother received total control over the religious education of young children. God gave mothers "a marvelous zeal in adapting the language of duty to the mind of her lisping child." Education began at the cradle on the mother's knee. She was expected to teach the child how to know, love, and serve God and to "lisp the sacred name of Jesus and the Holy Name of Mary." Mothers guided "the innocent hand to make the sign of the cross" and told the simple stories of the lives of the saints and "the history of Our Lord."[31]

Late nineteenth-century Catholics had their own version of Christian nurture. "How do you know what disposition of mind the child imbibes with its mother's milk?" asked the *Sacred Heart Review*. Since the connections between the soul and the body were "strange and mystical," the newspaper urged mother to "beware of her thoughts, her tempers, her inclinations" while her child depended on her. "What is the Christian mother?" queried Maurice d'Hulst. She is the one who has chosen "the slavery of home duties" and made "maternity a priesthood" by pouring the "faith of Christ into the very veins of her child as she nurses him at her breast."[32]

To direct home religious activities among older children or adults without threatening male authority, Catholic novelists often did away with fathers. Women led evening prayers since they were widows, and thus the maternal understanding of religion could be brought into harmony with a paternal understanding. In other cases Catholicism took on a strictly feminized quality as Protestantism did. Mother and daughter, according to the *Sacred Heart Review*, made charity boxes, bringing them out every Sunday to be passed around for contributions. "Choral leaflets" with music for piano or parlor organ were written by Misses Jordan and de Lande "to supply hymns for the Catholic family." Advertisers encouraged the purchases of "dainty little French novelties" of medals, statuettes, or holy water fonts for Christmas. Writers like Mary Sadlier might have resented this infringement on paternal religion, but by the turn of the century domestic religion seemed firmly in the hands of women.[33]

Such unrelenting devotion and pious duty toward the child's spiritual development endowed mothers with the ultimate in religious power—the power to save. Catholic women accomplished this in two ways. They could atone for male sins through the indulgences they gained from their prayers, or they could make everlasting impressions on their sons and husbands. In each case women succeeded in saving their loved ones where the church had failed.

According to Cardinal Gibbons, women were "angels of expiation" who by their "prayers and mortifications" atoned for the sins of "fathers, husbands, sons and brothers." A wonderful story in the *Catholic Girl's Guide* recounted the adventures of a carousing husband who made a bet with his buddies that his virtuous wife would willingly arise from her bed at midnight to make supper for the group. The wife did this without complaining. When asked why, she replied that since her husband's life "on the other side of the grave" will be rather dismal, "it is my duty at least to make his life here below as agreeable as possible." Her suffering not only lessened his time in purgatory; it eventually caused him to "reform his manner of life."[34]

Catholic examples of sons remembering their mothers and being "saved" are almost endless. One son wore a golden medal he took from his dead mother's neck. Looking at it moved him to say, "Mother I have kept my promise." Later in the century mothers no longer needed to give their sons religious symbols; the mere memory of the mother was religious. "Maternity, sweet sound!," went an 1887 article, "'tis our first love! 'tis of our religion." The religion had now become mother-love. In 1890 a Philadelphia newspaper carried a story called "A Mother's Look." The silent, "dumb look from her death-bed" of a mother motivated the "wretched youth" to become a Jesuit missionary. Likewise, the *Sacred Heart Review* explained in "A Mother's Influence" that the kiss "my mother gave me, has often proved the password to purity and honor in a young man's career and a shield against the many temptations in a young girl's life."[35]

Women not only directed their husbands and children to the paths of righteousness, they also converted Protestants. In *Mora Carmody,* the Protestant eventually becomes a Catholic, but too late to marry the virtuous Mora who dies as a nun during an epidemic. In *Bickerton; or the Immigrant's Daughter,* an article in a city newspaper warned young men to take heed if "they marry lovely Catholic wives and come to spend their honeymoon in Rome. There is more danger to their Protestantism in the experiment than they are aware of." Servant girls, usually indirectly through their good works, succeeded in converting whole families. Mary, in *The Governess; or, the Effects of Good Example,* converted a Protestant family via the child she taught (who eventually died). While men, especially priests, won converts through clever theological debates, Catholic women usually accomplished the same feat through their simple yet profound piety.[36]

Women's influence could also be put to evil use, especially if a Catholic man married a Protestant woman. In *Confessions of an Apostate,* Mary Sadlier had her main character Simon marry a Protestant woman not very subtly named "Eve." Eve, the daughter of "the deacon," hated housework and was determined to save Simon from "the abomination of desolation which abides in the Romish Church." Simon, who thought "religion was nothing" and Eve's love everything, gave up the true faith. On her deathbed Eve realized that Simon erred in selling "your God for a wife" and asked for forgiveness. Forgiven, she still died a Protestant. Simon, whose evil children deserted him, returned to Ireland where he lived to tell the story as a warning to all.[37]

Evil also hid within some Catholic women. Father Giradey in *Mission Book for the Married* reminded parents that "children, to a great extent, owe their passions and evil propensities to their parents, and especially to their mother." In *Aunt Honor's Keepsake* good Irish women were driven to drink and neglected to prepare dinner for their toiling husbands. Poor honest girls "who lived like demons through the night" had "lips foul with blasphemy" and "poisonous breath." Con O'Leary, the author of *The Lost Rosary,* showed no sympathy for these women, whose dress was "gay and fashionable twelve hours ago" and now was "broken, torn and faded." He thought they should choose death rather than "fall from the high estate of purity."[38]

Although this strain of woman as Eve existed in Catholic popular literature, the Blessed Virgin Mary was seen as a more adequate feminine archetype. Orestes Brownson ascribed "no little of the infidelity and immorality, the vice and crime of the age" to the woman and also assumed that she was a "being apart . . . to be worshipped as a star in the distant heavens." In advice literature such as Father Bernard O'Reilly's *The Mirror of True Womanhood,* Mary was presented as the kind of woman who set "the Eternal Father constantly before her eyes, studying to make every thought and aim and word and action most pleasing to that Infinite Perfection." Mary "ruled in this most blessed home" of Nazareth which was a model for all Catholics to emulate. Through Mary women were to learn "how to bring the light of heaven down into your home" which would "brighten your care and your suffering."[39]

In general, Mary served two functions for women. First, she legitimized their ability to "save" their families. "Just as Mary the mother of the New Life gave the Saviour and salvation to the world," O'Reilly wrote in 1877, "just as the Church, the spouse of Christ, ever more performs the divine office of motherhood here below toward the nations,—even so true woman in every home is the saviour and sanctifier of man." Mary as the "Mother of the Redeemer won salvation, deliverance and true spiritual life for the whole human race." Dying sons called out the names of both Mary and their mothers at their death. Mary was "Mother," and poets hoped that when life's voyage was over they would "meet again, no more to part."[40]

Mary also functioned as an ideal model for women. She was the ultimate true woman—an ever-virgin mother, obedient, suffering, unselfish, and pious. Father O'Reilly called her a "true mirror of maidenhood and womanhood!" Her love and devotion for her son not only moved him to crown her Queen of Heaven, but she "who had pillowed his infant head on her bosom" became "His Bride and our Mother." Mary was "no fashionable lady caring only for society and amusements, for dress and novels." Advice book writers stripped Mary of her more supernatural powers and presented her "in the peaceful house of Nazareth, industriously pursuing the ordinary avocations of a poor artisan's wife."[41]

In addition to Mary, Catholic mothers were presented a variety of saints to emulate. Saints such as Monica, Margaret Queen of Scotland, and Queen Blanche were noted for their ability to convert sinners or their insights into Christian education. Sometimes writers mentioned the names of the sainted husbands but not the virtuous wives. St. Giovanni Coloino was converted by his nameless wife. He had come home and found that his dinner was not ready. To stop him from upsetting and breaking furniture, his wife gave him a book on the lives of the saints to read while she helped the cook. A radical change came over him, and he eventually "died in the odor of sanctity." Advice book writers picked freely from many centuries of good Christian women, named and unnamed, who exemplified proper Christian virtues.[42]

Maternal Domestic Leadership

The nature of religious leadership within the home cannot be discussed without connecting it to a larger religious and cultural perspective. Trends in early evangelical Protestantism supported the greater role of women in religious leadership, first at home and then in the larger church organization. A decline in male Puritan church membership during the mid-seventeenth century and a rise in female membership encouraged mothers to replace fathers in catechizing and educating their children. Increases in female literacy, a decline in antinomian disturbances by women like Anne Hutchinson, and the rise of the idea of "separate spheres" led historians Gerald Moran and Maris Vinovskis to conclude that "by the mid-eighteenth century ministers commonly assumed the natural role of women in preparing their children spiritually."[43]

Even before the Great Awakening of the mid-eighteenth century, women in New England churches exceeded male communicants by more than two to one. By 1835 the percentage of women who belonged to Massachusetts Congregational churches was double the percentage of the male population. New England women also tended to join evangelical voluntary societies at a greater rate than men and responded to revivals with more enthusiasm. As men became more involved in nonreligious organizations—social, professional, or political groups—they lost interest in churches which condemned the "materialism of a new market economy and the divisiveness of new partisan politics." Evangelical Protestantism more and more concentrated on the private sphere of home, women, and children.[44]

Protestant women brought the religious enthusiasm generated by the Second Great Awakening, voluntary societies, and benevolent organizations into their homes. Where they might have been denied public leadership positions in the church or society, they easily assumed them in the home. Within the home women promoted a simplified and unifying Protestantism which seemed to be disappearing from male-controlled churches and seminaries. Proponents of the sacrality of the home presented the family as the foundation of the nation and of Christianity. Mothers thus became crucial in fulfilling America's religious and political destiny. Ministers and fathers were important figureheads but not the real guarantors of the faith. Dying sons called out their mother's name, not their minister's or father's.

The father's function as domestic priest took a backseat to the mother's position as domestic teacher. The paternal model of father leading his household in family worship did not fit well with an increasingly participatory, democratic, bourgeois society. Authority and formality were still valued as critical to the well-being of society, but the general American ethos supported a republican spirit of innovation. The teacher—in the home and in the school—symbolized the distribution of knowledge and the hope for an educated electorate. As formal theology faded into the background, informal religious instruction formed the primary means of bringing morality and Christian spirit to a growing nation. Educators like Catharine Beecher placed women in the center of this push for education.

Maternal domestic leadership in evangelical Protestantism can be summarized by a quick examination of an essay which appeared in the December 1886 issue of *Harper's Magazine*. Written by Lew Wallace, the author of *Ben Hur,* it was a speculation on the "boyhood of Christ." The family at Nazareth that Wallace proposed was not poor, but "comfortable." They had taken the gifts of gold the Magi brought, sold them, and lived off the income. Joseph's carpentry job "signifies nothing, as the law required every Israelite, rich or poor, to follow some occupation." Mary owned the house the family dwelt in. Wallace concluded that this middle-class life-style, "neither rich nor poor," allowed Jesus "marginal time in which to taste something of natural boyish freedom."[45]

Wallace portrayed Joseph as a "plain, serious" middle-aged man who had other children. Joseph played no important part in the story. Mary was about twenty-seven (when Jesus was twelve) and was "gentle, modest, sweet-spoken, of fair complexion, with eyes of violet-blue, and hair half brown, half gold." Although Jesus had divine instruction from the angels, it was Mary who taught him the alphabet and the Torah. "I delight in imagining the two at work," Wallace wrote. "The *torah* is spread upon her knee; he has a hand over her shoulder, she an arm about his waist; he is quick to apprehend; their voices are low and sweet; at times they turn to each other, and it is the old story— 'Soft eyes looked love to eyes that spake again.'" In the accompanying illustration, "Mary teaching Jesus the alphabet," Joseph is a mere shadow sawing away at wood in the background, while Mary and Jesus, wearing halos, are busy studying.[46]

For Wallace, as for many Victorian Protestants, domestic religion existed in a world dominated by mothers and children. The financial stability which provided for a secure home life appeared somewhat mysteriously; no true woman would have insisted her husband work *that* hard for mere money. Women "owned" their homes, and men were shadows busy in the background. Although love and emotions were crucial in creating a proper environment for Christian nurture, the maternal perspective understood domestic religion as a type of "intellectual ritual" based on teaching. Individuality, morality, and piety were virtues cultivated between mother and child.[47]

The situation for American Catholics was less explicit and has been less well-documented. There have been no statistical studies on male/female church attendance during the Victorian period. Orestes Brownson condemned women writers and promoters of women's rights, but he was silent on the ratio of participation by men and women in parish life. Cryptic comments in the popular presses, however, indicate a greater ratio of female to male participation. In an 1868 review of a new *Illustrated Catholic Sunday School Library*, the

Jesus and Mary Studying the Torah. Wallace, "The Boyhood of Christ," *Harper's Magazine* 74 (1886), p. 11.

author complained that all of the stories were about boys when "girls outnumber boys in our Sunday schools." We know that many women headed households as early death or desertion removed men from families. The general impression one receives is that women more enthusiastically participated in Catholic activities, but male participation was considered more important.[48]

Catholic concepts of maternal leadership derived from two distinct streams: a "Catholic" stream filled with ideals of true womanhood as defined by church and European authorities, and an "American" stream filled with concepts of true womanhood as defined by "secular" sources and American Catholic writers. Each of these streams must be taken seriously in order to understand the differences between, and similarities of, Protestant and Catholic views on maternal religious roles.

The Catholic concept of domestic religion rested on a hierarchical structure which placed religious power in the hands of a male clergy. Although the influence of the church had been eroding in Europe, it still commanded the attention of world authorities and, especially, of its members. There was no Catholic "clerical disestablishment"—a term used by Ann Douglas to describe Protestant American ministers—within the United States. American priests during the nineteenth century had important social and religious functions to perform for their parishioners and did not need to align themselves with women to assume moral power. For the Irish Catholic, the priest was a powerful spiritual and secular leader.

Although morality held an important place within Catholicism, a priest's major function was not to assure the establishment of a moral order. Whereas the Protestant minister and the mother could share their concern of creating a "Christian" nation, the priest could not share his ability to consecrate the bread and the wine with women. The sacramental life of the church was restricted from lay participation, and women were excluded from even peripheral activities. Victorian Catholicism, unlike Victorian Protestantism, had formal rituals which could not be taken over by women. Moral influence was important, but it was through faithful participation in the sacraments that one was saved.

Consequently, it was not difficult for European Catholics and some American writers to restrict women's domestic power. Catholic women did not hold the keys to salvation as did nurturing Protestant women. Although not all men were priests, all unmarried men possessed a "potential" priesthood which women could never possess. The authority and power invested in men and restricted from women were demonstrated each day at Mass. Whereas Protestant women (and their male supporters) redefined the nature of conversion as Christian nurture, Catholic women could not empower their domestic activities in the same way.

The strong position of the church functioned to draw attention away from the family and toward the parish. Religious professionals, priests and nuns, were assumed to be better educated in religion so that parents gave religious education over to them. The general structure of the church which put a high premium on authority, hierarchy, and formal ritual overwhelmed effort at informal, individual family worship and instruction. French views of spirituality, which emphasized a private and internal religious life, drew Catholics away from communal devotions. Even the existence of a Catholic sisterhood weakened maternal leadership. Women who felt themselves called to greater involvement in religion should become nuns and not overburden their families with religious activities.

The "Catholic" stream of domesticity also cast shadows over the perfectability of women. Catholic writers—both male and female—felt comfortable with the image of woman as Eve. As the weaker vessel, women could not be expected to function well in the wider world and should be sheltered within the home. Although the Protestant perspective in the early part of the century also echoed this view, by the 1870s women's education was being taken seriously. Irish Catholic women, because of their economic status and a general prejudice against female erudition, were relegated to convent school education. Convent school education, like the ladies' seminaries of the early nineteenth century, focused on creating true women and not intellectuals. The first degree awarded by a Catholic college to a woman was in 1899. Although Catholics cited the achievements of centuries of Catholic queens and saints, few used this as a justification for women's entrance into a wider world of social action and the professions.

This lack of formal educational opportunities for women combined with the general Catholic preference for imitation over instruction to shape the way that mothers taught their children. Catholic writers did not emphasize maternal education or individual instruction for children. Whereas Protestants enjoyed picturing a single child learning to read the Bible from the mother, Catholic writers infrequently mentioned such private instruction. Catholic women were given the lives of the saints, especially Mary, to imitate. Education, because of its association in America with Protestantism and in general with modernity, was held under suspicion during the nineteenth century.

American Catholic views of maternal religion assumed the "secular" attitude toward domesticity. Late-nineteenth-century newspapers and novels assumed that women were more religious than men, more attuned to the spiritual needs of their children, and that it was through leading a moral life that one was saved. Writers pictured Catholic mothers as mediating between heaven and earth just as Protestant mothers did. The formality of gaining indulgences allowed for a direct connection between the good works of the woman and those who had died. "Man may be the ruler," Elvira Hobson wrote in 1869, "but woman holds the light which is to guide him to glory or to shame." Like the Christ who suffered to redeem the world, the Catholic woman offered sacrifices for the redemption of her family.[50]

Catholic writers who hoped to promote the ascendancy of women as domestic redeemers drew from the great wealth of Marian imagery to secure the divine role of women. Mary's humble obedience and participation in the Incarnation was seen as the beginning of a "new era" for women. "Henceforth we see woman gliding through a renewed world," wrote one Victorian woman, "with gentle tear and joyful heart." Protestants might be able to picture a human Mary teaching her little boy how to read, but Catholics had available the rich traditions of almost two millennia of devotion to Mary to choose from. And if Mary was not enough, there was Helena, whose son changed the fate of European society, and Monica, who converted the great Augustine.[51]

While informal maternal influence gained greatly from the Victorian promotion of women, formal home worship was a relatively new phenomenon. By the last two decades of the century, the promotion of the family by Pope Leo XIII had shifted attention to home worship. The church was faced with a dilemma—whether to support a classical paternal understanding of domestic leadership or to follow more contemporary trends and underline the mother's importance in religious nurture. Church leaders remained silent on this issue and so permitted women—acknowledged by American culture as naturally more pious—to assume domestic religious leadership by default.

By the turn of the century the Catholic family had become a focus of papal attention, and in the United States the establishment of many diocesan parochial schools concentrated attention on children and their families. Second- and third-generation Irish American families gained economic stability and more awareness of the ways of adapting to American culture. The flux of Southern and Eastern Europeans threatened the Irish hold on the American church and the Irish definition of family structure, while greater pluralism in America shook the Protestant hegemony and caused strong reaction against the foreign influx. Liberal forces within Protestant circles and the rise of a "scientific" approach to understanding American life countered more conservative trends by trying to locate social problems not in the family or individual, but in the larger social order. The trends which began at the end of the nineteenth century were foundational for shaping twentieth-century attitudes toward religion and the family.

Conclusion

In 1967 Robert Bellah published an article which firmly established the concept of "civil religion" in the minds of scholars. Following classical sociological theory, Bellah saw religion not as individual piety but as a symbol system which binds together a community. Embodied in presidential inaugural addresses, Memorial Day celebrations, and the sense of national "election" was a religious system which existed alongside traditional American denominations. By using a language unique to civil religion, public figures evoked a common set of national symbols which both reflected the sentiments of the people and cemented a particular notion of America. Bellah provided an American example of Durkheim's conviction that "the collective ideal which religion expresses is far from being due to a vague innate power of the individual, but it is rather at the school of collective life that the individual has learned to idealize." Whether civil religion served as a legitimating ideology and ritual system or as a means of providing a transcendent judge for American society was of secondary interest to Bellah's insistence that public symbols define what is sacred in this country.[1]

Modifications of this Durkheimian perspective on religion took into account the tendency of modern Western society to push religion into the private, domestic sphere. Both Peter Berger in *The Sacred Canopy* and Thomas Luckmann in *The Invisible Religion* assumed that the pressures of modern society forced individuals to retreat to the private sphere where they cultivated autonomy, self-expression, and self-realization. Although admitting that "the segregation of religion within the private sphere is quite 'functional'" for the maintenance of modern society, they express dismay that the private sphere seized functions which are properly performed by the public sphere. Sexuality and its extension in the family are basically "innocuous from the point of view of a social order that is based, essentially, upon the functionally rational norms of the primary public institutions." For Berger and Luckman the family's role as a source of ultimate significance for its members was obvious, but regrettable.[2]

Although historians documented how the modern Western family lost many of its economic functions and became primarily a center for socialization and affection, this change was seen as unfortunate. Ann Douglas, in her *The Feminization of American Culture*, has been justly criticized for labeling domestic culture as sentimental and thus undesirable. Supporters of popular Victorian culture such as Barbara Welter and Nina Baym approved of domestic novels because they were "vehicles of protest" which commented on "temperance, women's rights, prolabor and antilabor, slavery and abolition." In other words, only when the private sphere (dominated by women) attempted to control the public sphere (dominated by men) was the private sphere worth noting.[3]

By taking seriously the Victorian concern for domestic matters we can see how a particular social and spiritual ideology developed within the private sphere. Domestic religion for Protestants and Catholics served to both uphold the traditions of the larger church and to provide an alternative to that church. We cannot generalize and say that domestic religion is merely minature church-religion or a unique, personal response to the divine. What should be clear is that domestic religion has its own intrinsic logic, leadership patterns, and symbols which provide a sense of the sacred. Studying the role of religion within the home and the sacralizing impact of domestic symbols and activities emphasizes the importance of the family as an institution, an institution which stands between the community and the individual, possessing characteristics of each.

I would modify Robert Bellah's argument for an American civil religion by insisting that running alongside of denominational religion in America is a domestic religion, as well as a civil religion. This domestic religion shares both the symbols of individual traditions—Protestantism, Catholicism, Judaism—and the symbols of American domesticity. By combining traditional religious symbols with a set of middle-class domestic values the Victorians rooted their home virtues in the eternal and allowed the more abstract traditional symbols to assume a real presence in everyday life. Domestic religion, in its uniquely religious and generally cultural forms, bound together what was truly meaningful in Victorian society. It also allowed the Victorians to separate and divide themselves from what they considered destructive to proper domestic sentiments. To understand the Christianity of this period we must look not only at public symbols of civil religion, or particular theologies, but at the sacramental character of the home.

Domestic Christianity provided Protestants and Catholics with a sense of stability in a climate of social and religious change. For Protestants the ideology and symbols of the home served as an alternative to sectarian splintering by presenting an agreed-upon notion of an eternal, God-given, Bible-based family life. For Catholics, domestic ideology not only vitalized lay life by connecting it to the sacred, but helped prepare immigrants for their lives in a new nation. The prevalence of Gothic architecture and designs, household religious articles, parlor organs, stained glass, and the publication of countless domestic novels, advice books, and magazines by religious presses underlined the fundamental significance of the home as the major center of Victorian piety.

The variations between Protestant and Catholic versions of domestic religion reflected both traditional differences and the unique social and religious setting of nineteenth-century America. Protestants maintained the virtue of home worship but slowly moved the father out of his position as the household priest while moving mother into her role as family minister and redeemer. Moral instruction—a teaching ritual—came to replace worship as the primary goal of Protestant family devotions. This instruction was child-centered, mother-directed, and individual. While paternal authority continued to be acknowledged, and male involvement desirable, fathers were increasingly edged out of a domestic Protestantism which stressed innocence, personal piety, individual education, and the sanctity of domestic sentiments.

The social and economic conditions of Irish American life kept Catholics from developing a middle-class domestic piety until almost the close of the century. Traditional Catholicism, with its preference for celibate life, church-centered rituals, and private piety worked against the establishment of family religion. The Catholic assertion of the primacy of the sacred space of the church and the mystical, adult-orientation of the Mass competed with the home and child-centered quality of domestic religion. With the rise of the American Catholic laity and the promotion by Rome of the sanctity of the home came a new acknowledgment of the importance of the family's religious roles. Greater affluency among Catholics enabled them to purchase suburban homes, furnish their rooms with religious articles, and read domestic advice literature. Led by novelists and advice book writers, Catholics called upon concepts of peasant purity and French sophistication to shape domestic sentiments appropriate to their new middle-class status.

Both Catholics and Protestants imprinted their domestic and religious feelings into the objects they made, bought, and displayed in their homes. In her book *Ladies of the Leisure Class,* Bonnie Smith recognized in late-nineteenth century northern France an attitude toward the home environment which I feel parallels that of America. Domestic articles rather than being neutral objects were imbued with sacred qualities. While Smith asserted that sensing the holiness of domestic objects was specifically a feminine trait, I would argue that both the men and women of Victorian America perceived the sacrality of certain household objects. Women might have made or purchased the objects—family Bibles, wax crosses, Angelus clocks—but popular literature often mentioned the object's emotional impact on men.[4]

Even if such emotional impact was absent, domestic objects helped establish the status of the family, facilitate social and household interaction, express individual roles and characters, and reveal the goals and expectations of the family. The display of specifically religious articles expressed the belief that the divine dwelt in the everyday world and could be experienced in the home. While theologians might insist on the abstract nature of faith and values, for the laity these needed to be embodied and made tangible in material objects. Religious articles linked the individual families to a larger pattern of cultural and ethnic traditions, abstract theologies, and mythical settings.

Although domestic ideology promoted the separate, private, isolated home as a restful alternative to the busy marketplace of the world, we must not ignore the accommodation of domesticity to public life. Privacy was valued, but the house needed to be built and landscaped so that passersby could see the character of the family in the physical embodiment of the home. Intimacy was promoted, so long as the sexes, ages, classes, and religions were kept separate either spatially in house design, ritually in family worship, or ideologically through advice literature. The cultivation of the individual was a family affair, but the character of "good" individuals was determined by novelists, ministers, and advice literature of the secular world. The Victorians were not a private people concerned with constructing a hiding place in the world, they were a public people who sought to define themselves through display of their sense of "election." The domestic environment was not only created for the good of the family, it had to be presented to the public as evidence for the goodness of the family.[5]

The vitality and enthusiasm of the popular literature and material culture of domestic Christianity attests to the viability of private, family religion in the nineteenth century. To imply that religion hastily retreated to the family to avoid being devoured by an uncompromising urban-industrial setting overgeneralizes the evolution of American religions. For Irish Americans, urban and industrial life permitted the establishment of Catholic culture in the United States. A set of teachings and symbols appropriate for universal Catholicism replaced the folkways of Irish rural life. Urban living allowed for the development of the parish system, and the industrial cash economy provided the funds for the creation of a visible Catholic culture at home and in the city. Strengthening public Catholicism in America permitted the strengthening of domestic Catholicism.

When Protestants and Catholics agreed on a set of home virtues, rituals, and symbols this overarching domestic religion gave them a common language to speak to one another. Domestic religion, even with the coloration of denominational differences, could bring people together under the truth of the eternal nature of a good home. Parlor organs, the symbol of middle-class respectability, family unity, and Christian sentiment were advertised and sold to Protestant and Catholic alike. Paintings of Madonna and Child graced the walls of Protestant and Catholic homes. Expectations of the piety of women and the religious authority of men were felt by both traditions. Following the lead of Bellah we may speak of a domestic Christianity which bound together both Protestants and Catholics. Especially in Victorian material culture there appeared a set of shared images which spoke of the virtue and piety of the Christian family.

On the other hand we must not underestimate the ways in which domestic religion divided Catholics from Protestants. With a drunken father, wild children, and a mother working in the mills, the Irish immigrant family was contrasted to the "proper" Protestant family. Likewise Catholic authors depicted Protestant mothers who neglected their children for social life, fathers who imposed dreary Sabbath devotions, and children who were spoiled and disobedient. Although Protestants and Catholics struck out at the family life of one another, they were equally harsh on their own group. Domestic Christianity served more as a way to judge and control the members of the same group than to criticize the actions of another. A set of domestic standards was presented as God-given, not man-made, and those who failed to uphold those standards were guilty on a religious level.

By the turn of the century the image of the ideal Victorian home came under attack from several directions. Feminists and social reformers called for Americans to expand their narrow family concerns to encompass more national and even global issues. As American Catholicism became more ethnically diverse, the definition of the good Catholic family was harder to articulate. In spite of such challenges, many religious writers continued to see the family as "a world in itself, no one entering except by permission, bolted and barred and chained against all outside inquisitiveness."[6] There would be an enduring legacy of Victorian domestic ideology, family worship, and leadership patterns, although modified by twentieth-century culture and religion. The rise of the laity after the Second Vatican Council, ecumenical overtures between the Christian denominations, the changing structure of the American family, and the strengthening of conservative Protestantism altered the character of domestic Christianity. It falls to future scholars to clarify the character of twentieth-century domestic Christianity and to include family beliefs, rituals, and values in their study of religion.

NOTES

Footnotes are cumulative and appear at the end of each paragraph. Works listed in the Bibliography are cited here by author and title only.

Preface

1. Catharine Beecher and Harriet Beecher Stowe, *The American Woman's Home*, 456–457. Bernard O'Reilly, *Mirror of True Womanhood*, 12.

1. Church, Homes, and Society

1. Thomas Moore, "God's University; or, The Family Considered As Government, A School, And A Church," *Home, School and Church: The Presbyterian Education Repository* 6 (1856), 2.

2. Elisabeth Schüssler Fiorenza, *In Memory of Her: A Feminist Theological Reconstruction of Christian Origins*, 175. Roland Bainton, *Christendom*, 9a.

On house churches see also F. V. Wilson, "The Significance of Early Christian House Churches," *Journal of Biblical Literature* 58 (1939), 105–112; Abraham Malherbe, "House Churches and Their Problems," in *Social Aspects of Early Christianity* (Baton Rouge, Louisiana: Louisiana State University Press, 1977), 60–91; Normand Provencher, "Vers une théologie de la famille: l'eglise domestique," *Eglise et Théologie* 12:1 (1981), 9–34; Hans-Josef Klauck, "Die Hausgemeinde als Lebensform im Urchristentum," *Münchener Theologische Zeitschrift* 32:1 (1981), 1–5.

For a discussion of family religion outside of Christianity see: Joachim Wach, *Sociology of Religion* (Chicago: University of Chicago Press, 1944), 58–70. H. J. Rose, "The Religion of a Greek Household," *Euphrosyne* 1 (1957), 95–116, and Marcel Bulard, *La Religion Domestique dans la Colonie Italienne de Delos* (Paris: E. de Boccard, 1926). Bulard writes, "La villa primitive, à la fois lieu de refuge et lieu consacré, forteresse et sanctuaire," p. 430.

3. Gillian Feeley-Harnik writes in *The Lord's Table: Eucharist and Passover in Early Christianity* (Philadelphia: University of Pennsylvania Press, 1981) that Jesus "does not celebrate Passover with his family as required by scriptures. He celebrates it with his disciples. They represent the relationship of 'family' or 'kin' as he conceived it under the 'new law'. . . . 'God's Household' (Ephesians 2:19) has been completely transformed," p. 144.

4. John Chrysostom, "De Virginitate," in J. P. Migne, *Patrologia Graeca (PG)* 48, 540.

The tenth Canon of the Council of Trent reads, "If anyone says that the married state surpasses that of virginity or celibacy, and that it is not better and happier to remain in virginity or celibacy than to be united in matrimony, *anathema sit.*" As quoted in Richard McBrien, *Catholicism*, vol. 2 (Minneapolis: Winston Press, 1980), 791.

On the impact of early Christian attitudes on virginity of women and the family, see Mary Daly, *The Church and the Second Sex* (New York: Harper Colophon, 1975), 79–90; Elizabeth Clark and Herbert Richardson, "Jerome: The Exaltation of Christian Virginity," and "Augustine: Sinfulness and Sexuality," *Women and Religion* (New York: Harper and Row, 1975), 53–68, 69–78; Rosemary Radford Ruether, "Mysogynism and Virginal Feminism in the Fathers of the Church," in *Religion and Sexism*, 150–183.

For a more positive view of marriage by celibate monks, see Jean Leclerq, *Monks on Marriage: A Twelfth-Century View* (New York: Seabury, 1982).

5. John Chrysostom, "In Genesim Sermo VI," *PG* 54, 607; "In Epistolam ad Ephesios Commentarius," *PG* 62, 143.

For a general introduction on the role of education in the early Christian church, see Henri Marrou, *A History of Education in Antiquity*, translated by George Lamb (New York: Sheed and Ward, 1956), especially 314ff.

6. On the development of the Catholic use of holy water, see the entry in the *New Catholic Encyclopedia* (New York: McGraw-Hill, 1967), vol. 14, 825–827. On house blessings, see Thomas Simons, *Blessings* (Saratoga, California: Resource Publications, 1981). During the Middle Ages the blessing of the rooms in a house, especially the couple's bed chamber, often occurred as a part of the marriage ritual. See Kenneth Stevenson, *Nuptial Blessing: A Study of Christian Marriage Rites*, 49–86; Jean-Baptiste Molin and Protais Mutembe, *Le Ritual du Marriage en France du XIIe au XVIe Siècle* (Paris: Beauchesne, 1974), 27–28, and Ch. XII, "La Bénédiction de la Chambre Nuptiale," 255–270.

7. The best analysis of the relationship between the extended family and the church during this period is John Bossy, "The Counter-Reformation and the People of Catholic Europe," *Past and Present* 47 (1970), 60. The French "Annales" school has produced some important monographs on peasant life which include descriptions of domestic religious traditions. See Emmanuel Le Roy Ladurie, *Montaillou: The Promised Land of Error*, translated by Barbara Bray (New York: G. Braziller, 1978), 306–326; Peter Burke, *Popular Culture in Early Modern Europe* (New York: Harper and Row, 1978), 207–243.

For carry-overs of pre-Tridentine Catholicism into nineteenth-century France, see Martine Segalen, *Love and Power in the Peasant Family*, translated by Sarah Matthews (Chicago: University of Chicago Press, 1983), 121–123.

8. Lawrence Stone, *The Family, Sex and Marriage*, 139. The Reformation's impact on the family is also discussed in Jean-Louis Flandrin, *Families in Former Times*, translated by Richard Southern (New York: Cambridge University Press, 1979), 103–111, 120–122; and Steven Ozment, *When Fathers Ruled*, 1–50.

9. Jane Dempsey Douglass, "Women and the Continental Reformation," in Ruether, ed., *Religion and Sexism*, 294–295. On Luther's role in defining family religion, see Gerald Strauss, *Luther's House of Learning*, and Roland Bainton, *Here I Stand: A Life of Martin Luther* (New York: Abingdon-Cokesbury Press, 1950), 300ff.

It is interesting to note Ozment mentions only the catechizing of children (pp. 132–177) and nothing of formal family worship.

10. Bossy, 68; Stone, 140.

On pre-Reformation Catholic home worship and Puritanism, see Christopher Hill, "The Spiritualization of the Household," in *Society and Puritanism in Pre-Revolutionary England*, 446; Levin Schücking, *The Puritan Family*, 61–63.

11. Stone, 141.

The failure of the Tridentine Church to integrate the family into Catholicism is described in John Bossy, "The Counter-Reformation and the People of Catholic Europe." For another argument on the rise of the individual (over the family), see Louis Dumont, "A Modified View of Our Origins: The Christian Beginnings of Modern Individualism," *Religion* 12 (1982), 1–27.

12. Stone, 245.

13. Edmund S. Morgan, *The Puritan Family*, 87–88. Cotton Mather, *A Family Well-Ordered* (Boston: B. Green & J. Allen, 1699), 36.

14. Charles E. Hambrick-Stowe, *The Practice of Piety*, 148, 150.

15. Cotton Mather, *Magnalia Christi Americana*, edited and abridged by Raymond J. Cunningham (New York: Frederick Ungar, 1970), 27.

The existence of family religious activities in the eighteenth century is mentioned in Jan Lewis, *The Pursuit of Happiness*, 40–68 and Russell L. Blake, "'The Private Sanctuary of Home': Evangelical Protestantism in the Shaping of Antebellum Planter Life," *Working Paper Series of the Center for the Study of American Catholicism* (Spring 1979), 9ff.

16. Tamara Haveran, "Family Time and Industrial Time," *The Journal of Urban History* 1 no. 3 (May 1975), 365–389. See also E. P. Thompson, "Time, Work-Discipline, and Industrial Capitalism," *Past and Present* 38 (1967), 56–97.

17. Daniel Rodgers, *The Work Ethic in Industrial America 1850–1920*, 1–29.

18. The level of "leisure" of middle-class women depended on many variables, including where they lived and what their husbands did. To get a more specific idea of the economic and social life of nineteenth-century women, see Mary Ryan, *Womanhood in America*, 139–191; Gerda Lerner, ed., *The Female Experience* (Indianapolis: Bobbs-Merrill, 1977), 121–147; Carl Degler, *At Odds*, 362–394; Eli Zaretski, *Capitalism, The Family, and Personal Life*, 36–55.

19. Mary Ryan, *Cradle of the Middle Class*, 204; 172–173.

20. Barbara Welter, "The Cult of True Womanhood: 1800–1860," *Dimity Convictions*, 21–41. Donald M. Scott and Bernard Wishy, eds., *America's Families* (New York: Harper Colophon, 1982), 271–334. Nancy Cott, *The Bonds of Womanhood*.

21. Carl Degler, 181. See also Robert Wells, "Women's Lives Transformed: Demographic and Family Patterns in America," in Carol Ruth Berkin and Mary Beth Norton, eds., *Women of America: A History* (Boston: Houghton Mifflin, 1979), 16–33.

22. Statistics and conclusions on American economic change have been drawn from Edgar Martin, *The Standard of Living in 1860;* Richard Brown, *Modernization and the Transformation of American Life 1600–1865;* H. L. Ingle and James A. Ward, *American History* (Boston: Little, Brown, 1978); Blake McKelvey, *The Urbanization of America 1860–1915;* Thomas Cochran, *Frontiers of Change: Early Industrialism in America* (New York: Oxford University Press, 1981); Rodgers, *The Work Ethic in Industrial America* and Sam Bass Warner, *Streetcar Suburbs*.

23. Advice books also flourished. Two recent commentaries on Victorian advice books are Ronald Walters, ed., *Primers for Prudery: Sexual Advice to*

Victorian America, and Barbara Ehrenreich, *For Her Own Good: 150 Years of the Experts' Advice to Women* (Garden City, New York: Anchor Books, 1978).

24. The discussion of the social situation of the American Irish is based on Patrick Blessing, "Irish," in Stephan Thernstrom, ed., *The Harvard Encyclopedia of American Ethnic Groups,* 524–545. The quote is from page 531.

25. Blessing, 529–532. Hasia R. Diner, *Erin's Daughters in America,* 46–50.

26. Same-sex bonding is prevalent among many immigrant working class groups. The relationship between same-sex bonding and male dominance is described in Marjorie Fallows, *Irish Americans: Identity and Assimilation,* 101. Diner, 20–26, 58–60.

27. Carol Groneman, "Working-Class Immigrant Women in Mid-Nineteenth-Century New York: The Irish Woman's Experience," *Journal of Urban History* 4, no. 3 (May 1978), 260, 263. Diner writes that "married Irish women abandoned their jobs with the same zeal and ardor with which they had rushed into them as single women," p. 52.

28. Blessing, 531–532. For this process in one city see Denis Clark, *The Irish in Philadelphia.*

29. Helen Cowan, *British Emigration to British North America: The First Hundred Years* (Toronto: University of Toronto Press, 1961), 178.

30. Jay Dolan, *The Immigrant Church,* 56.

31. Emmet Larkin, "The Devotional Revolution in Ireland: 1850–1875," *The American Historical Review* 77, no. 3 (June 1972), 625–652.

32. James Hennesey, *American Catholics,* 119. Julia McNair Wright (1840–1903), a popular domestic writer, also feared the power of "Papism" to ruin the family. See her novels *Priest and Nun* (1868) and *Secrets of the Convent and Confessional* (1872).

33. Brownson used less neutral terms to describe sentimental Protestantism. He called it the "religion of gush" and assumed that it is "only by a return to the Church and Catholic principles and influences, that we can overcome its evils." *Brownson's Quarterly Review* 3, no. 3 (1875), 380.

34. On Protestant hegemony, see Martin E. Marty, *Righteous Empire* and Robert Handy, *A Christian America.*

35. Sydney Ahlstrom, *A Religious History of the American People,* 458.

36. Handy, 161.

37. H. Shelton Smith et al., *American Christianity,* vol. 2, 66–74.

38. Ahlstrom, 420.

39. Barbara Welter, "The Feminization of American Religion 1800–1860," in *Dimity Convictions,* 83–102; Ann Douglas, *The Feminization of American Culture;* Richard D. Shiels, "The Feminization of American Congregationalism, 1730–1835," *American Quarterly* 33, no. 1 (Spring 1981), 46–61. Cedric Cowing, "Sex and Preaching in the Great Awakening," *American Quarterly* 20 (Fall 1968), 624–644; Mary Farrell Bednarowski, "Outside the Mainstream: Women's Religion and Women Religious Leaders in Nineteenth-Century America," *Journal of the American Academy of Religion* 48, no. 2 (June 1980), 207–231.

40. Horace Bushnell, *Christian Nurture,* 50. The first, second and fourth chapters of *Christian Nurture* were written in 1847; the other thirteen chapters were completed for the final publication in 1861. The work was copyrighted by Mary A. Bushnell in 1888, and a slightly revised edition was put together by Dotha Bushnell Hillyer in 1916 in connection with the estab-

lishment at Yale Divinity School of the Horace Bushnell Professorship of
Christian Nurture.

41. Walter Rauschenbusch, *Christianity and the Social Crisis*, 279.

2. *Domestic Architecture and the Protestant Spirit*

1. Clifford Clark, "Domestic Architecture as an Index to Social History:
The Romantic Revival of the Cult of Domesticity, 1840–1870," *The Journal of
Interdisciplinary History* 7, no. 1 (1976), 35.

The American Institute of Architects (AIA) was founded by A. J. Davis in
1857. The first academic program for architects was the Massachusetts Institute of Technologies School for Architecture founded in 1867.

2. Clark, 35.

3. Andrew Jackson Downing, *The Architecture of Country Houses*, 407. Andrew Jackson Downing's books were very popular during the 1840s and
1850s, going through five and six editions. According to Edna Donnell, they
were "in the library of every country gentleman." From "A. J. Davis and the
Gothic Revival," *Metropolitan Museum Studies* 5, pt. 2 (1936), 190. George
Hersey, "Godey's Choice," *Journal of the Society of Architectural Historians* 18, no.
3 (1959), 104.

4. Kenneth Clark, *The Gothic Revival*, 201, 192–193.

5. William Ranlett, *The Architect*, 3; Oliver Smith, *The Domestic Architect*, iii.

6. Orson Fowler, *The Octagon House*, 11; Smith, iii.

7. Downing, 262, 263.

8. Downing, 40, 43, 138, 257–258.

9. Downing, 42; Andrew Jackson Downing, *Rural Essays*, "The Moral Influence of Good Houses," 212–213.

10. Downing, *Rural Essays*, 210; Cleveland and Backus, *Village and Farm
Cottages*, 2 (to be cited as "CB").

11. Downing, *Country Houses* xix; CB, 4, 3.

12. Fowler, 14; Smith, iv.

13. Ranlett, 3; CB, i; Fowler, 184–185.

14. Downing, 268; Smith, 37.

15. CB, 13, 14; Downing, 258.

Cleveland and Backus, although writing about a "home in the country,"
were referring to what we now call the suburbs. Downing was aware of the
difference between a rural and suburban home. "An industrious man," he
wrote in 1850, "who earns his bread by daily exertions, and lives in a snug and
economical little home in the suburbs of a town has very different wants from
the farmer . . ." *Country Houses*, 40.

16. Gervase Wheeler, *Rural Homes*, 276; Ranlett, 3; Smith, iv.

17. Downing, 341, 258.

18. Downing, 403; Fowler, 65.

19. David Handlin, *The American Home*, 167–231.

20. Norma Prendergast, "The Sense of Home: Nineteenth-Century Domestic Architectural Reform," 88.

21. Smith, 22.

22. Clark, 125–126.

23. Clark, 140, 129. The controversy over who designed the British Parlia-

ment buildings began after the death of Charles Barry, the accredited architect. Kenneth Clark sides with the supporters of Pugin, ". . . I believe we can say that every visible foot of the Houses of Parliament is the work of Pugin," p. 130, 129–133.

24. Clark, 175–176.

25. Clark, 195–196.

26. See Calder Loth and Julius Sadler, *The Only Proper Style*, 95ff., 121ff.; Phoebe Stanton, *The Gothic Revival and American Church Architecture*.

27. James Early, *Romanticism and American Architecture*, 67ff.

28. Downing, 41.

29. Mary Foley, *The American House*, 149.

30. David Arnot, *Gothic Architecture Applied to Modern Residences*, 31.

31. Downing, 37.

32. Early, 92.

33. Downing, 258; Edgar Martin, *The Standard of Living in 1860*, 98.

34. Downing, 113, 263.

35. Downing, 79.

36. Downing, 295.

37. Catharine Beecher and Harriet Beecher Stowe, *The American Woman's Home*, 456–457. In 1870 the same publisher produced *Principles of Domestic Science* which contained most of what was in *American Woman's Home*. The information on the house church is in chapter 31, "Christian Neighborhood," 338–345. Most scholars think that Catharine Beecher was primarily responsible for these books, especially the architectural chapters; see Kathryn Sklar, *Catharine Beecher*. Beecher saw the house church as a type of missionary outpost for "the grand ministry of salvation" (*American Woman's Home*, 455). Beecher is not clear on how a family made up of women, adopted orphans, and servants would relate to a more traditional nuclear family. It is possible that she saw the house church only as a stopgap institution in "destitute settlement[s]." On the other hand, Beecher promoted the salvation qualities of the home. She concluded her discussion of the house church by saying that eventually all of the "darkened nations" would be converted, and "the 'Christian family' and 'Christian neighborhood' would become the grand ministry, as they were designed to be, in training our whole race for heaven," 459.

38. Hersey, 111.

39. Sampler by Ann Briton, 1842 (New York Library Picture Collection).

40. Bookmarker, *Godey's Lady's Book* 51 (1855), 459; motto-cases, Henry T. Williams and Mrs. C. S. Jones, *Household Elegancies*, 256–257.

41. Hair art, Henry T. Williams and Mrs. C. S. Jones, *Ladies' Fancy Work*, 49–51; mourning gifts, 190.

42. Home crosses, Williams and Jones, *Household Elegancies*, 180–181; *Fancy Work*, 67ff., 97ff.

43. Bishop's hat, *Godey's Lady's Book* 89 (1874), 274–275; pincushion churches *Godey's Lady's Book* 90 (1875), 560; Mary shrine, *Fancy Work*, 151ff.; prie-dieus, *Godey's Lady's Book* 85 (1872), 467; brackets, *Household Elegancies*, 83, 96–98.

44. Kenneth Ames, "Material Culture as NonVerbal Communication: A Historical Case Study," *Journal of American Culture* 3 (1980), 620, 223.

45. Ames, 632.

46. J. R. Miller, *Weekday Religion*, 269, 272.

47. Alan Gowans, *Images of American Living: Four Centuries of Architecture and Furniture as Cultural Expression,* 289. Mircea Eliade, *Patterns in Comparative Religion,* 455.

48. John Ware, *Home Life: What It Is, and What It Needs,* 15. For an excellent article on how Victorians used space and furniture to control their private lives, see Kenneth Ames, "Meaning in Artifacts: Hall Furnishings in Victorian America," *Journal of Interdisciplinary History* 9 (1978), 19–46.

49. CB, 14.
The image of a middle ground between the decadent city and the howling wilderness is discussed in a different context in Leo Marx, *The Machine and the Garden.*

50. Prendergast, 114.

51. Clifford Geertz, *The Interpretation of Cultures,* 127; Hiram Orcutt, *The Parent's Manual, or Home and School Training,* 10.

52. Bushnell, *Christian Nurture,* 12; Ware, 132.

53. Bushnell, 39.

54. Martin E. Marty, *The Righteous Empire,* 204–209.

55. Jeffrey Kirk, "The Family as Utopian Retreat from the City," *Soundings* 55 (1972), 21–41.

56. Timothy Titcomb, *Titcomb's Letters to Young People, Single and Married,* 237.

57. Bushnell, 77.

58. Smith, iii; Fowler, ii; Bushnell, 82.

59. For discussions of the use of middle-class values in urban social reform see Jan Cohn, *The Palace or the Poorhouse: The American House as a Cultural Symbol;* Marlene Stein Wortman, "Domesticating the Nineteenth Century American City," in Jack Slazman, ed., *An Annual of American Cultural Studies: Prospects* 3 (1977), 531–571, and Gwendolyn Wright, *Moralism and the Model Home.*

3. Catholic Domesticity

1. Mary Sadlier, *Con O'Regan or Emigrant Life in the New World,* 325.
The "Cult of True Womanhood" is chapter two of Barbara Welter's, *Dimity Convictions.* For a discussion of poverty and Irish-American life see Jay Dolan, *The Immigrant Church,* 27–44; Denis Clark, *The Irish in Philadelphia,* 44–52; Oscar Handlin, *Boston's Immigrants,* 150ff. On the Irish family see Lynn Hollen Lees, *Exiles of Erin,* 123–163; Thomas Curran, "The Irish Family in Nineteenth Century Urban America: The Role of the Catholic Church," *Working Paper Series of the Center for the Study of American Catholicism,* Notre Dame (1980). For the role of Irish women see Hasia Diner, *Erin's Daughters in America* and Carol Groneman, "Working-Class Immigrant Women in Mid-Nineteenth-Century New York: The Irish Woman's Experience," *Journal of Urban History* 4 (May, 1978), 255–273.

2. There is a great need for a full biography of Mary Sadlier. Summaries of her life are found in *Notable American Women,* vol. 3, 219–220; James White, *The Era of Good Intentions* and Willard Thorp, *Catholic Novelists in Defense of Their Faith, 1829–1865,* 98–113.

3. *Notable American Women,* 220. Miss Buckley in "Ornaments of the Home,"

Sacred Heart Review (SHR) (February 1, 1890), 11, plagiarizes Father O'Reilly's *Mirror of True Womanhood*, 12.

Willard Thorp writes that Mary Sadlier's novels were kept in print for fifty years or more. In 1895 Sadlier's publishing house was purchased from Mrs. Sadlier by P. J. Kenedy and Sons, and early in the twentieth century they reprinted several of Mary Sadlier's novels. Thorp remarks that Mary Sadlier's early novels, "were evidently read to pieces," p. 98–99.

4. The prices of the books were collected from advertisements in Catholic almanacs and books. Newspaper subscriptions come from their own advertising. The dedication to Rose Donahue was found in the copy of *Mirror of True Womanhood* at St. Charles Seminary Archives, Philadelphia.

5. As late as 1883 an editor of the *Catholic World* would comment " . . . in the United States, among non-Catholics quite as among Catholics, women and the clergy are the chief readers of books—not counting professional and technical books. The American man reads the newspaper, and the bookseller depends upon libraries and the clergy principally for his sales of serious works." 37 (1883), 431. Diocesan newspapers are a particularly American phenomenon. The first diocesan newspaper to be published in Dublin appeared in 1888.

6. *Catholic World* 36 (1882–1883).

7. William Lucey, "Catholic Magazines, 1865–1880," *Records of the American Catholic Historical Society of Philadelphia* (June 25, 1952), 105, (March, 1952), 25; *SHR* (October 25, 1890), 1.

Local parish calendars encouraged parishioners to buy "good" newspapers. A brief note in *Our Parish Calendar* from Laurence, MA, explained how one barber refused to give the "pink-colored paper, usually teeming with filth" to customers, but preferred to offer the *Sacred Heart Review* which cost "about one shave a month." (December 1886), 12.

Other less successful family magazines included *Christian Family Magazine* (one issue, 1842), *Home Magazine* (one issue, 1892), *Monthly Messenger for the Catholic Home* (eighteen issues, 1907–1908), *Our Own* (five months, 1869).

8. French authored advice books published in the United States include *Madame de Lavalle's Bequest* (1875); *Madame Recamier and Her Friends* (1875); Madame Froment, *Real Life* (1876); Madame de Gentelles, *Appeal to Christian Young Women* (1870); Bishop Dupanloup, *Studious Woman* (1869); *The Child* (1875); Rev. Auguste Riche, *The Family* (1875); Archbishop Fenelon, *Letters to Women* (1878); *Letters to Men* (1878); Monsignor Landriot, *The Valiant Woman* (1874), *Household Duties* (1868).

9. O'Reilly, *Mirror*, 12; Maurice Lesage d'Hautecoeur d'Hulst, *The Christian Family*, 14.

10. O'Reilly, *Mirror*, 62, 57; Mrs. I. J. Hale, *Catholic Home Journal* (January 1, 1886), 8; *St. Agatha's Parish Calendar*, Philadelphia, "Home Life" (June, 1889), 7; D'Hulst, 9.

11. Mary Carroll, *Glimpses of Pleasant Homes*, "A Washerwoman's Household", 196–197. The Catholic Publication Society originally published this in 1869.

12. *SHR* (January 25, 1890), 9, "French Home Life," *Catholic World* 25 (1877), 767.

The Council of Trent stated this position succinctly: "If anyone says that the married state surpasses that of virginity or celibacy, and that it is not better and happier to remain in virginity or celibacy than to be united in matrimony, anathema sit." This Tridentine perspective remained normative for Catholic theology, canon law, and pastoral practice until Vatican II. Richard McBrien, *Catholicism,* vol. 2, 791.

13. *SHR* (October 2, 1889), 11.

14. *Philadelphia Catholic Standard and Times* (April 23, 1892), 8; (November 22, 1890), 8; (December 17, 1892), 8.

15. For a discussion on the relationship between the private and the social body see Mary Douglas, *Purity and Danger.*

16. *SHR* (October 2, 1889), 11.

17. Carroll, 177. R. O'K., "A Peasant Home," *Catholic World* 51 (1890), 175, 179, 183.
The reality, of course, of the Irish peasant cottage was quite different. The Lawrence Collection of 19th- and early 20th-century photography in the National Library, Dublin, show very "untidy" cottages. Poorly thatched roofs, faded whitewash walls, yards littered with broken furniture, peat baskets, animals, and barefoot children seemed more normal. As in America, late 19th-century Irish housing reformers sought to remedy this. An illustration from a supplement to the October 6, 1883, *Weekly Irish Times,* showed two houses, one a typical broken down thatched cottage and the other a new Gothic-style house. The cottage was "the cabin of the past" and the house the "home of the future."

18. *Boston Pilot* (February 2, 1867), 4; Edward Maguire, ed., *O'Hanlon's Irish Emigrant's Guide for the United States,* 240.

19. Some of these include Ronald Walters, ed., *Primers for Prudery,* 1974; David Pivar, *Purity Crusade, Sexual Morality and Social Control 1868–1900* (Westport, CT: Greenwood, 1973); Walter Houghton, *The Victorian Frame of Mind, 1830–1870;* Carroll Smith-Rosenberg, "Beauty, the Beast and the Militant Woman: A Case Study in Sex Roles and Social Stress in Jacksonian America," *American Quarterly* 23 (October, 1971), 574–575.
John Maguire, *The Irish in America,* 333–334; R. Matignon, *Duties of Christian Parents,* 81; *SHR* (July 12, 1890), 9.

20. *St. Agatha's Parish Calendar,* January, 1899, 5.

21. *New York Irish American* (February 29, 1894), 2. Catholic parishes seemed well aware that children worked. *St. Agatha's Parish Calendar* noted in December, 1895, without fuss that "children who are not employed during the day should come to confession in the afternoon," p. 7.

22. *Baltimore Catholic Mirror* (March 12, 1881), 4.

23. *Baltimore Catholic Mirror* (January 14, 1881), 3; Mary Sadlier, *Old and New; Taste Versus Fashion,* 10–59.
Irish-American women, as much as their men, felt the strains of working in America. Hasia Diner writes in *Erin's Daughters in America* that "statistics accumulated particularly by state labor departments indicated that work and labor force participation was an experience that just about all Irish women had at one time or another. The woman who had never worked rarely figured in the Irish-American social portrait," p. 74. Married Irish women, however, more frequently than other native immigrant women, did not work outside of the home.

24. *Baltimore Catholic Mirror* (December 31, 1881), 2; O'Reilly, 408; Xavier Sutton, *Crumbs of Comfort for Young Women Living in the World,* 150. For an

excellent explanation of why Irish women worked as domestics see Diner, *Erin's Daughters*, 80ff.

25. Mary Sadlier, *The Blakes and the Flanagans*, 11, 125.

26. Sadlier, *Old and New*, 77.

27. Ibid.; Mary Sadlier, *Confessions of an Apostate;* Anna Dorsey, *Nora Brady's Vow*, 21.

28. Maurice Francis Egan, "How Perseus Became a Star," Eleanor Donnelly, ed., *A Roundtable of the Representative Catholic Novelists*, 127, 42; Con O'Leary, *The Lost Rosary;* Charly O'Grady is a characer in Mary Sadlier's, *Aunt Honor's Keepsake*.

29. Matignon, 18.

30. Stephen V. Ryan, introduction to W. Cramer, *The Christian Father*, 4; D'Hulst, 23.

31. Mary Hughs, *The Two Schools*, 181. *Two Schools* was first published in 1835. In 1869 the Catholic Publication Society brought out another edition. This edition was reviewed by the *Catholic World* which points to its popularity and acceptability in Catholic circles. *Catholic World* 9 (1869), 859. Mary Hughs herself is not cited in any of the major biographical resources and the 1869 edition is not mentioned in *NUC*.

32. The emphasis on conversion loosens with the second generation of writers. Ella Dorsey, daughter of Anna Sadlier and granddaughter of Mary Ann Madden Sadlier, has the mother in *Pauline Archer* tell her daughter not to talk to her Presbyterian nurse about religion because it might hurt her feelings, p. 14.

33. S. J. Connolly, *Priests and People in Pre-Famine Ireland 1780-1845;* David Miller, "Irish Catholicism and the Great Famine," *Journal of Social History* 9 (Fall, 1975), 81–98; Sheridan Gilley, "The Roman Catholic Church and the Nineteenth-Century Irish Diaspora," *Journal of Ecclesiastical History* 35 (April, 1984), 188–207; Patrick Corish, *The Catholic Community in the Seventeenth and Eighteenth Century;* John Brady and Patrick Corish, *The Church Under the Penal Code*.

34. Emmet Larkin, "The Devotional Revolution in Ireland, 1850–1875," *The American Historical Review* 77 (June, 1972), 625–652.

35. Lees, 164. John Bossy, *The English Catholic Community 1570–1850;* James Hennesey, *American Catholics*, 176–187.

36. For a discussion of private devotions which took place in church and at home see Ann Tave's review of her dissertation research, "Lay Catholic Piety in Midnineteenth-Century America," in the *American Catholic Studies Newsletter* (Spring, 1983).

37. Rural Irish simplicity was a result of both poverty and intention. See Henry Glassie, *Passing the Time in Ballymenone*. After the devotional revolution in Ireland, Catholics began to decorate their homes with religious iconography. This can be seen in the cottages at the Glencolumbkille Folk Museum in Donegal. The pre-famine cottage has no religious art except a crucifix, the 1850s cottier's cabin has a crucifix and a statue of Mary (as well as a misplaced 1893 house blessing), and the 1900 cottage has house blessings, holy pictures, statues, and a crucifix.

38. Anna Dorsey, *The Student of Blenheim Forest*, 48. Sadlier, *Old and New*, 131. Dorsey, 153. Lamb's oratories were advertised in the 1875 *Illustrated Catholic Almanac*. This fascination for things Gothic may have strong Irish, as

well as continental associations. One British landlord, Lord Thomas Bellingham, built Gothic Revival style homes on his land near Dundalk, Ireland. These homes were later Romanized by their Catholic owners by placing porcelain icons of the Madonna and Child on the outside walls. Gothic in Ireland may have been associated with social status (and not British occupation) as well as with Catholic tradition.

39. *SHR* (February 2, 1989), 1; "A Peasant Home," *Catholic World* 51 (1890), 179.

40. Sadlier, *Blakes and Flanagans*, 311–312; *Philadelphia Catholic Standard* (February 10, 1877), 2.

41. *Boston Pilot* (February 29, 1876), 8, (February 5, 1876), 8; *Philadelphia Catholic Standard* (April 21, 1866), 8.

42. *Philadelphia Catholic Standard* (March 21, 1866), 8. The ad begins: "Something new for your albums! Photographs worth preserving."

Cartes-de-visite began in France in 1857 when the Duke of Parma decided to have a photographer place his picture on his calling cards. They arrived in the U.S., via London, a few years later and became very popular between 1860 and 1890. Photographers also produced these cards, not for individual use, but for collecting. Elaborate albums were made to hold the cards. Although the albums were most likely set in the parlor, erotic carte-de-visite could be collected, but were probably kept in the gentlemen's study. The Library Company of Philadelphia has a large collection of family carte-de-visite albums under the care of Ken Finkle.

43. On the Sacred heart see Louis Verheylezoon, *Devotion to the Sacred Heart*, (1954; reprint Rockford, IL: TAN Books & Pubs., 1978), 129–140. For an anthropological perspective see Raymond Firth, *Symbols*, 230–237, 411–414.

44. A. A. Lambing, *The Sacramentals of the Holy Catholic Church*, 114, 116.

45. Conversation with Dennis Clark on Irish religious articles. *SHR* (February 15, 1980), 11.

46. *Philadelphia Catholic Standard* (November 29, 1884), 3; William Shannon, *The American Irish*, 143. On parlor organs see Kenneth Ames, "Material Culture as NonVerbal Communication: A Historical Case Study." *Journal of American Culture* 3 (Winter, 1980), 619–641.

47. *SHR* (July 26, 1980), 3.

48. Advertisements for religious articles appeared in Catholic newspapers in the last part of the century. I collected the calendar from the *Philadelphia Catholic Standard* (December 6, 1890); the pedestals from the January 1, 1877, edition; charity boxes from the *SHR* (December 12, 1890). Temperance pledges, etc., may be seen at the St. Charles Seminary Archive, Philadelphia. A beautiful Irish Catholic sampler complete with stitched altars is on display at the Balch Institute in Philadelphia.

49. Fred Israel, ed., *1897 Sears Roebuck Catalogue*, 328.

50. Dorsey, 136.

51. Dorsey, 151.

52. Hughs, 70. This definition is quiet similar to *Godey's Lady's Book's* statement that religion is "pure, peaceable, gentle, unselfish, exalting the tastes and pursuits, and brings glory to God and good-will to man," 50 (1855), 51.

53. Donna Merwick, *Boston Priests 1848–1910*, 120.

54. On the French influence in Catholic schooling see Sister Catharine

Frances, *The Convent School of French Origin in the United States 1727–1843;* the ads in the Catholic almanacs and directories; and Agnes Repplier, *In Our Convent Days* (1905). Madame Marlier advertised in *SHR* (December 20, 1890), 8.

The quote on language comes from *Catholic World* 31 (1890), 143. The editor was reviewing Bishop Mermillod's book, *The Mission of Women,* and deserves to be quoted in full. "There is something about the French language that makes it particularly well-adapted for conveying religious instruction to women. Religion and its duties are never more attractive to the gentler sex than when presented in the polite and elegant language of France. This is evidenced by the fact the ladies of other nationalities who are familiar with the French generally like to use it in religious exercises in preference to their mother-tongue." Three volumes later, the reviewer of *Household Science: or, Practical Lessons In Home Life. By the author of Golden Sands* explained that "there are no time-worn platitudes [in the book], but a great deal of very useful information such as an accomplished Catholic Frenchwoman might be expected to possess as to all that concerns home and its surrounding." *Catholic World* 34 (January, 1882), 576.

55. Dennis Clark, "The Irish Catholics," in Randall Miller, ed., *Immigrants and Religion in America,* 59; Lynn H. Lees, John Modell, "The Irish Countryman Urbanized: A Comparative Perspective on the Famine Migration," *Journal of Urban History* 3 (August, 1977), 391–408; E. P. Thompson, "Time, Work-Discipline, and Industrial Capitalism," *Past and Present* 38 (1967), 56–97; Peter Laslett, *The World We Have Lost,* 57.

56. The best source of women domestics contains only a few pages on religion. Faye E. Dudden, *Serving Women,* 67–71, 202–203.

Hasia Diner in *Erin's Daughters* appears to agree with this conclusion. She writes that Irish women who knew they would not return to Ireland began "immediately the process of acculturation on their own terms and domestic service provided perhaps the most intimate glimpse of what middle-class America was really like. Throughout the literature on Irish America the domestic servant emerges as the civilizer of the Hibernians in their new home. The servant girls in novels, sermons, and sociological studies provided the model to which the Irish were aspiring. They were the ones who set the tone that the immigrants were to emulate." She finishes by saying that "American homes provided a school for the Irish women, a school where they could learn lessons that they would pass on to their daughters, who might therefore be spared the necessity of being a Bridget" (p. 94).

57. The "feminization" of American Catholicism begins after the 1880s and will be described in chapter five. The connection between schools and families is from Garry Wills, *Bare Ruined Choirs,* 23. "It [the 1884 requirement of a Catholic education] meant Catholicism would be in large measure child-centered, its piety of a feminine sort—the church (with its rectory) would have to spend a great deal of its time and energy keeping open the school (with its convent)."

4. Rituals of the Hearth

1. Erastus Hopkins, "The Family A Religious Institution," *Home, School and Church: The Presbyterian Education Repository* 1 (1850), 2, 13.

2. James Wood, "Household Religion," *Home, School and Church: The Presbyterian Education Repository* 8 (1858), 7; James McGill, *'Enter Into Thy Closet' or Secret Prayer, and its Accompanying Exercises* 22, 21, 25. For a discussion on the origin of the term "closet" see the *Oxford English Dictionary*.

3. Directions for constructing a prie-dieu, *Godey's Lady's Book* 85 (1872), 467. James Miller, *Weekday Religion*, 77.

4. Thomas Moore, "God's University; Or, The Family Considered as a Government, a School, and a Church," *Home, School and Church: The Presbyterian Education Repository* 3 (1856), 23; J. P. Thompson in *Home Worship*, xv. This page also cites: Acts XX:8; Colos. IV:15; Rom. XVI:5; I Cor. XVI:18; Philemon 2; Rom. XVI:23.

5. Sarah Hale, "Family Devotions," *Godey's Lady's Book* 24 (1842), 241. James Alexander, *Thoughts on Family Worship*, 26. Victorian Protestant ministers did not draw upon any classical Protestant theologians—Luther, Calvin, Schleiermacher—to validate their promotion of the family or home worship.

6. Alexander, 191, 190.

7. Hale, 241.

8. Protestant Episcopal Church in the U.S.A., *A Family Liturgy*, 5–16.

9. Charles Deems, *The Home Altar*, 85.

10. Samuel Fisher, *The Family Assistant*; Benjamin Jenks, *Prayers and Offices of Devotion for Families*; Louise Houghton, *The Sabbath Month*; see especially S. G. Winchester, *The Importance of Family Religion With a Selection of Prayers and Hymns*.

11. James Weir, *Prayers for the Family Circle*, 13; Alexander, 194–195.

12. Alexander, 195, 212; Lydia Maria Child, *Mother's Book*, (Boston: Carter and Hendee, 1831), 69.

13. James Miller, *Home-Making*, 269–270; Alexander, 213. Horace Bushnell in *Christian Nurture* (pp.332–351) did not elaborate on the details of family worship. He was concerned that families prayed with sincerity, and that their prayers reflected their general Christian life style. In spite of his focus on the positive character of children, he still assumed that the father would pray "in the morning that his children may grow up in the Lord" and that the children were passive actors in family devotions (p. 345).

14. Deems, 93. B. B. Hotchkin, *Manliness For Young Men*, 94. *My Own Hymn Book*, 38.

15. J. P. Thompson, *Home Worship*, 793, 822.
For the development of a domestic heaven see Ann Douglas, *The Feminization of American Culture*, 200–226. The role of domestic imagery in hymns is best described in Sandra Sizer, *Gospel Hymns and Social Religion*, 83–110.

16. John Power, *Discourse on Domestic Piety and Family Government in Four Parts*, 62; Caroline Fry, *Daily Readings*, v; Deems, vii.

17. Henry T. Williams, *Beautiful Homes*, 200–201; Williams and Jones, *Household Elegancies*, 126; Helen Chapman, *Jennie Prendle's Home*, 79.

18. *Household Elegancies*, 96.

19. Alexander, 216; Catharine Sedgwick, *Home*, 6, 11.

20. Henry Boardman, *Bible in the Family*, 233; Wood, 14; Power, 70.

21. John Carter, "Religious Instruction at Home," *Home, School and Church: The Presbyterian Education Repository* 2 (1852), 13.

22. Mary Sadlier, *Old and New*, 131, 140.

23. *Catholic World* 26 (1877), 767; Mary Sadlier, *Willy Burke*, 34–35.

24. Mary Carroll, *Glimpses of Pleasant Homes,* 183; Anna Dorsey, *The Student of Blenheim Forest,* 153–154.

25. Cardinal Gibbons, "The Duties of Parents," *Baltimore Catholic Mirror* (January 10, 1891), 1.

26. Sadlier, *Old and New,* 132; Mary Sadlier, *Bessy Conway,* 205.

In 1871 Father George Deshon was quite specific about Catholic domestics not participating in family worship. "Do not engage anywhere where attendance at family prayers is required, for it is unjust for them to demand it and improper for you to comply. Say to all such, 'I say my own prayers, and will try to discharge my duties faithfully; more than that I cannot and will not do.' If this is not satisfactory, go somewhere else." *Guide for Catholic Young Women,* 165.

27. A. A. Lambing, *The Sacramentals of the Holy Catholic Church,* 140, 142.

28. *St. Agatha's Parish Calendar,* Philadelphia (January, 1889), 4; *The Sacred Heart Review* (October 4, 1890), 4.

29. Tom Barclay, *Memories and Medleys,* 7.

30. Sadlier, *Willy Burke,* 123; *Catholic Anecdotes,* 680, 697; *Baltimore Catholic Mirror* (November 28, 1891), 14.

31. Patrick Blessing in his article on the Irish writes: "The rate of literacy was high. From the earliest years of the 19th century unskilled rural peasants were common in the movement to the New World . . . Nevertheless, at mid-century about 75% and by 1910, 97% of all the Irish admitted to the United States could read and write English." *The Harvard Encyclopedia of Ethnicity,* 529; Mary Sadlier, *Aunt Honor's Keepsake,* 171.

32. Gerald Fogarty, "The Quest for a Catholic Vernacular Bible in America," in Nathan Hatch and Mark Noll, eds., *The Bible in America,* 172; *Baltimore Catholic Mirror* (March 19, 1881), 4.

33. Lambing, 165–175; *Baltimore Catholic Mirror* (June 17, 1882), 4; *Boston Pilot,* several issues including (February 26, 1876), 7.

34. Such Stations of the Cross can be seen at St. Charles Seminary Archives and the scroll type described by Dennis Clark in an oral interview. Lambing, 716, 82–85.

35. Although there are no studies of the Victorian sabbath in America, Winton Solberg, *Redeem the Time* and John Wigley, *The Rise and Fall of the Victorian Sunday* are important contributions. Neither, however, give attention to the domestic activities of the sabbath. Winton Solberg attributes the saying about the Puritan who hung his cat for killing a mouse on Sunday to Richard Brathwaite in 1638, p. 80.

36. Sedgwick, 59, 65, 66.

37. Julia Corner, *Sabbath Day Readings, or Children's Own Sabbath Book,* v; *Children of the Bible,* 5, 7. The Methodist Sunday School literature at Drew University numbers over 350 items.

38. Lydia Sigourney, "Mothers, As Christian Teachers," *Godey's Lady's Book* 18 (1839), 2; Mary Hughes, *Family Dialogues, or Sunday Well-Spent,* 14; and for fathers, A. W. Mitchell, *Conversations of a Father with His Children.*

39. Moore, 2; Carter, 9.

40. *Catholic World* 23 (1876), 559–561. John Wigley discusses in *The Rise and Fall of the Victorian Sunday* how in Britain the sabbath was used as a way of separating the virtuous middle class who had the opportunity to enjoy a leisurely Sunday of no work from the less-than-righteous workers who had no

labor-free sabbath.

41. *Ibid.*, 551, 555, 564.

42. On Catholic missions see Jay Dolan, *Catholic Revivalism*, esp. 57–112.

43. In a survey of Catholic books found in Swiss Victorian homes, the essential books were the Goffine, a catechism, lives of the saints, a book about the Mass, and a good prayer book. Ursula Brunold-Bigler, "Das Lektüreangebot für Katholiken des 19. Jahrhunderts dargestellt am Beispiel der Schweizerischen Kirchenzeitung," *Jahrbuch für Volkskunde* 5 (1982), 169–212.

44. Leonard Goffine, *Explanation of the Epistles and Gospels for the Sundays, Holydays and Festivals Throughout the Ecclesiastical Year, to which are added The Lives of Many Saints,* acknowledgment page.

45. Emmet Larkin, "The Devotional Revolution in Ireland, 1850–1875," *The American Historical Review* 77 (June, 1972), 636.

46. *Baltimore Catholic Mirror* (January 14, 1882), 6. Catholics who married Protestants were not allowed to marry in a church, but still had to be married by a priest. For a description of such a celebration see Lelia Harding Bugg, *The People of Our Parish,* 64ff.

47. Since baptism is considered a sacrament by most Protestant denominations, while marriage is not, most denominations required baptisms to be performed either during a service or in the church. Catharine Sedgwick in *Home* describes a pre-baptismal ceremony at home and concludes "How easy it is to interweave the religious with the domestic affections, and how sadly do those sin against the lights of nature, who neglect to form this natural union!" (p. 54).

48. *Sacred Heart Review,* "Christian Funeral Christian Burial," (July 27, 1889), 9. Writings on Irish funeral customs include Sean O'Suilleabhain, *Irish Wake Amusements;* Lynn Lees, *Exiles of Erin,* 186–188.

The church, via local parish publications, tried to control the funeral activities of Irish Catholics. In 1886 the *Our Parish Calendar* of Laurence, MA, noted the archdiocesan restriction of the number of hacks used in funeral processions to five and the prohibition of flowers and exposure of the dead body in church (September, p. 31; November, p. 16).

In 1897 it enjoined Catholics to have a Requiem Mass, pay the church for its services well in advance, invite only relatives and dear friends to the services, and spend money on masses for the dead rather than on profane trappings and merriments (January, p. 29).

49. Writings on Victorian funeral customs include: Charles Jackson, *Passing: The Vision of Death in America* (Westport, CT: Greenwood Press, 1977); James Farrell, *Inventing the American Way of Death, 1830–1920;* John Morley, *Death, Heaven and the Victorians* (Pittsburgh: University of Pittsburgh Press, 1971); a good description of mourning attire is found in Karen Halttunen, *Confidence Men and Painted Women: A Study of Middle-Class Culture in America, 1830–1870* (New Haven, Yale University Press, 1982), 137ff.

50. Edmund Morgan, *The Puritan Family,* 87–88; Carter, 11; Deems, vii.

51. Mitchell, iii; Miller, *Home-Making,* 251.

52. The role of fiction as a means of the theologizing is developed in Ann Douglas, *The Feminization of American Culture;* Barbara Welter, *Dimity Convictions;* David Reynolds, *Faith in Fiction;* Gayle Kimball, *The Religious Ideas of Harriet Beecher.*

53. The evolution of women's fiction is recounted in Nina Baym, *Women's Fiction;* Reynolds, 49.

54. Barbara Welter, "She Hath Done What She Could: Protestant Women's Missionary Careers in Nineteenth-Century America," 111–125 in Janet Wilson James, ed., *Women in American Religion.*

55. "St. Aloysius of Gonzaga," Alban Butler's *Lives of the Saints* (London: Burns, Oates & Washbourne, n.d.), 324, 327. Sheridan Gilley writes in "The Roman Catholic Church and the Nineteenth-Century Irish Diaspora," *Journal of Ecclesiastical History* 35 (April, 1984), 188–207, that during the devotional revolution "in the school-books of the Christian Brothers, St. Patrick and St. Brigid ceased to be the mass-miracle workers of Irish folklore, and became the stained-glass-window exemplars of a Victorian virtue." He does not elaborate on this conclusion (p. 192).

56. For instance see Mary Sadlier, *New Lights; or, Life in Galway* (New York: D. & J. Sadlier 1853); Anna Dorsey, *The Heiress of Carrigmona* (Baltimore: John Murphy Company, 1887); Maurice Egan, *The Flower of the Flock and the Badgers of Belmont* (New York: Benziger Brothers, 1895).

57. *Boston Pilot* (January 8, 1876), 6; Anna Dorsey, *Palms.*

58. Sizer, 121.

59. Power, 184.

5. Leaders at the Domestic Altar: The Paternal Model

1. S. G. Winchester, *The Importance of Family Religion, with a Selection of Prayers and Hymns,* 14; Sarah Hale, "Family Devotions," *Godey's Lady's Book* 24 (1842), 241. On Protestant paternal authority during the Reformation period see Ozment, *When Fathers Ruled.*

2. The doctrine of the offices of Christ is rooted in patristic theology but was rediscovered by Calvin. After the Counter-Reformation it saw a revival in Catholic theology as well. See D. R. Grabner, "Jesus Christ, Offices," *New Catholic Encyclopedia* (New York: McGraw-Hill, 1967), vol. 7, 941.
On Cotton Mather see Morgan, *The Puritan Family,* 138. On Francis Wayland see Philip Greven, *The Protestant Temperament,* 38–43.

3. John P. Carter, "Religious Instruction at Home," *Home, School and Church: The Presbyterian Education Repository* 2 (1852), 11, 12. The best discussion of changing views of conversion is Barbara Leslie Epstein, *The Politics of Domesticity,* 11–65.

4. James Alexander, *Thoughts on Family Worship,* 209. Charles Deems, *The Home Altar,* 99.

5. T. S. Arthur, *Our Homes,* frontispiece; T. S. Arthur, *Steps Toward Heaven* 390–391.

6. Henry Boardman, *The Bible in the Family,* 231; "The Religion of the Family," *Ladies' Repository* 31 (1871), 296; William Thayer, *Pastor's Wedding Gift,* 66.

7. John Power, *Discourse on Domestic Piety,* 69; Davis Newton, *Apples of Gold in Pictures of Silver,* 346.

8. Power, 72; J. P. Thompson, *Home Worship,* xx; Annie Wilson, *The Family Altar,* 6; Horace Bushnell, *Christian Nurture,* 343.

9. Thompson, xix; Alexander, 193.

10. Thomas Moore, "God's University; or, the Family Considered as a Government, a School and a Church," *Home, School and Church: The Presbyterian Home Repository* 6 (1856), 8; "Religion of the Family," 374.

11. Samuel Phillips, *The Christian Home* 217; Moore, 14, 10.

12. James Wood, "Household Religion," *Home, School and Church: The Presbyterian Education Repository* 8, (1858), 11. Philip Greven in *The Protestant Temperament* clarifies the process of "breaking the will" by distinguishing child rearing patterns in Evangelical, Moderate, and Genteel families. Although the dates of his sources are earlier than my period, his discussion of discipline is particularly helpful in understanding the varieties of paternal authority.

13. Thayer, 70; William Alcott, *Young Man's Guide*, 106.

14. Thayer, 70; Hale, "Family Devotions," 241.

15. James Miller, *Weekday Religion*, 80; Wilson, 6; J. S. Mills, *A Manuel of Family Worship With an Essay on The Christian Family*, 53.

16. "A Beautiful Story—A Child at Prayer," *The Ladies Garland and Family Wreath* 4 (1850), 188–189.

17. T. S. Arthur, *The Home Mission*, frontispiece.

18. Catharine Beecher, *Religious Training of Children in the School, the Family and the Church*, 101–202.

19. For citations on the feminization of religion see chapter one, note 39. For criticism of this concept see David S. Reynolds, "The Feminization Controversy: Sexual Stereotypes and the Paradoxes of Piety in Nineteenth-Century America," *The New England Quarterly* 53 (1980), 96–106, and David Schuyler, "Inventing a Feminine Past," *The New England Quarterly* 51 (1978), 291–308.

20. Janet Forsythe Fishburn, *The Fatherhood of God and the Victorian Family*, 102–111, 138–144.

21. Muscular Christianity was strongly promoted in England by author Thomas Hughes (*The Manliness of Christ*, 1879) and by Charles Kingsley, chaplain to Queen Victoria. An avid sportsman, Kingsley promoted a "healthful and manly Christianity, one which does not exalt the feminine virtues to the exclusion of the masculine." Walter Houghton, *The Victorian Frame of Mind 1830–1870*, 202–204. For the development in America see Louis Schneider, *Popular Religion*, 87–93; Leo P. Ribuffo, "Jesus Christ as Business Statesman: Bruce Barton and the Selling of Corporate Capitalism," *American Quarterly* 33 (Summer, 1981), 206–231.

22. Maurice d'Hulst, *The Christian Family*, 57.

23. Father Hyacinthe (Charles Loyson), *The Family and the Church*, 194.
Charles Loyson, the Carmelite superior of the Paris convent, left the Catholic priesthood and the church after the First Vatican Council in 1870. *The Family and the Church* published by Putnam and Sons includes a lengthy introduction detailing Loyson's departure from Catholicism. It implies that Loyson rejected Rome's condemnation of the modern world as contained in the *Syllabus of Errors*. The addresses on the family were presented in December of 1866 when, it is assumed, Loyson was still a member in good standing within the church. His unusual, for a Catholic, support of extreme patriarchal dominance and family prayer could, however, be used as evidence for alienation from Catholic tradition.
R. Matignon, *Duties of Christian Parents*, 16; Hyacinthe, 197.

24. "Women's Novels," *Brownson's Quarterly Review* 8 (1875), 271, 372, 373, 380.

25. *The Catechism of the Council of Trent* (New York, n.d.), 234; Joseph Curr, *Familiar Instructions*, 88.

26. Hyacinthe, 199; Abbot Gasquet, "The Christian Family in Pre-Reformation Days," *Catholic World* 84 (1906), 146–160; Richard Whytford, *A Werek for*

Householders (London: Wynkyn de Worde, 1530).

27. As quoted in *Philadelphia Catholic Standard and Times*, February 15, 1890, 2. The text from a more recent translation reads: "This is a suitable moment for us to exhort especially heads of families to govern their households according to these precepts, and to be solicitous without failing for the right training of their children." *The Papal Encyclicals*, Claudia Carlen, ed., *Sapientiae christianae*, no. 42.

"The Duty of Parents," *Baltimore Catholic Mirror*, January 10, 1891, 1.

28. Mary Sadlier, *The Blakes and the Flanagans*, 54, 115, 347, 104.

29. Mary Sadlier, *Old and New; Taste Versus Fashion*, esp. 194–205, 458.

30. Con O'Leary, *The Lost Rosary*, 118.

31. Mary Carroll, *Glimpses of Pleasant Homes*, "Franklin, the Heir of Elm Grove," 55, 56, 64, 61, 62, 64.

32. *Sacred Heart Review* (October 26, 1889), 9. The comment on the necessity of fathers to be present at the baptism of their children was standard in the parish calendars from the Philadelphia diocese in the late-nineteenth century. *St. Agatha Parish Calendar*, Philadelphia, April, 1903, 1.

33. Tom Barclay, *Memoires and Medleys*, 10.

34. Marina Warner, *Alone of All Her Sex*, 189.

35. *Catholic Home* (June 4, 1887), 1.

36. Francis X. Lasance, *The Catholic Girl's Guide*, 413.

37. Bernard O'Reilly, *True Men As We Need Them*, 210.

38. *Quamquam pluries*, sec. 6. Prayer for the Holy Family (1893) as seen on a house blessing found at the Glencolumbkille Folk Museum, County Donegal, Ireland.

39. *Ave Maria*, 20 (1886), 270–271.

40. Beecher, 33; Erastus Hopkins, *The Family a Religious Institution or Heaven Its Model*, 59. T. S. Arthur, *Our Homes*, 277; Catharine Sedgwick, *Home*, 54ff.

41. On Mass attendance in Ireland see David Miller, "Irish Catholicism and the Great Famine," *Journal of Social History* 9 (Fall, 1975), 81–98. Descriptions of popular Irish Catholicism can be found in Patrick Corish, *The Catholic Community in the Seventeenth and Eighteenth Centuries*, 82–115; S. J. Connolly, *Priests and People in Pre-Famine Ireland*, 74–174. John Bossy, "The Counter-Reformation and the People of Catholic Ireland, 1596–1641," *Historical Studies* 7 (1971), 155–169.

42. Two books by Sean O'Suilleabhain are useful in describing Irish rites of passages such as wakes: *Irish Folk Custom and Belief* and *Irish Wake Amusements*.

For theoretical discussions of various roles of men and women in rituals see Michelle Zimbalist Rosaldo, "Women, Culture, and Society: A Theoretical Overview," in Michelle Zimbalist Rosaldo and Louise Lamphere, *Women, Culture, and Society*, 17–42; and Rayna R. Reiter, "Men and Women in the South of France: Public and Private Domains," in Rayna R. Reiter, ed., *Toward an Anthropology of Women*, 252–282.

43. Connolly, 98.

6. Leaders at the Domestic Altar: The Maternal Model

1. Ann Douglas, *The Feminization of American Culture*, 121–164; Barbara Welter, *Dimity Convictions*, 103–129; Nina Baym, *Women's Fiction*, 41ff. Gayle H.

Kimball, *The Religious Ideas of Harriet Beecher Stowe: Her Gospel of Womanhood,* 88–102.

2. Catharine Beecher and Harriet Beecher Stowe, *Principles of Domestic Science,* 191; James Miller, *Weekday Religion,* 82; Beecher and Stowe, *Principles,* 19.

3. John Power, *Discourse on Domestic Piety,* 73–74. Lydia Sigourney, *Letters to Mothers,* 165; Davis Newton, *Apples of Gold in Pictures of Silver,* 38.

4. Sarah Hale, "Family Devotions," *Godey's Lady's Book (GLB)* 24 (1842), 241; "Maternal Instructions," *GLB* 30 (1845), 108; James Miller, *Homemaking,* 267; Samuel Goodrich, *Fireside Education,* 125.

5. "Maternal Influence," *GLB* 11 (1835), 73; Sarah Hale, "Woman's Sabbath Mission," *GLB* 34 (1847), 210.

6. Ann Douglas discusses the relationship between Mary and Aunt Winifred in *The Feminization of American Culture,* 223–226. For examples of mothers and daughters reading the Bible see the illustrations for "Maternal Instructions," *GLB* 30 (1845), 108; Lydia Sigourney, ed., "Teaching the Scriptures," *The Religious Souvenir for 1840,* opposite 154; "Reading the Bible," *Bible in the Family; Hints on Domestic Happiness,* page after frontispiece.

7. T. S. Arthur, *Our Homes,* 267; Frank Walters, "Woman's Power," *GLB* 40 (1850), 118. The complete stanza is "But o'er Woman's gentler nature,/Finer sense and purer soul,/Moulded by an angel stature,/Earth has never held control." Hale, "Woman's Sabbath Mission," 210; Amy, "The Christian Woman," *GLB* 51 (1855), 539.

8. Kathryn Sklar's biography *Catharine Beecher,* discusses Beecher's attitudes towards self-sacrificing, especially pages 247–249. Also see Beecher and Stowe, *Principles,* 17–21; 334–336. "The Little Children," *GLB* 84 (1872), 380. Two of the more important stanzas read:

> O Divine compassion
>   For the human race!
> Christ was made of woman,
>   and His loving face
> Drew her little children,
>   Like sweet music's tone,
> to His arms—His blessing
>   Made them all His own.

> Suffer little children
>   When the Saviour comes,
> They are of His Kingdom,
>   He will bless their homes!
> O divine compassion
>   to the mother given,
> Christ will keep her jewels
>   In the light of Heaven.

Hale, "Sabbath Mission," 210; Alice Neal, "The Christian Mother," *GLB* 41 (1850), 67.

9. Catharine Beecher, *Religious Training of Children in the School, The Family and the Church,* 35–39.

10. M. T. R., "The Bible the Mother's Study," *Mother's Journal and Family*

Visitant 17 (1852), 63, 11, 12; Lydia Sigourney, "Mothers, as Christian Teachers," *GLB* 18 (1839), 1.

11. "Maternal Instruction," 108.

12. M. T. R., "The Bible the Mother's Study," 109, 89.

13. A good visual example of the difference between mother reading and father reading can be seen in Davis Newton's *Apples of Gold in Pictures of Silver.* On page 37 ("The Mother Imparting Heavenly Wisdom") a smiling mother reads to her son. She has her arm on his shoulder, and he has his hand on the Bible. On page 73 ("The Happy Family—A Heaven Below") a rather hefty father sits at a table with the Bible and a gas lamp. His five children stand in the background listening intently. Goodrich, 124.

14. Editor's Table, *GLB* 34 (1847), 51.

15. Goodrich, frontispiece; Lydia Sigourney, *Letters to Mothers,* 16.

16. Many of the hymns which were sung in families extolled the virtues of home and motherhood. See Mary Gosselink De Jong, "Meeting Mother in 'that home beyond the skies': Maternal Influence in Late Nineteenth-Century Popular Hymns" unpublished manuscript presented at the American Studies Association Meeting, November, 1983.

17. *The Faithful Mother's Reward: Narrative of the Conversion and Happy Death of J. P. B.,* 179–190.

18. T. S. Arthur, *The Home Mission,* 140–141; Sigourney, "Mothers, As Christian Teachers," 1; J. S. Mills, *A Manual of Family Worship With an Essay on The Christian Family,* 53.

19. Sigourney, 1; Arthur, 140; M. R. LeWahl, "To My Mother," *GLB* 84 (1872), 857.

20. "The Little Children," 380, includes this stanza:

> Buds of life from Heaven,
> Little children come
> To be nursed and ripened
> In a human home.
> Screen the flower, unfolding,
> From the blight of sin:
> Watch the rich fruit growing
> Lest the worm creep in.

GLB 6 (1833), 268, "Childhood" explains that "There is in childhood a holy ignorance, a beautiful credulity, a sort of sanctity, that one cannot contemplate without something of the reverential feelings with which one should approach beings of a celestial nature." Newton, *Apples of Gold,* 75.

21. Hiram Orcutt, *The Parents Manual,* 112, 113. Cf. Mark 2:27, "The Sabbath was made for man, not man for the Sabbath."

22. The best guide for Victorian Catholic magazines is Eugene Paul Willging and Herta Hatzfeld, *Catholic Serials of the Nineteenth Century in the United States: A Descriptive Bibliography and Union List* (Washington, D.C.: Catholic University, 1954).

23. A vigorous critique of the relation between priests and women in Victorian France is Jules Michelet, *Priests, Women, and Families* (London: Longman, Brown, Green, and Longmans, 1846), 97–124.

24. "Home Heroes," *Catholic Home Journal* (November 1, 1886), 8.

25. "Notes and Remarks," *Ave Maria* 31 (1890), 235.

26. The Von Wiegels are characters in Mary Sadlier's *Old and New; Taste Versus Fashion;* Eleanor Donnelly, "A Lost Prima Dona" from *A Round Table of American Catholic Novelists,* 46.

27. Mary Sadlier, *The Blakes and the Flanagans,* 108.

28. Landriot, *The Valiant Woman,* 22–23.

29. *The Catholic Home* (December 13, 1886), 148; "The Dignity of Women," *Philadelphia Catholic Standard and Times* (February 29, 1894), 2. Cardinal Gibbons was an often quoted Catholic authority, and his speeches frequently appeared simultaneously in several Catholic journals. He also seemed to reuse a few basic themes on the role of women in the church.

30. Francis X. Lasance, *The Catholic Girl's Guide,* 403. Father Lasance quotes "a French writer" who sagely noted that if you "take religion away from woman . . . she is deprived of morality also; in that case she is nothing but a whited sepulchre, wherein abide corruption and decay." He then concludes: "Especially does the housewife need religion to accomplish her lofty task, namely, to cultivate religion in her family, to instruct her children in its truths, and thus to become the priestess of the domestic shrine," p. 403; Mary Carroll, *Glimpses of Pleasant Homes,* 18–19.

31. Maurice d'Hulst, *The Christian Family,* 66; "Early Education," *Sacred Heart Review (SHR)* (November 11, 1889), 3.

32. *SHR* (December 28, 1889), 2; D'Hulst, 69.

33. Charity boxes: *SHR* (December 13, 1890), 9; hymns: *SHR* (July 26, 1890), 3.

34. "The Dignity of Women," *Philadelphia Catholic Standard and Times* (February 29, 1894), 2; Lasance, 406.

35. "A Mother's Last Request," *Philadelphia Catholic Standard and Times* (February 15, 1868), 6; "Maternal Affection," *Catholic Home Journal* (May 1, 1887), 3; "A Mother's Look," *Philadelphia Catholic Standard and Times* (December 13, 1890), 7; "A Mother's Influence," *SHR* (July 12, 1890), 13.

36. Summaries of *Mora Carmondy, Bickerton,* and *The Governess* are found in Willard Thorp, *Catholic Novelists in Defense of Their Faith.* The quotation from *Bickerton* is found on p.60.

37. Mary Sadlier, *Confessions of an Apostate,* 167, 241.

38. Ferrol Giradey, *Mission Book for the Married,* 28; Mary Sadlier, *Aunt Honor's Keepsake,* 25; Con O'Leary, *The Lost Rosary,* 179.

39. "Religious Novels, and Woman Versus Woman," *Brownson's Quarterly Review* 1 (1873), 59, 62; Bernard O'Reilly, *Mirror of True Womanhood,* 11, 12.

40. O'Reilly, 322; Lasance, 146; G. M., "A Thought," *The Catholic Home* (May 28, 1887), 1. The poet takes a common theme, the reunion of mother and child in heaven, and adapts it to the reunion of Mary with her devotee. Never mentioning the word "Mary," only referring to her as "Mother," the poet makes it clear that it is reunion with Mary which is hoped for.

> In this life, should you consider
>   That our paths, to lead to Thee
> Must diverge, we ask this favor,
>   Dearest Mother, let it be
> Thy sweet will when life is closing
>   Draw those chains close round Thy Heart
> That we may, life's voyage over
>   Meet again, no more to part.

41. O'Reilly, 358; Lasance, 189.

42. O'Reilly, 39–40.

43. Gerald F. Moran and Maris A. Vinovskis, "The Puritan Family and Religion: A Critical Reappraisal," *Working Paper Series of the Center for the Study of American Catholicism,* Notre Dame (Spring, 1980), 33.

44. Cedric Cowing, "Sex and Preaching in the Great Awakening," *American Quarterly* 20 (Fall, 1968), 625. Richard Shiels, "The Feminization of American Congregationalism, 1730–1835," *American Quarterly* 3 (Spring, 1981), 52.

45. Lew Wallace, "The Boyhood of Christ," *Harper's New Monthly Magazine* 74 (December, 1886), 8.

46. Wallace, 14, 10.

47. A complete description of intellectual rituals may be found in Bernhard Lang, ed., *Das tanzende Wort: Intellektuelle Rituale im Religionsvergleich,* 15–48.

48. *Catholic World* 8 (1867), 286. "We find one fault, however. Considering how far girls outnumber boys in our Sunday schools, we think it hardly fair that but one volume should be devoted to the joys and sorrows, the temptations and triumphs, of girlhood."

49. Douglas, 17–43.

50. Elvira Hobson, "On the Influence of Woman," unpublished valedictorian speech, St. Mary's Academy, 1869. Found at the Heritage Center Archives, Denver, Colorado.

51. Hobson.

Conclusion

1. Robert Bellah, "Civil Religion in America," *Daedalus* 96 (1967), 1–21. For a bibliographic survey of the sociological literature on civil religion see Gail Gehrig, "The American Civil Religion Debate: A Source for Theory Construction," *Journal for the Scientific Study of Religion* 20 (1981), 51–63; Emile Durkheim, *Elementary Forms of the Religious Life,* 470.

2. Peter L. Berger, *The Sacred Canopy,* 134; Thomas Luckmann, *The Invisible Religion* (New York: Macmillan 1967), 112.

3. David S. Reynolds, "The Feminization Controversy: Sexual Stereotypes and the Paradoxes of Piety in Nineteenth-Century America," *The New England Quarterly* 53 (1980), 97–98.

4. Bonnie G. Smith, *Ladies of the Leisure Class: The Bourgeoises of Northern France in the Nineteenth Century* (Princeton: Princeton University Press, 1981), 102ff.

For a sociological explanation of contemporary domestic articles and an excellent methodological essay on the significance of material culture, see Mihaly Csikszentmihalyi and Eugene Rochberg-Halton, *The Meaning of Things: Domestic Symbols and the Self* (New York: Cambridge University Press, 1981).

5. A recent summary of the Victorian concept of domestic privacy which ignores the equal fascination with public display is Maxine van de Wetering, "The Popular Concept of 'Home' in Nineteenth-Century America," *Journal of American Studies* 18 (1984), 5–28.

6. Francis X. Doyle, *The Home World: Friendly Counsels for Home-Keeping Hearts* (New York: Benziger, 1922), 10.

BIBLIOGRAPHY

The following bibliography contains only books of major significance to this study. Journal and newspaper articles are cited in full in the text.

Protestant

Alcott, William. *Young Man's Guide.* 1833. Reprint. Boston: Marvin, 1843.

Alexander, James. *Thoughts on Family Worship.* Philadelphia: Presbyterian Board of Publication, 1847.

Arnot, David. *Gothic Architecture Applied to Modern Residences.* New York: D. Appleton, 1849.

Arthur, Timothy Shay. *The Home Mission.* 1853. Reprint. Philadelphia: J.W. Bradley, 1858.

———. *Our Homes: Their Cares, and Duties, Joys and Sorrows.* Cincinnati: H. C. Peck and Theo. Bliss, 1856.

———. *Steps Towards Heaven; or Religion in Common Life.* 1858. Reprint. Philadelphia: G. G. Evans, 1859.

Beecher, Catharine. *Religious Training of Children in the School, the Family and the Church.* New York: Harper and Bros., 1864.

———. *Treatise on Domestic Economy For the Use of Young Ladies at Home, and at School.* Boston: Marsh, Capen, Lyon, and Webb, 1841.

Beecher, Catharine and Harriet Beecher Stowe. *The American Woman's Home, Or Principles of Domestic Science.* New York: J. B. Ford, 1869.

Boardman, Henry. *Bible in the Family; or, Hints on Domestic Happiness.* Philadelphia: Lippincott, 1854.

Bushnell, Horace. *Christian Nurture.* 1888. Reprint. New Haven: Yale University Press, 1967.

Chapman, Helen. *Jennie Prindle's Home.* Philadelphia: Presbyterian Board of Publication, 1877.

Children of the Bible. Philadelphia: Fisher and Bros., 1853.

Cleaveland, Henry W., and William and Samuel Backus. *Village and Farm Cottages.* New York: Appleton, 1856.

Corner, Julia. *Sabbath Day Readings, or Children's Own Sabbath Book.* Philadelphia: Presbyterian Board of Publication, 1853.

Deems, Charles. *The Home Altar: An Appeal in Behalf of Family Worship.* New York: M. W. Dodd, 1851.

Downing, Andrew Jackson. *The Architecture of Country Houses.* 1850. Reprint. New York: Dover Publications, 1969.

———. *Rural Essays.* 1853. Reprint. New York: Leavitt, 1869.

The Faithful Mother's Reward: Narrative of the Conversion and Happy Death of J.P.B. Philadelphia: Presbyterian Board of Publication, 1853.

Fisher, Samuel. *The Family Assistant, or, Book of Prayers for the Use of Families.* Philadelphia: Reformed Church Board, 1873.

Fowler, Orson. *The Octagon House: A Home For All.* 1856. Reprint. New York: Dover Publications, 1973.

Fry, Caroline. *Daily Readings. Passages of Scripture.* Philadelphia: Presbyterian Board of Publication, 1852.

Goodrich, Samuel G. *Fireside Education.* Albany: E. H. Pease, 1851.

Hopkins, Erastus. *The Family A Religious Institution, Or Heaven Its Model.* Troy, NY: n.p., 1840.

Hotchkin, Beriah Bishop. *Manliness for Young Men.* Philadelphia: Presbyterian Board of Publication, 1864.

Houghton, Louise. *The Sabbath Month: Devotional Thoughts for Young Mothers.* Philadelphia: Presbyterian Board of Publication, 1879.

Hughes, Mary. *Family Dialogues, or Sunday Well-Spent.* Philadelphia: Tract and Book Society of the Evangelical Church of St. John, 1828.

Jenks, Benjamin. *Prayers and Offices of Devotion for Families.* London: W. Rogers and B. Tooke, 1697.

McGill, James. *'Enter Into Thy Closet' or Secret Prayer, and its Accompanying Exercises.* Philadelphia: Presbyterian Board of Publication, 1843.

Miller, James. *Home-Making.* Philadelphia: Presbyterian Board of Publication, 1882.

———. *Weekday Religion.* Philadelphia: Presbyterian Board of Publication, 1880.

Mills, J. S. *A Manual of Family Worship With an Essay on the Christian Family.* Dayton, OH: W. R. Funk, 1900.

Mitchell, A. W. *Conversations of a Father with His Children.* Philadelphia: Presbyterian Board of Publication, 1849.

My Own Hymn Book. Philadelphia: Presbyterian Board of Publication, 1852.

Newton, Davis. *Apples of Gold in Pictures of Silver.* New York: By Author, 1869.

Orcutt, Hiram. *The Parent's Manual, or Home and School Training.* Boston: Thompson, Brown and Co., 1874.

Phillips, Samuel. *The Christian Home.* New York: Gurdon Bill, 1865.

Power, John. *Discourse on Domestic Piety.* 1851. Reprint. Cincinnati: Swormstedt and Power, 1854.

Protestant Episcopal Church in the U. S. A. Book of Common Prayer. *A Family Liturgy; Wholly Selected from the Book of Common Prayer.* New York: D. Dana, 1851.

Ranlett, William. *The Architect.* 2 vols. New York: W. H. Graham, 1847–1849.

Rauschenbusch, Walter. *Christianity and the Social Crisis.* 1907. Reprint. New York: Harper and Row, 1964.

Sedgwick, Catharine. *Home.* 1835. Reprint. New York: J. Munroe, 1850.

Sigourney, Lydia. *Letters to Mothers.* 1838. Reprint. New York: Harper and Bros., 1839.

———. *The Religious Souvenir for 1840.* New York: Scofield and Voorhies, 1839.

———. *The Western Home and Other Poems.* Philadelphia: Parry and McMillan, 1854.

Smith, Oliver. *The Domestic Architect.* 1852. Buffalo: Derby and Co., 1857.

Thayer, William. *Pastor's Wedding Gifts.* 1854. Reprint. Boston: Crosby, Nichols, Lee, and Co., 1861.

Thompson, Joseph Parrish and Charles Haddon Spurgeon. *Home Worship . . . For Daily Use in Family and Private Devotions.* 1882. (Entered According to Act of Congress 1871) New York: A. C. Armstrong and Sons, 1883.

Titcomb, Timothy. (Josiah G. Holland) *Titcomb's Letters to Young People, Single and Married*. New York: Charles Scribner's, 1858.

Ware, John. *Home Life: What it is, and What it Needs*. Boston: W. V. Spencer, 1866.

Weir, James. *Prayers for the Family Circle*. Philadelphia: Presbyterian Board of Publication, 1879.

Wheeler, Gervase. *Rural Homes*. New York: Charles Scribner's 1851.

Williams, Henry T. and Mrs. C. S. Jones. *Beautiful Homes*. New York: H. T. Williams, 1878.

———. *Household Elegancies: Suggestions in Household Art and Tasteful Home Decorations*. New York: H. T. Williams, 1875.

———. *Ladies' Fancy Work*. New York: H. T. Williams, 1876.

Wilson, Annie (Anneliza). *The Family Altar: Helps and Suggestions for Family Worship*. Richmond, VA: Presbyterian Committee of Publication, 1898.

Winchester, Samuel Grover. *The Importance of Family Religion with a Selection of Prayers and Hymns*. 1835. Philadelphia: Lippincott, 1840.

Catholic

Barclay, Tom. *Memories of a Bottle-Washer*. Leicester, England: Edgar Backus, 1934.

Bugg, Lelia Harding. *The Correct Thing for Catholics*. Boston: Benziger, 1891.

———. *The People of Our Parish*. Boston: Marlier, Callanan and Co, 1900.

Cannon, Charles. *Bickerton, or, The Immigrant's Daughter*. New York: P. O'Shea, 1855.

———. *Mora Carmody; or, Women's Influence*. New York: E. Dunigan, 1844.

Carroll, Mary Teresa Austin. *Glimpses of Pleasant Homes*. New York: Catholic Publication Society, 1869.

Catholic Anecdotes; or, The Catechism in Examples. Of the Brothers of the Christian Schools. Translated by Mary Sadlier. New York: D. J. Sadlier, 1870.

Conway, Katherine. . . . *Bettering Ourselves*. Boston: Pilot Publishing Co., 1899.

———. *The Christian Gentlewoman and the Social Apostolate*. Boston: Flynn and Co., 1904.

———. *Questions of Honor in Christian Life*. Boston: Pilot Publishing Co., 1896.

———. *The Way of the World and Other Ways*. Boston: Pilot Publishing Co., 1900.

Cramer, Wilhelm. *The Christian Father: What He Should Be and What He Should Do*. Translated by L. A. Lambert. New York: Benziger, 1883.

Curr, Joseph. *Familiar Instructions*. Boston: Donahoe, n.d.

Deshon, George. *Guide For the Catholic Young Woman, Especially Those Who Earn Their Own Living*. 1863. Reprint. New York: Columbus Publishing Co., 1893.

Donnelly, Eleanor ed. *A Roundtable of the Representative Catholic Novelist*. New York: Benziger, 1897.

Dorsey, Anna. *The Flemmings; or, Truth Triumphant*. New York: O'Shea, 1870.

———. *Nora Brady's Vow*. New York: Benziger, 1869.

———. *Palms*. Baltimore: J. Murphy, 1887.

———. *The Student of Blenheim Forest; or, The Trials of a Convert*. Baltimore: J. Murphy, 1867.

Giradey, Ferrol. *Mission Book for the Married.* New York: Benziger, 1897.

Goffine, Leonard. *Explanation of The Epistles and Gospels for the Sundays, Holydays, and Festivals Throughout the Ecclesiastical Year, to Which are Added the Lives of Many Saints.* Translated by Gerard Pilz. 1859. Reprint. New York: F. Pustet, 1880.

Hughs, Mrs. *The Two Schools: A Moral Tale.* Baltimore: F. Lucas, 1835.

d'Hulst, Maurice Lesage d'Hautecoeur. *The Christian Family: Seven Conferences.* (Conferences given in 1891–1896). Translated by Bertrand L. Conway. New York: J. F. Wagner, 1905.

Lambing, Andrew Arnold. *The Sacramentals of the Holy Catholic Church.* New York: Benziger, 1892.

Landriot, Jean François. *The Valiant Woman . . . Intended For the Use of Women Living in the World.* Translated by Helena Lyons. 1873. Reprint. Boston: Donahoe, 1874.

Lasance, Francis. *The Catholic Girl's Guide: Counsels and Devotions for Girls in the Ordinary Walks of Life.* New York: Benziger, 1906.

Loyson, Charles. *The Family and the Church.* New York: G. P. Putnam and Sons, 1870.

Maguire, Edward. *Reverend John O'Hanlon's The Irish Emigrant's Guide for the United States.* 1851. Reprint. New York: Arno, 1976.

Maguire, John. *The Irish in America.* 1868. Reprint. New York: Arno, 1969.

Matignon, R. *Duties of Christian Parents.* Translated by Constance Bellingham. London: R. Washbourne, 1869.

O'Leary, Con. *The Lost Rosary: Or, Our Irish Girls, Their Trials, Temptations, and Triumphs.* Boston: P. Donahoe, 1870.

O'Reilly, Bernard. *Mirror of True Womanhood.* 1878. New York: P. J. Kenedy, 1892.

———. *True Men As We Need Them.* New York: P. J. Kenedy, 1878.

Pellico, Silvio. *On the Duties of Young Men.* Translated by R. A. Vain. New York: D. J. Sadlier, 1872.

Repplier, Agnes. *In Our Convent Days.* Boston: Houghton, Mifflin and Co., 1905.

Sadlier, Anna. *Pauline Archer.* New York: Benziger, 1899.

Sadlier, Mary. *Aunt Honor's Keepsake: A Chapter From Life.* New York: D. J. Sadlier, 1866.

———. *Bessy Conway; or, The Irish Girl in America.* New York: D. J. Sadlier, 1863.

———. *The Blakes and the Flanagans, a Tale Illustrative of Irish Life in the United States.* New York: D. J. Sadlier, 1855.

———. *Confessions of an Apostate.* New York: D. J. Sadlier, 1864.

———. *Con O'Regan; or, Scenes From Emigrant Life.* New York: D. J. Sadlier, 1864.

———. *Old and New; or, Taste Versus Fashion.* New York: D. J. Sadlier, 1862.

———. *Willy Burke; or, The Irish Orphan in America.* New York: D. J. Sadlier, 1850.

Scott, Martin. *You and Yours: Practical Talks on Family Life.* New York: P. J. Kenedy, 1921.

Sutton, Xavier. *Crumbs of Comfort for Young Women Living in the World.* Philadelphia: H. L. Kilner, 1898.

Secondary Sources

The following is a list of scholarly books and articles which I found the most
helpful in interpreting the relationship between American Christianity
and domesticity.

Ahlstrom, Sydney. *A Religious History of the American People.* New Haven: Yale
University Press, 1972.
Ames, Kenneth. "Material Culture as Non Verbal Communication: A Histor-
ical Case Study." *Journal of American Culture,* 3 (1980), 619–641.
———. "Meaning in Artifacts: Hall Furniture in Victorian America." *Journal
of Interdisciplinary History,* 9 (1978), 19–46.
Bainton, Roland. *Christendom.* 2d Revised Edition. New York: Harper
Torchbooks, 1966.
Barbour, Ian. *Myths, Models, and Paradigms.* New York: Harper and Row, 1974.
Baym, Nina. *Women's Fiction: A Guide to Novels by and about Women in America
1820–1970.* Ithaca, NY: Cornell University Press, 1978.
Bedharowski, Mary Farrell. "Outside the Mainstream: Women's Religion and
Women Religious Leaders in Nineteenth-Century America." *Journal of the
American Academy of Religion,* 48 (1980), 9–18.
Bellah, Robert. "Civil Religion in America." *Daedalus* 96 (1967), 1–21.
Berger, Peter. *The Sacred Canopy: Elements of a Sociological Theory of Religion.*
Garden City, NY: Doubleday, 1967.
Bossy, John. "The Counter-Reformation and the People of Catholic Europe."
Past and Present, 47 (1970), 51–70.
———. "The Counter-Reformation and the People of Catholic Ireland, 1596–
1641." *Historical Studies,* 8 (1971), 155–169.
———. *The English Catholic Community 1520–1850.* London: Oxford Univer-
sity Press, 1975.
Brady, John and Patrick Corish, *The Church Under the Penal Code.* Dublin: Gill
and Macmillan, 1971.
Brown, Richard. *Modernization and the Transformation of American Life 1600–
1865.* New York: Hill and Wang, 1976.
Carlen, Claudia, ed. *The Papal Encyclicals.* Raleigh, NC: McGrath, 1981.
Clark, Clifford. "Domestic Architecture as an Index to Social History: The
Romantic Revival and the Cult of Domesticity, 1840–1870." *The Journal of
Interdisciplinary History,* 7 (1976), 33–56.
Clark, Dennis. *The Irish in Philadelphia: Ten Generations of Urban Experience.*
Philadelphia: Temple University Press, 1974.
Clark, Kenneth. *The Gothic Revival.* New York: Harper and Row, 1962.
Cohn, Jan. *The Palace or the Poorhouse: The American House as a Cultural Symbol.*
East Lansing: Michigan State University Press, 1979.
Connolly, Sean. *Priests and People in Pre-Famine Ireland 1780–1845.* New York:
St. Martin's, 1982.
Corish, Patrick. *The Catholic Community in the Seventeenth and Eighteenth Century.*
Dublin: Helicon, 1981.
Cott, Nancy. *The Bonds of Womanhood: Women's Sphere in New England.* New
Haven: Yale University Press, 1977.

Cowing, Cedric. "Sex and Preaching in the Great Awakening." *American Quarterly,* 20 (Fall 1968), 624–644.

Curran, Thomas. "The Irish Family in Nineteenth Century Urban America: The Role of the Catholic Church." *Working Paper Series of the Center for the Study of American Catholicism,* Notre Dame (1980).

D'Antonio, William and Joan Aldous. *Families and Religion: Conflict and Change in Modern Society.* Beverly Hills, CA: Sage Publications, 1983.

Degler, Carl. *At Odds: Women and the Family in America from the Revolution to the Present.* New York: Oxford University Press, 1980.

Diner, Hasia. *Erin's Daughters in America: Irish Immigrant Women in the Nineteenth Century.* Baltimore: Johns Hopkins University Press, 1983.

Dolan, Jay. *Catholic Revivalism: The American Experience: 1830–1900.* Notre Dame, IN: University of Notre Dame Press, 1978.

———. *The Immigrant Church: New York's Irish and German Catholics 1815–1865.* Baltimore: Johns Hopkins University Press, 1975.

Donnel, Edna. "A. J. Davis and the Gothic Revival." *Metropolitan Museum Studies* 5, pt. 2 (1936), 183–233.

Douglas, Ann. *The Feminization of American Culture.* New York: Knopf, 1977.

Douglas, Mary. *Purity and Danger: An Analysis of Concepts of Pollution and Taboo.* London: Routledge and Kegan Paul, 1966.

Dudden, Faye E. *Serving Women: Household Service in Nineteenth-Century America.* Middleton, CT: Wesleyan University Press, 1983.

Durkheim, Emile. *The Elementary Forms of the Religious Life.* Translated by Joseph Ward Swain. New York: The Free Press, 1954.

Early, James. *Romanticism and American Architecture.* New York: A. S. Barnes, 1965.

Eliade, Mircea. *Patterns in Comparative Religion.* New York: Harper and Row, 1958.

———. *The Sacred and Profane.* New York: Harcourt and Brace, 1959.

Epstein, Barbara. *The Politics of Domesticity: Women, Evangelism, and Temperance in Nineteenth-Century America.* Middleton, CT: Wesleyan University Press, 1981.

Fallows, Marjorie. *Irish Americans: Identity and Assimilation.* Englewood Cliffs: Prentice-Hall, 1979.

Farrell, James. *Inventing the American Way of Death, 1830–1920.* Philadelphia: Temple University Press, 1980.

Fiorenza, Elisabeth Schüssler. *In Memory of Her: A Feminist Theological Reconstruction of Christian Origins.* New York: Crossroads, 1983.

Firth, Raymond. *Symbols: Public and Private.* Ithaca, NY: Cornell University Press, 1973.

Fishburn, Janet Forsythe. *The Fatherhood of God and The Victorian Family: The Social Gospel in America.* Philadelphia: Fortress Press, 1981.

Foley, Mary. *The American House.* New York: Harper and Row, 1980.

Galvin, Sister Frances Catharine. "The Convent School of French Origin in the United States 1727–1843." Thesis. University of Pennsylvania, 1936.

Geertz, Clifford. *The Interpretation of Cultures.* New York: Basic Books/Harper, 1973.

Glassie, Henry. *Passing the Time in Ballymenone.* Philadelphia: University of Pennsylvania Press, 1982.

Gowans, Alan. *Images of American Living: Four Centuries of Architecture and Furniture as Cultural Expression.* Philadelphia: Lippincott, 1964.

Greven, Philip. *The Protestant Temperament: Patterns of Child Rearing, Religious Experience, and the Self in Early America.* New York: Meridan, 1977.

Groneman, Carol. "Working-Class Immigrant Women in Mid-Nineteenth-Century New York: The Irish Woman's Experience." *Journal of Urban History,* 4, no. 3 (1978), 255–273.

Hambrick-Stowe, Charles. *The Practice of Piety: Puritan Devotional Disciplines in Seventeenth-Century New England.* Chapel Hill, NC: University of North Carolina Press, 1982.

Handlin, David. *The American Home: Architecture and Society 1815–1915.* Boston: University of Massachusetts Press, 1979.

Handlin, Oscar. *Boston's Immigrants.* New York: Athenaeum Press, 1970.

Handy, Robert. *A Christian America: Protestant Hopes and Historical Realities.* New York: Oxford University Press, 1971.

Hatch, Nathan and Mark Noll, eds. *The Bible in America.* New York: Oxford University Press, 1982.

Hennesey, James. *American Catholics: A History of the Roman Catholic Community in the United States.* New York: Oxford University Press, 1981.

Hersey, George. "Godey's Choice." *Journal of the Society of Architectural Historians,* 18, no.3, (1959), 104–111.

Hill, Christopher. *Society and Puritanism in Pre-Revolutionary England.* New York: Schocken, 1967.

Houghton, Walter. *The Victorian Frame of Mind 1830–1870.* New Haven: Yale University Press, 1957.

Israel, Fred, ed. *1897 Sears Roebuck Catalogue.* New York: Chelsea House, 1968.

James, Edward T., et. al. *Notable American Women.* Cambridge: Belknap Press of Harvard University Press, 1971.

James, Janet, ed. *Women in American Religion.* Philadelphia: University of Pennsylvania Press, 1976.

Jeffrey, Kirk. "The Family as Utopian Retreat from the City." *Soundings,* 55 (1972), 21–41.

Kimball, Gayle. *The Religious Ideas of Harriet Beecher: Her Gospel of Womanhood.* New York: Mellen Press, 1982.

Kuhn, Anne. *The Mother's Role in Childhood Education: New England Concepts.* New Haven: Yale University Press, 1947.

Lang, Bernhard, ed. *Das tanzende Wort: Intellektuelle Rituale im Religionsvergleich.* Munich: Kösel, 1984.

Larkin, Emmet. "The Devotional Revolution in Ireland: 1850–1875." *The American Historical Review,* 77 no. 3 (1972), 625–52.

Laslett, Peter. *The World We Have Lost: England Before the Industrial Age.* New York: Charles Scribner's, 1965.

Leach, Edmund. *Culture and Communication.* New York: Cambridge University Press, 1976.

Lees, Lynn H. *Exiles of Erin.* Ithaca: Cornell University Press, 1979.

Lees, Lynn H. and John Model. "The Irish Countryman Urbanized: A Comparative Perspective on the Famine Migration." *Journal of Urban History,* 3 (1977), 391–408.

Lewis, Jan. *The Pursuit of Happiness: Family and Values in Jefferson's Virginia.* Cambridge: Cambridge University Press, 1983.

Loth, Calder and Julius Sadler. *The Only Proper Style: Gothic Architecture in America.* Boston: New York Graphic Society, 1975.

McKelvey, Blake. *The Urbanization of America 1860–1915.* New Brunswick, NJ: Rutgers University Press, 1963.

Mainero, Lina, ed. *American Women Writers.* New York: Frederick Ungar, 1979.

Martin, Edgar. *The Standard of Living in 1860.* Chicago: University of Chicago Press, 1942.

Marty, Martin E. *Righteous Empire: The Protestant Experience in America.* New York: Harper Torchbooks, 1970.

Marx, Leo. *The Machine and the Garden.* New York: Oxford University Press, 1964.

Merwick, Donna. *Boston Priests 1848–1910: A Study of Social and Intellectual Change.* Cambridge: Harvard University Press, 1973.

Messbarger, Paul. *Fiction With a Parochial Purpose: Social Uses of American Catholic Literature 1814–1905.* Brookline, MA: Boston University Press, 1971.

Miller, David. "Irish Catholicism and the Great Famine." *Journal of Social History,* 9 (1975), 81–98.

Miller, Randall, ed. *Immigrants and Religion in America.* Philadelphia: Temple University Press, 1977.

Morgan, Edmund. *The Puritan Family.* New York: Harper Torchbooks, 1966.

O'Suilleabhain, Sean. *Irish Wake Amusements.* Cork: Mercier, 1967.

———. *Irish Folk Custom and Belief.* Dublin: n.p., n.d.

Ozment, Steven. *When Fathers Ruled: Family Life in Reformation Europe.* Cambridge: Harvard University Press, 1983.

Porterfield, Amanda. *Feminine Spirituality in America.* Philadelphia: Temple University Press, 1970.

Prendergast, Norma. "The Sense of Home: Nineteenth-Century Domestic Architectural Reform." Unpublished dissertation, Cornell University, 1981.

Reiter, Rayna, ed. *Toward an Anthropology of Women.* New York: Monthly Review, 1975.

Reynolds, David. *Faith in Fiction: The Emergence of Religious Literature in America.* Cambridge: Harvard University Press, 1981.

———. "The Feminization Controversy: Sexual Stereotypes and the Paradoxes of Piety in Nineteenth-Century America." *The New England Quarterly,* 53 (1980), 97–98.

Rodgers, Daniel. *The Work Ethic in Industrial America.* Chicago: University of Chicago Press, 1974.

Rosaldo, Michelle Zimbalist and Louise Lamphere. *Women, Culture, and Society.* Stanford, CA: Stanford University Press, 1974.

Ruether, Rosemary, ed. *Religion and Sexism.* New York: Simon and Schuster, 1974.

Ryan, Mary. *Cradle of the Middle Class: The Family in Oneida County New York, 1790–1865.* Cambridge: Harvard University Press, 1981.

———.*Womanhood in America.* New York: New Viewpoints, 1975.

Shannon, William. *The American Irish.* New York: Macmillan, 1966.

Schneider, Louis. *Popular Religion*. Chicago: University of Chicago Press, 1958.

Schücking, Levin. *The Puritan Family*. Translated by Brian Batter Shaw. London: Routledge and Kegan Paul, 1969.

Shiels, Richard D. "The Feminization of American Congregationalism 1730–1835." *American Quarterly*, 33, no. 1 (1981), 46–61.

Sizer, Sandra. *Gospel Hymns and Social Religion*. Philadelphia: Temple University Press, 1979.

Sklar, Kathryn. *Catharine Beecher: A Study in American Domesticity*. New York: Norton, 1973.

Smith, H. Shelton, et al. *American Christianity*. New York: Charles Scribner's, 1963.

Solberg, Winton. *Redeem the Time: The Puritan Sabbath in Early America*. Cambridge: Harvard University Press, 1977.

Stanton, Phoebe. *The Gothic Revival and American Church Architecture*. Baltimore: Johns Hopkins University Press, 1968.

Stevenson, Kenneth. *Nuptial Blessing: A Study of Christian Marriage Rites*. New York: Oxford University Press, 1983.

Stone, Lawrence. *The Family, Sex and Marriage: In England 1500–1800*. New York: Harper and Row, 1977.

Strauss, Gerald. *Luther's House of Learning: Indoctrination of the Young in the German Reformation*. Baltimore: Johns Hopkins University Press, 1978.

Thernstrom, Stephan, ed. *The Harvard Encyclopedia of American Ethnic Groups*. Cambridge: Harvard University Press, 1980.

Thompson, E. P. "Time, Work-Discipline and Industrial Capitalism." *Past and Present,* 38 (1967), 56–97.

Thompson, John. *The American Catholic Family*. Englewood Cliffs, NJ: Prentice-Hall, 1956.

Thorp, Willard. *Catholic Novelists in Defense of Their Faith: 1829–1865*. New York: Arno Press, 1978.

Walters, Ronald, ed. *Primers for Prudery: Sexual Advice to Victorian America*. Englewood Cliffs, NJ: Prentice-Hall, 1974.

Ward, James. *The Urbanization of America 1860–1915*. New Brunswick, NJ: Rutgers University Press, 1963.

Warner, Marina. *Alone of All Her Sex*. New York: Knopf, 1976.

Warner, Sam Bass. *Streetcar Suburbs*. Cambridge: Harvard University Press, 1962.

Welter, Barbara. *Dimity Convictions*. Athens, OH: Ohio University Press, 1976.

Wetering, Maxine van de. "The Popular Concept of 'Home' in Nineteenth-Century America." *Journal of American Studies,* 18 (1984), 5–28.

White, James. *The Era of Good Intentions*. New York: Arno Press, 1978.

Wigley, John. *The Rise and Fall of the Victorian Sunday*. Manchester: Manchester University Press, 1980.

Wills, Garry. *Bare Ruined Choirs: Doubt, Prophecy, and Radical Religion*. Garden City, NY: Doubleday, 1972.

Wright, Gwendolyn. *Building the Dream: A Social History of Housing in America*. Cambridge: MIT Press, 1981.

————. *Moralism and the Model Home*. Chicago: University of Chicago Press, 1980.

Zaretsky, Eli. *Capitalism, The Family, and Personal Life*. New York: Harper Colophone Books, 1976.

Index

Colleen McDannell received her doctorate in religious studies from Temple University and currently teaches for the University of Maryland, European Division. She has published in both the United States and Germany in the fields of American religions and women's studies.